P9-AGJ-956

The Secret Life of Kids

QUEST BOOKS
are published by
The Theosophical Society in America,
Wheaton, IL 60189-0270,
a branch of a world organization
dedicated to the promotion of brotherhood and
the encouragement of the study of religion,
philosophy, and science, to the end that man may
better understand himself and his place in
the universe. The Society stands for complete
freedom of individual search and belief.
In the Classics Series well-known
theosophical works are made
available in popular editions.

Cover art by *Jane A. Evans*

Children's illustrations adapted to line
drawings by Susan Maffet Peterson

55.4
P 4422

WITHDRAWN

The Secret Life of Kids

An Exploration into Their Psychic Senses

James W. Peterson

LIBRARY ST. MARY'S COLLEGE

*This publication made possible with
the assistance of the Kern Foundation*

The Theosophical Publishing House
Wheaton, Ill. U.S.A.
Madras, India / London, England

WITHDRAWN

© Copyright 1987 by James W. Peterson
A Quest original. First Edition 1987

All rights reserved. No part of this book may be reproduced in any manner without written permission except for quotations embodied in critical articles or reviews. For additional information write to:

The Theosophical Publishing House
306 West Geneva Road
Wheaton, IL 60187

A publication of the Theosophical Publishing House, a department of the Theosophical Society in America.

Library of Congress Cataloging in Publication Data

Peterson, James W. (James William), 1949-
    The secret life of kids.

    Bibliography: p.
    Includes index.
    1. Psychical research and children. I. Title.
BF1045.C45P48   1987   133.8'088054   87-40126
ISBN 0-8356-0620-1 (pbk.)

Printed in the United States of America

Contents

Acknowledgments

There are many, many people who helped to bring this book about and many others who offered continual encouragement and love from behind the scenes.

Murshida Ivy O. Duce first encouraged me to pursue this research in 1969, and in 1972 Dr. Larry Lowery and Dr. John David Miller of the University of California at Berkeley suggested that I might expand the data I had collected into a Master's Degree research project.

As early as 1975, a cherished friend and counselor, Virginia Hanson, planted the seed of this book in my mind. She was the editor of Quest Books at that time.

I wish to thank the following people for sharing ideas and stories with me which were eventually incorporated into these pages: Dr. Allan Cohen, Dr. Pascal Kaplan, Charmian Knowles, Dr. Pauli Nemanic, Dr. Charles Thomas Cayce, Dr. Lee Sannella, and René Querido.

Many thanks to Susan Isaacs, fellow author and valued friend, for helping me get started on this manuscript and to her friend, Rose Falanga, for helping me find many of the references cited throughout the text.

It was in 1975 that I first heard Joseph Chilton Pearce present his "Magical Child" material in a seminar, and since then we have met on several occasions and discussed issues of mutual interest relating to the development of children and their paranormal perceptions. I am very happy and grateful that Joe graciously offered to pen a few words of introduction to this volume.

Acknowledgments

My thanks and love to my wife JoAnn and my dear
friend Bob Holcomb for their unflagging support in spur-
ring me on during the two years I have been preparing this
book for publication.

Shirley Nicholson and William Metzger, my editors, de-
serve my heartfelt gratitude for their infinite patience with
me and continuous and valuable help in refining the
manuscript.

I also am very grateful to my sister-in-law, Susan Peterson, who so beautifully rendered the children's crayon
drawings into accurate and precise black and white
sketches. And I must not forget my mother, Marian Peterson, whose pride and faith in her son kept me going and
who, incidentally, typed several of the chapters in rough
draft form.

And, of course, I wish to thank the hundreds of children
and adults who acted, knowingly and unknowingly, as
sources for the anecdotes I have told.

Finally, I wish to thank my teacher and friend, Murshid
James MacKie, without whose loving help this book could
not have come into being.

Foreword
by Joseph Chilton Pearce

Some twelve years ago I came across Jim Peterson and his work with children. I was delighted with both. His fresh insight into the mind and world of children became a key part of my book *Magical Child* (1976). Since then Jim's work has expanded and matured (as I would like to think mine also might have).

This book of Jim's explores what might be called our natural intuitions. Jean Piaget noted that a form of intuition became available for development in children between ages four and seven, but I have found that this genetically given intelligence is more extensive in scope than Piaget suggested. Developed, this capacity would give access to information, guidance, nurturings, and knowings not present to or available through our physical five senses. This intuitive intelligence is preverbal, not thinking as such, but a precursor to thought. The child's intuitions, toward which Piaget pointed and which Peterson explores, generally relate to the child's actual well-being. Not casual entertainments of mind, these intuitions enter into the direct shaping of the child's relationships with self and world. They help determine the emotional-relational *feeling tone* which is the basis of the child's life. These emotional-relational qualities are not directly available through those sensorimotor parts of our brain, but are given through higher evolutionary structures such as the limbic system and neocortex. These inner senses, acting on the outer senses, give rise to a far richer experience of self and world.

The world/self view built up in our early years rests on an esthetic evaluation, a qualitative judgment or feeling tone superimposed on experience by the inner psychic machinery of brain-mind. What the child relates with is less important than the relationship itself as a qualitative, esthetic experience. We boast of a high "standard of living" given our children. But this standard is based on the value we adults have placed on certain kinds of material surroundings and is largely quantitative. The child's experience is qualitative, based on the emotional tone generated between child and that to which he or she relates. These emotional tones are the foundation of intelligence, and they can be richly provided in the apparent deprivation of a poverty-ridden, dirt-floored grass shack which is filled with a loving, responsive, nurturing family, and seriously missing from the richest of our high-standard well-fed technologically equipped American homes.

An integral part of this emotional-relational foundation of intelligence is this "paranormal sensitivity" Peterson discusses. Though few writers in this genre recognize the light, playful character of these inner senses, Jim sees this side. In this brilliant yet extremely readable and enjoyable study, he avoids the arbitrary seriousness we adults tend to place on natural functions we have failed to develop (and so consider mysterious and exotic). I was surprised to find my own stock of prejudice-filters through which I unknowingly looked at the psychic phenomena of children. In my book *Magical Child,* for instance, I saw "great powers" inherent within us, blocked by the evil machinations of culture. Peterson puts the psychic aspect of children into a clearer and more meaningful framework. I am particularly grateful that he supports and so splendidly adds to our growing awareness that the development of a true intelligence rests squarely on a spiritual foundation. Rudolph Steiner's Waldorf Schools clearly demonstrate that when the spiritual foundation of life is acknowledged and nurtured, a true intelligence and happiness results. This, I

believe, is why children love Waldorf schools so much,
and thrive so in them. (Interestingly, the word "spiritual"
virtually never appears in Waldorf curriculum. When the
state or condition is nurtured, one doesn't need the verbal
substitute.) The spiritual foundations of Sister Grace
Pilon's remarkable *Workshop Way* is also made evident by
function, not semantics, and is the reason that this stunning
educational development is being embraced by more and
more public school systems.

Peterson is too knowledgeable to make the common error of mistaking psychic phenomena for spiritual experience or growth, but he does show how psychic capacities
are an integral and early part of a general development
which is always by nature spiritual. When we grasp how
these early psychic abilities are designed by nature to be
integrated into and put to the service of higher realms of
intelligence later in life, the mature spiritual intuitions, we
are then well on the road to realizing what this divine play
of development of consciousness is all about.

Recently, "ultradian rhythms" within the brain have
been discovered, and they manifest from birth. Though
eventually distorted or even lost to most of us, these bio-
rhythms are designed to maintain a proper integration of,
and balance between, the various parts of the brain, and
between brain-mind, body, soul, and Self. My belief (and
recent experience through Siddha Yoga) is that this balanced state is our natural birthright and is what we refer to
when we speak of meditation. This natural meditation includes, peripherally as a side effect, those subtle prompt-
ings, knowings, and guidances Peterson explores here. If
fostered, nurtured and *allowed* in early childhood (or if
rediscovered and nurtured in our adult life, as I did
through Siddha meditation), this meditative state unfolds in
ever greater cycles of creative power, leading ultimately
(we trust) to the integration of individual self with universal Self. At that point of union of ego-intellect with creative intelligence we (would) realize *Tat Tvam Asi:* Thou
Art That. Of course, we are always That, the universal
Self, that God who dwells in the heart of all, but real-

ization and eventual exercise of this unity is what development is all about.

At any rate, it is with delight that I urge the reader to plunge into Jim Peterson's absorbing account of the inner life of the child. May we all discover this inner power resonating from that "cave of the heart wherein God dwells."

1

A Widely Shared Secret

Almost seven percent of young children have psychic experiences on a daily basis, according to a graduate study conducted on both coasts of the United States. This surprising information came as part of my Master's degree project for the University of California at Berkeley. If this percentage holds true for the country as a whole, it would mean almost two and a half million children under the age of nine frequently experience some sort of paranormal phenomena. And of course, a much larger percentage may experience an occasional glimpse into another world.

Many adults, if they reflected carefully on their early childhood years, might recall some unusual experiences. Even though I do not consider myself at all psychic, I remember some extraordinary occurrences from my childhood.

My most vivid recollection is of an experience I had often as a child, usually in the afternoons when I was sent upstairs for a nap, although I remember it repeating in the evenings sometimes as well. I would be lying wide awake in bed when my body would start to tingle and my head feel light and dizzy. At this point, if I closed my eyes, I would immediately find myself in another world, falling dreamily through space—a very black space with no stars or lights of any kind. Although I seemed to have no control over the falling, I was not frightened, nor was it an unpleasant feeling. I felt myself drifting in a very safe world of cushioning darkness.

As I fell, I would ask myself, "Who is this person whose body I inhabit and who claims to be me? Who's ME?" My mind would then suddenly rise above the body and realize, "No, that body is not me!" But then I seemed to find myself in some new body which claimed with equal certainty that it was me. As I began to feel safe and secure in this new body, again the question would arise. "Who's me?" And once again my mind would lift out of this body and realize, "No, that's not me, either." After repeating this process five or ten times, I would burst into a dizzying feeling of intense and expansive peacefulness. At this point I would usually open my eyes and ponder the experience for a few minutes before going to see what was on T.V. At other times the expanded feeling simply gave way to sleep.

This experience was a regular staple of my childhood. I loved it and felt nurtured by it, though I never thought about it except when it was happening, nor did I ever mention it to anybody. I guess the experience somehow carried its own explanation for me. Or perhaps it just didn't hold any meaning while I was still fully immersed in the unconscious tasks of childhood growth and development. Thirty years later, that childhood state holds much more significance for me, and I am beginning to appreciate and understand it.

During my seventeen years of exploring the psychic world of children, I discovered that various forms of paranormal experience are surprisingly common, much more than in adult life. In fact, most of the psychic children I have known seemed to lose touch with the unseen world as they grew older. They became average, dense adults who experience thoughts, feelings, and activities only as they relate to the physical realm. Yet I am quite sure that if they reflected on their earlier years, they would remember unusual experiences. This is no doubt true for many other adults as well as it is for me.

Many of history's wisest beings have acknowledged how common unusual states of consciousness are in childhood and how children are often especially close to the inner spiritual world. Ancient and contemporary spiritual figures have described this secret life of children as almost a oneness with nature and God.

Two thousand years ago, Jesus told his disciples to "Let the children come to me, and do not hinder them; for to such belongs the kingdom of God" (Luke 18:16). Many people assume this was a poetic and symbolic way to characterize the innocence and joy with which children approach life. This innocence, arising naturally from minds not yet cluttered with the stuff of the world, gives rise to a simple and pure love. Children have the ability to love all things and beings with such abandon that it prompted another spiritual figure, Kahlil Gibran, to write, "You may strive to be like them, but seek not to make them like you" (Gibran 1964).

But when Jesus stated one should be like a child if one wants to enter the kingdom of heaven (Matthew 18:3), he may have had more than symbolism in mind. Of course, there can be many interpretations of what is meant by "the kingdom of heaven." But if it refers to the subtle, interpenetrating vibratory fields or planes of mental and emotional energy, then the findings presented in this book suggest that not only does this kingdom of heaven belong to children, but many of them seem able to enter it at will. Indeed, for many children in this country, the veil between the physical world and the inner spiritual world is so thin that they often are confused about which world they are inhabiting. They live almost with "one foot in heaven." Luminous beings from other dimensions visit them, music unheard by others rings in their ears, and living things in the outer material world often seem to be bathed in swirling, multicolored fountains of energy. The kingdom of heaven can indeed be said to belong to children. A journey into this kingdom as described by children is a fascinating one.

But this book is not about psychic sensitivity or the characteristics of inner planes of consciousness. It is about children. It is not possible fully to understand the consciousness of children or their perceptual processes without

3

examining the paranormal perceptions that many, perhaps most, have at least intermittently. By focusing on these psychic perceptions, it is not my intent to advocate or encourage their development in adults or children. The natural and innate abilities often found in small children are completely different in range and mechanism from the psychic faculties some adults seek artificially to induce. Indeed, one of the most important and interesting aspects of this present work has been the opportunity to examine the differences between childhood and adult psychic experiences.

This topic leads to the question: Why do children tend to be psychic? Is there some special anatomical mechanism, either physical or superphysical, that allows paranormal impressions to enter a child's waking consciousness? And why does sensitivity to such impressions seem to fade between the ages of nine and fourteen? Such questions are not simple. The answers take the reader into realms of esoteric philosophy and occult investigation. The theories offered in this book have helped me to understand the secrets of the inner life of kids, and suggest new ways of understanding normal growth processes in child development. As these ideas are presented and this more spiritual view of the growing child emerges, perhaps Gibran's advice will become clearer: "You may strive to be like them."

2
The Beginnings of the Research

The problem in pursuing research into the world of psychic children is that children who have these perceptions almost never talk about them. These two and a half million kids really know how to keep a secret! When one of them does offer a report of his abilities more often than not he is humiliated and condemned by family and friends.* Like a turtle retreating into its shell, the child facing such harshness finds solace in his secret and private world.

The story of how I was able to penetrate this secret inner world of children seems to be an account of my own professional and spiritual growth—almost an autobiographical study. Bound up with discovering more about the hidden lives of children was my own search for an identity. During the years of this research, I was establishing myself, first as a university researcher in educational psychology, then as an elementary teacher in the public schools. Overshadowing these more mundane identities was my own spiritual quest. In many ways, the world of psychic children served to link my worldly pursuits with my spiritual quest.

As my research took increasingly concrete form, I was often asked to lecture or write on the subject. The task of articulating the psychic experiences of children and understanding them in the context of psychological and occult

---

*The masculine pronoun is used for ease of expression and is intended to include girls and women as well.

processes of child development forced me to clarify my own spiritual philosophy and the way in which psychic development fit with that philosophy. This book is the culmination of a process of inner discovery that has continued for almost twenty years. Uncovering the deeper nature of children and the reasons they often are sensitive to unseen currents of life became for me an exploration into the most fundamental mysteries of life: Who we are, and how and why do we incarnate on the earth?

Since the psychic life of children has become such a significant and meaningful topic for me, I make no apologies for the personal, almost autobiographical treatment of the subject in these pages. I freely offer my own theories as to how paranormal abilities work and how they articulate with an integrated vision of spirituality in our life on earth. When objectivity is needed, I attempt to be scientific, but so little research has been done and so little has been written on childhood psychism that my own formulations seem as valid as any others.

Since children rarely come out and speak about their unusual perceptions, it should come as no surprise that I literally stumbled into a discovery of these abilities. I had just turned twenty and had come to realize that I did not want to continue the premedical training which my father had encouraged me to pursue. I was taking all sorts of courses and enjoying every minute of my academic uncertainty. Summers during this period were equally open, so I accepted a job as a camp counselor for underprivileged children from Philadelphia.

I had never worked with children before, but I suddenly found myself in charge of twenty kids, six to nine years old, of every racial mix. I did not know how to talk to children, how to discipline them, or how to comfort them when they were homesick. Every aspect of working with children was new to me. While I gradually realized this was the most difficult job of my life, it also was the most rewarding. An educator was born that summer, and my whole life took a new direction.

This camp was the setting for my initial discovery that children sometimes live in a secret world filled with marvelous and magical sights. This discovery came spontaneously and unexpectedly.

Camp counselors put in long hours. In a fourteen hour stretch of duty, we had only one hour off. I cherished this period. For the first few minutes I would rest on my bed in the far corner of a long, army-style bunk house. Then I would use the remainder of the hour for my daily meditation. I had been doing a simple form of mantra yoga, using a name for God as my mantra. Since the children were at the swimming pool, I had no concern about being disturbed during this time alone.

Yet one day my meditation was disturbed. I was sitting quietly when I heard some kids suddenly run through the door seven or eight minutes earlier than usual. Determined to complete my meditation, I kept my eyes closed. Apparently the two boys, eight-year-old Drew and nine-year-old Eric, saw something peculiar in the meditating figure at the far end of the bunk house. I heard them tentatively approach, one whispering, "Do you see what I see?" The other responded, "Yeah, it's weird." Then they began to describe to each other the swatches of color they saw floating around various portions of my body. As Drew later dictated into my tape recorder:

> Well, one day when we came back from swimming, Jim was meditating and we saw colors coming out of his stomach. And the outside was purple, and then it was blue, then it was a dark yellow, and then...reddish and light yellow in the middle.

Apparently the colors were arranged in more or less concentric circles, and not only did they range from purple to yellow, but they also seemed constantly to be changing in shade.

Listening to them describe what they saw was far more interesting to me than finishing my meditation. I had been a student of comparative religion and esoteric studies since my senior year in high school, so when I heard Drew and Eric talking, I never doubted that they were describing levels of radiating psychological energy, generally invisible to ordinary, external vision. They claimed to see a phenomenon that is called an ''aura,'' and I had no reason to be skeptical of this claim.

I was more than merely sympathetic to their claim; I really became excited by it. This was the first time I had spontaneous confirmation that some of the topics I had been studying were truly part of the real world. It is one thing to believe that an aura exists, but it is quite another to have people (and children at that) describing what your aura looks like.

Later I asked these boys more about their visions, and they were able to describe many clairvoyant experiences. The term ''clairvoyant'' refers to the perception of nonphysical dimensions of life, specifically through the visual sense. Through my discussions with the boys, I learned that they had seen colors around people's bodies since earliest childhood, although these visions came only intermittently. Often an adult's intense emotion (such as anger or happiness) would precipitate the boys' clairvoyant perception of an adult's aura. Even then, the paranormal perception would come and go, completely beyond their control. Although the boys accepted these visions as a natural ability, they also realized they were somehow special, and both told me they had never mentioned it to any other person before that summer. Later I became well acquainted with Drew's parents, and though they both came to accept his clairvoyance and my interest in it, they confirmed that he had never mentioned it to them before meeting me.

Yet Drew and Eric almost immediately accepted each other's paranormal vision, though neither had previously encountered anyone who shared these experiences. The meditation incident seemed to them a natural occurrence. They accepted my interest in their perceptions without reservation or hesitation.

In the days that followed, I felt I had been transformed into a parapsychological researcher. Because members of my family communicated during this time through "talking letters," I was in the habit of carrying a portable tape recorder with me. Now this became my research tool. I cannot say why I became so obsessed with getting every detail of the boys' clairvoyant descriptions onto tape. Perhaps I wanted to make sure people would believe me when I told them about these children. Perhaps I was simply fascinated by their reports of the swirling, ever-changing patterns of energy they described, or the tiny flying beings they said inhabited the woods around camp. Or perhaps some part of me knew these tapes would create the foundation for a research project and the early chapters of a book.

Many six to nine year olds came to camp that summer, as every two weeks one group left and another arrived. I decided to question others about their visual perceptions. I found, much to my surprise, that one boy in fifteen claimed to have clairvoyant visions, seemingly identical to those reported by Drew and Eric.

I quickly discovered that one can never interview children in a group setting. They are chameleons and imitate their surroundings. Whenever unusual perceptions of lights or colors were mentioned in a group, suddenly almost every child became "clairvoyant." Many of these under-privileged kids just wanted to please me, and if I gave special attention to those who were clairvoyant, then that is certainly what they must be too. Also, the one time I foolishly pursued a discussion of such visions with a group, I noticed that many of the children seemed not to distinguish between their imaginary visions, their dreams, and their daydreams. Most thought we were playing a game in which we imagined seeing all sorts of weird things.

I did not need formal research training to figure out that the only way I could get truthful and candid data from children about their paranormal perceptions was in a private setting where I could question each child alone. Also,

I learned to be unemotional and matter-of-fact in my line of questioning, so as not to encourage particular responses. I tried to ask open-ended, non-threatening questions that were not leading in tone. In this setting, most kids told me frankly they had no idea what I was talking about when I asked about colors around people's bodies or lights in the woods. However, almost seven percent of the ones I spoke to that summer knew precisely what I meant and shared fascinating perceptions. These responses were all tape-recorded.

I returned to camp the next two summers and continued the interviews, sometimes with children I knew from earlier years, and sometimes with new ones. I felt I was studying an unacknowledged aspect of childhood psychology. But though this paranormal childhood perception seemed unknown to the academic community, it certainly was not rare.

Not only had I developed an interest in child psychology, but I was equally enthusiastic about every other aspect of my work with the children at camp. This enthusiasm led me to graduate work at the University of California at Berkeley in elementary education and child psychology. While there, I never encountered any reference to the subject of paranormal abilities in children, and none of my professors knew anything of the subject. Still I continued to discover children who claimed to have such perceptions. Convinced that this field needed investigation, I undertook a Master's project to study clairvoyant children, the results of which eventually were published as "Some Profiles of Non-ordinary Perceptions of Children."

The study, conducted in my first year as a second-grade teacher, was primarily a continuation of my interviews with children. My technique was more academically rigorous, but still included the open-ended, non-judgmental approach I had been using for years. Now my data included video as well as audio tape recordings, and colored pictures drawn by the children.

The study yielded some fascinating conclusions. The clairvoyant visions described by children in California were virtually identical in content to those reported at the Pennsylvania camp. Though each child's experience seemed unique in certain details, many common patterns of clairvoyant perception emerged. Furthermore, the basic statistic I had discovered in Pennsylvania, that one child in fifteen below the age of nine is clairvoyant, held true for the kids in California.

My interest in this study continued after I completed my graduate work. In the succeeding years, I accumulated case after case of children who not only were clairvoyant, but who had other psychic abilities as well. I have written articles on the subject and have lectured widely. This book allows me the opportunity for the first time to present all the data accumulated over the years, as well as my theories about possible causes of childhood psychism. I hope this book is but the beginning of a greater recognition of the existence of this secret life of kids, and that it will stimulate further study.

3
The Seven Psychic Senses

Before presenting case studies and anecdotes concerning the secret life of kids, it is necessary to sketch in a conceptual framework into which these intriguing incidents fit, and to clarify some important terms. Just a catalogue of cases would not be very meaningful or helpful to the reader. I have found a workable way to classify psychic senses. Through the years I have also come across many sources that offer partial explanations of psychism. I have pieced these together into an overall picture which I offer for consideration, in the belief that it will put childhood psychism into a meaningful perspective. The colorful stories that follow this chapter will be more valuable to the reader when they can be seen in the light of these concepts. I introduce this philosophic framework in this chapter and further develop it in Chapters 11 and 12, after discussing the data on childhood psychism.

The Indian teacher J. Krishnamurti often said that the key to answering any fundamental question of human existence lies in careful analysis of the question itself. Since my days at the Pennsylvania summer camp, the key to understanding the secret life of kids has not only involved clarifying questions about childhood psychic sensitivity, but also finding a precise vocabulary to describe the processes of consciousness involved. It seemed to me that if a distinct vocabulary could be evolved, then the underlying processes of consciousness would be revealed and understood.

I felt that if I could *name* these processes, I would somehow come to *know* them.

Naming the facets of human consciousness, however, is no mean feat. It would have been simpler had I limited myself to a given list of terms from a single spiritual perspective. But since so little has been written on this subject, I had to gather information from a wide variety of sources. This eclectic approach eventually made it necessary to integrate the vocabularies of modern psychology, experimental parapsychology, Western occult philosophy, and Eastern mystical traditions.

It seems astonishing that psychic phenomena, which have been reported and studied for thousands of years, should yet involve such a jumble of conflicting theories, loose concepts, and imprecise vocabularies. I recently came across an ad for a particular spiritual group, which promised to help the reader ''...tap into the sixth sense phenomena, such as intuition, telepathy, precognition, telekinesis and astral projection, among others.'' Now how could telepathy, intuition and astral projection all be different aspects of the same psychic ability, and what could be more imprecise than calling all of these faculties ''sixth sense abilities''? To make matters even more confusing, parapsychological researchers coin new terms, such as ''out-of-body experience,'' ''psi,'' and ''transpersonal,'' terms that are beginning to seep into contemporary idiom. In addition some gurus or leaders of spiritual groups have taken to making up idiosyncratic terms to describe processes of consciousness. So trying to correlate terms from different sources is a surprisingly complex task.

Another aspect of the problem is that different writers or teachers use the same terminology to refer to different phenomena. Many commonly used terms, when used in differing contexts, have a confusing variety of meanings. Take the term ''clairvoyance.'' I have used this term to refer to specific, unusual visual perceptions of ''other dimensions'' normally invisible to ordinary sight. As the clairvoyant Geoffrey Hodson has defined it, clairvoyance is ''an extension of the normal range of visual response to include both physical rays beyond the violet and, beyond them again, the light of the superphysical'' (Hodson 1970, 10).

This definition of clairvoyance, however, is not the most widely accepted use of the term. People in the field of the paranormal use the term in an astonishing variety of ways. C. W. Leadbeater, another clairvoyant and author, expanded the definition to include clairvoyance in time. Someone who could tune into events of the remote past, such as in reading past lives, or someone who could prophesy events of the future would equally be termed ''clairvoyant'' (Leadbeater 1971 [1903], 30).

Parapsychologists use the term to describe an ability to see something which is physically removed or hidden from the vision of a research subject. This is also sometimes called ''remote viewing.'' Thus if a child can correctly guess hidden symbols on E.S.P. cards better than just by chance, he would be considered to have clairvoyant ability. According to this view, clairvoyance is ''the mind's ability to be aware of *external, material things* or to perceive *external* events other than by our ordinary visual sensory organs'' (Moncrieff 1951, 98). By ''external, material things'' parapsychologists mean ordinary physical things, not unusual or invisible objects or events on some imperceptible superphysical plane.

Furthermore, these ''precise'' uses of this particular word have practically nothing to do with the manner in which the popular media uses the term. Magazines, tabloid newspapers, and television programs often loosely describe virtually anybody with any sort of psychic ability as ''clairvoyant.'' It is no wonder that research into paranormal abilities has received such bad press in scientific circles. Scientists look for precision and repeatability in their work, but in psychic investigation, one cannot even rely on the meaning of a simple term such as ''clairvoyance.''

This variety of usages illustrates the importance of clarifying the definitions of terms to be used in this book. The actual vocabulary chosen represents a personal integration of the terms I have encountered in my research, and the definitions offered will be my personal "working definitions." My occasional digressions into the esoteric meaning of certain terms represent further integrations of concepts culled from many different sources. This eclectic approach seems helpful in understanding the processes underlying childhood psychism. If it is to be a help to the reader as well, however, it all must be carefully articulated.

The terms used in this book seemed to me to best express the concepts under consideration. Many of them might be considered "esoteric terminology" and not as scientific as some alternate terms might be, but I use the vocabulary I have found most illuminating, whatever its source. Esoteric terminology has evolved over the epochs of recorded history to name and define aspects of nonmaterial processes of consciousness. So it seems logical to take advantage of these specific names and terms where appropriate. Ancient traditions held that knowing the correct name of something placed that thing under one's control. The tale of Rumpelstiltskin illustrates this belief.

If I am to write about psychic children, the word "psychic" must be clearly defined. One could hardly find a word in the English language more loaded with prejudice or misconception. For some it conveys lofty heights of spiritual attainment, while for others it calls to mind only sensational chatter in tabloid newspapers. Followers of Sri Aurobindo define "psychic" as "belonging to the soul or psyche," and consider the psychic level of consciousness to be a refined spiritual state beyond the domain of mind (Pavitra 1961, 66). For Jungian psychologists, it connotes the emotional side of one's nature; for others it usually refers to E.S.P. and paranormal abilities. Some feel becoming "psychic" in this latter sense is an important first step in spiritual development, while others emphatically denounce psychic sensitivity as an egotistical and dangerous distraction from true spiritual growth. Still others suggest that psychic abilities have a neutral quality—neither good nor bad, helpful nor unhelpful. Rather, their value is relative to the character of the person with such faculties.

At present the relative value of psychic abilities is not the issue, although it will be addressed in detail in Chapter 15. But a clear working definition of the term is needed. In the present context "psychic" will denote *the ability, through whatever means, to collect sensory information from non-physical realms*. If a sensory perception is psychic, it would indicate (by definition) that the impressions registered in waking consciousness could not have been received through the ordinary use of the physical senses.

Psychic perception should not be confused with imagination, delusion, or hallucination. Hallucinations and delusions are frequently associated with pathological conditions or with drug-induced physiological states. Hallucinations refer to pictorial or symbolic expressions of impaired mental structures, and by definition they manifest to each hallucinator in a unique way (Leuner 1964, 2). A psychic impression, by contrast, must involve the reception of actual sense data from the outside environment.

Any treatise on paranormal perceptions must start with the assumption that this "outside environment" that we see with our normal senses is merely the outer crust of a vibratory reality that contains worlds within worlds of objective existence that are physically imperceptible. The sensory receptivity of one who is psychic involves a much wider range of possibilities than is available to one without such faculties.

It is necessary not only to distinguish psychic experience from hallucination, but also to suggest that this expansion of the senses can be distinguished from what is called a "spiritual" experience. This present work does not concern children's spiritual or religious experiences. But the problem is that the dividing line between what is called a "psychic experience" and what is called a "spiritual" or "mystical experience" is often hazy or ill-defined.

For one thing, confusion can result from the use of the phrase "spiritual world" by many esoteric groups to denote any of the subtle inner dimensions of non-physical existence. In this view any perception of this "spiritual world," therefore, could be viewed as a spiritual experience. The drawback to this terminology is that it makes no attempt to distinguish levels of consciousness or sources of experience, which, as will be seen, are vitally important. If there is no concept of gradations or levels, the etheric forces affecting physical vitality appear as much a part of the "spiritual world" and "spiritual experience" as forces that underlie inner reality at its deepest levels. It is therefore necessary to classify types of inner experiences according to the level of human consciousness that gives rise to them.

Our inner being exists in different stages of expression and manifestation, corresponding to different dimensions or levels of objective existence. In the same way that the physical body simultaneously exists as atoms, as chemical combinations, as organs, each level with its corresponding environment, other aspects of our being are constructed of different degrees of subtle matter and exist in correspondingly subtle environments, each of which interpenetrates the physical world.

A sensory perception of one of these inner environments is called a "psychic experience." Such a perception involves an enhanced awareness of one of these objective, supersensible spheres of existence that is closely connected with earthly life. One perceives that what he is experiencing is not merely subjective but comes from an external stimulus. So an experience of this type might amplify one's sense of being an objective observer, detached and separate from the field of perception (although it is most difficult not to project one's preconceptions onto what one sees). Psychic experiences, therefore, often tend to be somewhat ego-centered and can lead to a sense of exaggerated self-importance. This is one reason that many spiritual leaders warn against developing psychic faculties.

A spiritual experience has characteristics quite opposite to those of a psychic experience. A spiritual experience is a subjective feeling that tends to unite one to the objective environment in a wave of expansiveness. Such a sense of unity with life forces could not arise from objective realms of sensorial separateness, but must have its roots in higher spheres where life energies flow and intermingle with far less differentiation. A psychic experience seems localized within some kind of sensory apparatus, and tends to enhance a feeling of separateness from the outer objective world. A spiritual experience usually involves one's entire being, mental, emotional, and spiritual, and evokes a feeling of blissful love for all life, which often profoundly affects or changes one's character long after the experience itself has faded away.

Although others (e.g., Armstrong 1985) have written about childhood spiritual experiences, they are more rare than the psychic variety. Experiences of psychic senses in childhood are tied to normal sensorial and emotional growth processes and are extremely common in children under seven. The forces that precipitate a genuine spiritual experience function quite differently, and in many ways are in opposition to the natural forces of childhood growth and development. This is an important point to understand since so many "New Age" educators attempt artificially to induce spiritual experiences in children through the trendy practices of meditation and yoga. I suggest in Chapter 15 that such practices for children may in fact be quite dangerous.

By referring to the "psychic senses," I am attempting to unravel and organize many different abilities which often are lumped together as "E.S.P." In the early 1970s, when I first began to present my research on psychic children in public lectures, I had already discovered that a child might well have one type of psychic faculty without possessing other types. Since the physical senses of man seem distinct and independent of each other, I began to assume the psychic senses may be similarly independent. It seemed reasonable, then, to evolve an extrasensory model which separates the various psychic abilities.

Fortunately, about this time, I encountered Dr. Allen Cohen of the Consciousness Studies Department of John F.

Kennedy University in California. He had been offering a
course at the university entitled "The Psychic Senses,"
and the model he used to organize paranormal sensibilities
corresponded to my own thoughts on the subject, though
Dr. Cohen had developed a more concrete and systematic
approach. The data I had gathered by interviewing psychic
children seemed to fit so well within his model that I have
used it ever since. Many other researchers have organized
data on psychic sensitivity in different ways. But the system presented here seems to fit better with my data than
any other system I have encountered.

According to this model, there are seven distinct psychic
senses, each functioning in complete independence of the
others—even as physical sight functions independently of
physical hearing. However, I cannot discuss these psychic
senses and the way they are expressed in children without
carefully defining more terms. Part of my understanding of
unusual childhood perceptions has come through clarifying
the terms and concepts needed to describe psychic processes and the inner structures of consciousness which
underlie these processes. At this point it would make little
sense merely to offer isolated definitions without providing
at least a general philosophical framework or model to
which the reader can relate the terms. This requires a
sketch of the entire inner structure of human consciousness, which will help explain the anecdotes in the next few
chapters. As I attempt to unravel the profound mysteries of
existence which underlie the hidden processes of childhood
growth, I need to make certain theoretical assumptions.
These assumptions about the inner being of man represent
the foundation of all the concepts presented in this book.
Although they are my personal and somewhat idiosyncratic
formulations and may seem to be a digression, they are
essential background for the data and theories which come
later.

I must begin with the Source of life—the divine essence
of all—that is the core of a human being. This divine
essence focused in human consciousness is referred to as

"monad," *"atma,"* "soul," or "spirit." It projects itself into realms of manifested reality in stages. (The purpose of this manifestation falls into the domain of religious philosophy and as such is not crucial in the context of the present outline of esoteric psychology.) The *atma* wraps around itself increasingly complex and solid sheaths of consciousness or levels of being. These levels assist in the process of developing and expressing myriad aspects of the unfolding consciousness of the atma. At the same time, each succeeding sheath, more dense than the previous one, inevitably dulls and deadens the person to the simple, flowing, open levels of life represented by the subtler levels. In a general way, the more subtle of these inner levels relate one to aspects of being which exist beyond normal waking consciousness, while everyday awareness of subjective mental and emotional states works through denser and more material sheaths.

Different systems refer to the sheaths of consciousness in different ways. My own quest has been to integrate these terminologies in a single vocabulary for public presentations.

The first, most refined vehicle of manifested life expression is often called the "causal body," though the word "body" seems inappropriate as this sheath has little form or substance from a concrete perspective. It is created out of coded units of mind called in Sanskrit *sanskaras.** Sanskaras represent the residue of all one's life experiences from this and previous incarnations. At this highest level of mind (sometimes called *buddhi manas*), these mental

---

Practical Sanskrit Dictionary (MacDonell, 1924): A sanskara is a "...mental impression left by causes no longer operative, dating from a previous birth" (326). Madame H.P. Blavatsky stated, "...the term is used to denote the impression left upon the mind by individual actions or external circumstances, and capable of being developed on any future favorable occasion— even in a future birth. The sanskara denotes, therefore, the germs of propensities and impulses from previous births to be developed in this, or the coming...reincarnations,...and as such is connected with karma and its working" (Blavatsky 1952 [1892], 287-88).

impressions are in a nonactivated, latent state. This aspect of being creates the "causes" of future mental expression, hence the name "causal body."

This sheath of consciousness, from the ordinary psychological perspective, could be described as the deepest layer of the unconscious mind. A person is aware of sanskaras only when they somehow erupt into conscious expression. This highest mental aspect, then, does not represent the "mind" of concrete or even abstract thinking that we ordinarily experience, but it can be said to be the root source or cause of the mind.

Man's consciousness is further expressed through what is termed the "lower mind" or, in Sanskrit, *kama manas,* which denotes mind impregnated with desire and intimately bound to earthly life (Blavatsky 1952 [1892], 66). Previously unmanifested sanskaras gain energy at this level and project into partial manifestation, gaining a fuller range of expression. But rather than considering this denser material to be "matter," it is more helpful to consider this level of mind simply as energy. Thus the pure mind of the causal body consolidates into the energy of the *kama manas,* where it is partially expressed.

The "mind" referred to here is not the intellectual functioning commonly associated with the word, but rather the essence of conscious life. The Buddha remarked that man is nothing but Mind. From this perspective, the denser, "lower" sheaths simply are different expressions of Mind. At the level of the kama manas, this mind-plus-energy expresses itself as concrete thoughts combined with emotion. Since thoughts and emotions are not really separate from one another, the thinking aspect of the mind is reflected energetically and concretely, along with desires and emotions, in this layer of consciousness.

The lower three vehicles, which are constructed of subtle mind-energy now solidified as particles of matter (physical and superphysical), represent the expression of essential Mind as a manifested personality in incarnation on earth. Therefore, while the higher sheaths have a certain permanent existence, the lower three vehicles come and go as birth and death connect them to or disconnect them from earthly fields of expression.

These three "lowest" sheaths are generally called the "astral body," the "etheric body," and the "physical body." These three work in close harmony, expressing mental and emotional impulses in external activity in the physical world. They also (and this often is not emphasized) work together to sustain physical life processes.

Even though the astral and etheric bodies are closely bound up with physical processes, particularly in the endocrine, circulatory, and nervous systems, a human being usually is only indirectly aware of the astral and etheric aspects of such mechanisms. In a sense, our awareness of these levels of life is subjective, unrelated to concrete, sensory experiences. However, these levels can be very objective to children, especially before the astral and etheric bodies have reached full maturity. These two superphysical bodies grow and develop in step with the physical body. Through an understanding of these phases of astral and etheric growth, we can discover the causes underlying childhood psychism.

Now I return to the subject of the seven psychic senses which constitute the sensory apparatus of the astral body. Since we usually experience the astral vehicle only subjectively, we are ordinarily blocked from direct consciousness of the astral environment through the senses. An unusual linking between the astral and physical sheaths would be necessary for one to become "psychic." The psychic senses, which are aspects of higher sheaths of consciousness usually do not filter into physical awareness, though they are available on the astral level. Under normal conditions, sensory information from this subtle astral sheath does not flow directly into the physical system. Rather, this sense data is psychically screened at the "threshold of waking consciousness," a level bridging the physical and astral, called the "etheric sheath" (Bendit and Bendit

1977, 98). To be aware of any of these astral senses, there must be some special link or direct channel (sometimes requiring a biochemical modification of physical tissue, according to this theory) into the physical nervous and glandular systems which would allow astral sense data to precipitate into consciousness, a process explored in Chapter 12.

If a person has use of one of the seven psychic senses, it in no way guarantees any other psychic abilities. However, even as every human being possesses each of the physical senses, so everyone possesses the seven psychic senses, though they do not often break into conscious awareness. The delineation of these senses, especially the numerical designations I assign, may seem arbitrary, but this system adequately expresses the distinct and separate nature of these "paranormal" abilities, which are of course "normal" at the astral level.

The first of the senses, supposedly the most common, is telepathy. This is the ability to receive the thoughts and feelings of others. The second is the ability to "see" into the past, to "read" past lives, and is sometimes referred to as "clairvoyance of the past." Clear memories of one's own recent past lives are an indirect aspect of this sense. This kind of "far-memory" would probably not require as complex a "hook-up" to the astral sheath as would be needed to read impersonal events from some remote historical period.

The third psychic sense is the ability to look into the future, sometimes referred to as "clairvoyance of the future" or prophetic vision. Media reports of "psychic" predictions may suggest that this ability is a common one, but those who claim to see the future have a strikingly low accuracy rate. An aspect of this third sense is the prophetic dream, a more indirect ability to "see" the future. As with far memory, the connections to the astral sensory mechanism for such an indirect ability would not need to be as strong as for bringing regular and clear prophetic perceptions into waking consciousness.

The fourth psychic sense, reportedly the most rare, is the

ability to do medical diagnosing. A diagnoser using this sense can tell the state of a person's health simply by being near that person—and sometimes even physical proximity is not necessary. No "visions" are involved; the diagnoser "just knows." I knew a Chinese doctor specializing in herbal medicine who could consistently sense the health problems of a new patient when the patient walked through his office door. The doctor would then use his normal diagnosing technique of checking the patient's twelve pulses to confirm that immediate diagnosis. He claimed the earlier diagnosis has always been confirmed by the pulses. He never thought he was using a "psychic ability," but assumed he was simply extremely intuitive. In recent years, he has come more fully to trust and use his unusual diagnostic ability.

The most common and in some ways most complex of the supernormal senses, and the one most easily "brought through" to the physical nervous system, is the fifth sense. Clairvoyance and clairaudience belong to this sense, as does the ability for astral travel or "out of body" experiences. Healing also is a part of this fifth sense, especially healing by the "laying on of hands."

According to this model of the psychic senses, reading into the past and reading into the future are considered separate and distinct senses, while clairvoyance, clairaudience, astral travel, and healing are all included as part of the fifth psychic sense. C. W. Leadbeater wrote at the turn of the century that one who is clairvoyant is almost invariably clairaudient as well (Leadbeater 1971 [1903], 2). But why include astral travel, which surely seems an unrelated ability? I asked Dr. Cohen this question, and he told me there seems to be some connection among these four sensibilities, possibly through a specific biochemical characteristic of the physical body. Although clairvoyance seems distinct from healing by touch, the link to the astral sheath for these abilities is similar, and a person with one of these fifth sense faculties could easily cultivate the others.

The sixth psychic sense, psychometry, involves the ability to receive impressions through the sense of touch. A person possessing this gift could, for example, hold an antique vase in his hands, describe when it was made and by whom, and discuss temperaments of the various owners of the vase. This sixth sense also includes the ability to "see" color through touch, a faculty often reported among blind people.

The final ability is a somewhat dangerous one in that it can easily be selfishly misused. In this schema the seventh sense is called "mind control," but it really is more the ability to project the mind. Someone with this sense actually can move physical objects merely by focusing mental energy (often termed "psychokinesis" or P.K.) and can sometimes levitate and do materializations. Poltergeist phenomena also often fall within this category.

Having listed these seven distinct senses and the faculties associated with them, I must point out an important point relating to their use. These psychic abilities can unfold within a person's consciousness and function in at least two different ways. They may open up as a byproduct of spiritual development, related to the expansion and refinement of the human mind (sometimes termed the "unwinding of sanskaras"). Or they may function simply as a talent, a developed propensity which can occur in anyone with normal consciousness of the physical world. This second type of psychic functioning (by far the more common of the two) has nothing to do with spiritual advancement or permanent expansion of consciousness.

A bit of philosophical background might help clarify this second type of psychic ability. Many spiritual teachers suggest that the purpose of the atma's (or soul's) continual reincarnations is to have as wide a variety of life experiences as possible. Once the momentum to gain constant stimulation in life begins to wane for a person, the possibility arises to journey back in consciousness to the Source of life. Although the urge to gain as much life experience as possible implies trying out many professions and many personality traits in myriad different cultures during the rounds of reincarnations, nevertheless each individual tends to have propensities for specific activities lifetime after lifetime. These propensities, developed and nurtured through the ages, are called "talents."

According to this premise, every human being has an array of major and minor talents. With each incarnation, one pulls through at least one of these for use. They represent inborn gifts, the innate capacities, knowledge, or abilities that are frequently cited as arguments for the theory of reincarnation. Without the notion of talents developed through repeated reincarnations, how else could one account for the innate genius of, say, a Mozart? In any event, an individual usually will work with the specific talents needed for the karmic lessons of a given life. The sanskaras associated with other major talents of the individual may remain latent in the causal body and be unavailable for expression for an entire lifetime, or indeed, for several lifetimes. But given the sweep of many reincarnations, an individual would have a tendency to work with a specific group of talents. In the arts, for example, an individual might repeatedly work with painting but never pursue an interest in music.

According to this concept, psychic faculties are considered talents like any others. Just as a talent such as for sculpture, design, or engineering would not necessarily imply advanced spiritual status, so a psychic talent would not. Much of the popular literature on the subject suggests that the development of psychic and occult powers is an important, even necessary, step in spiritual evolution. The view that psychism is an innate, inborn propensity, however, would imply that these faculties have little to do with spiritual evolution and would be quite difficult to open up at all unless they were at least among one's minor talents.

There is, however, an entirely different type of occult ability that is intimately connected to spiritual development and the refinement of the mind. This type of psychic awareness might appear to an external observer as similar—even identical—to the psychic perceptions of someone who possesses these abilities as a talent. But the mechanics and implications of this second type of psychism are utterly different. Perhaps an analogy would help illustrate this difference: A normal, physically conscious human being with a strong psychic talent is like someone who is able to peer through a window of an elegant mansion (here representing the inner planes and worlds) and describe the activities occurring within the mansion. In contrast, one who acquires these abilities as a byproduct of moral purification and expansion of consciousness is like one who actually lives within the mansion, completely and utterly absorbed in the activities and life within it. Even though the physical body of such a one usually appears outwardly unexceptional, the internal state of consciousness is permanently united with the particular level of life experience that his purified sanskaras manifest for him. (See Donkin 1969). Such individuals do not experience external consciousness of the physical world at all, but rather experience all of life's activities from the perspective of one of the higher planes of consciousness. A person united with such a realm of expanded awareness would be clairvoyant, clairaudient, telepathic, and indeed might manifest any or all of the psychic abilities. But such abilities would have little similarity to those possessed by normal individuals who happen to have a psychic talent. One example of a person often mistakenly referred to as a "psychic" but who actually was focused on higher planes would be H.P. Blavatsky, one of the founders of the Theosophical Society and author of *The Secret Doctrine.* Paranormal faculties such as hers obviously are extremely rare, and as such will not be of much concern in this book. I have heard of children with this type of psychic expansion of consciousness, but I have never met any.

Now that the distinction has been drawn between spiritually advanced psychism and psychism as a talent, I shall confuse the issue again by stating that neither of these types of psychic ability has much relevance to children. Although it is certainly important to understand how psychism functions in adulthood, with children such faculties generally work in a completely different way and fall into yet another category. Children can be highly telepathic, psychokinetic, or clairvoyant without the existence of either psychic talent or occult advancement. Their ability comes instead as a byproduct of normal growth processes and is referred to as "atavistic psychism." But rather than attempt to define this type of paranormal sensitivity in this chapter, already filled with too many concepts and definitions, I shall save this discussion for Chapters 11 and 12, after I have thoroughly reviewed the sights, sounds, and experiences of this "secret life of kids."

The anecdotes I have gathered of children's paranormal experiences are arranged according to the particular psychic sense involved. However, I do not necessarily discuss each type in its numerical order, but rather according to how prevalent and common an ability is; thus telepathy is discussed first, clairvoyance second, and so on.

There is one more matter to be mentioned, however, before these anecdotes can be presented. When I was doing my original research, I was surprised at how little material was available on the subject of childhood psychism. If the existence of psychic sensibilities in children was as common as I had begun to suspect, why had so little been written? Surely I was not among the first to discover it. Inquiries led me to a distant past in which pyramids and stone circles were the secret doorways into the inner, invisible realms, and the psychic world of children was a common part of everyday life. I now turn to the history of childhood psychism.

4
Psychic Children—
A Retrospective

When I began my Master's degree study in 1973 at the University of California in Berkeley, I asked a professor of educational psychology if he had ever come across childhood psychism. The professor told me that not only had he never heard of a child with such perceptual abilities, but he had never seen any scientific or psychological treatment in the literature on such a phenomenon.

Only in recent times could such a statement be made. In ancient times the existence of a subtle non-material world and the possibility of perceiving it was taken for granted. Indeed, some researchers claim that the modern separation of scientific knowledge from a natural, intuitive understanding of psychic forces in life only began to manifest as a pattern of human consciousness after the fifteenth century (Steiner 1982).

In ancient times the belief in paranormal phenomena was tied to an understanding of nature and the gods. The gods were not distant forces in some faraway heaven, but active in the natural world. For the ancients the world of psychism was not one of seances, mind-reading or the bending of spoons on television (as Uri Geller has done), but was intimately bound up with a knowledge of how plants grow, of the times to harvest or sow, and of how powerful cosmic forces, such as those of the sun and the moon, work through the elements of air, earth, fire, and water (Steiner 1982). Of course, people did not analyze these forces, but revered them (Douglas 1977). In civilizations such as those of ancient Egypt, Greece, or the Yucatan, priests or oracles served as communicators with the subtle forces of nature. The oracles, with their psychic abilities, were greatly honored in the community (Douglas 1977).

The sensitivity and openness of children were probably acknowledged facts in these cultures, for it was believed that the training of a new priest or oracle must begin in earliest childhood while the child is naturally most open to the spiritual worlds. Often the sensitivity of a child was tested before training for priesthood could begin. In Greece, for instance, seven- or eight-year-old boys and girls were taken to the temple, where sheep were cut open and their viscera spread out before the children. The priest would then ask the children what they could see revealed there. The ones showing the most aptitude for prophecy and revelation would be given the opportunity of beginning their apprenticeship in the temple. The psychic openness of youngsters in general was so well respected in Greece that children were routinely initiated into the secrets of the Eleusinian Mysteries (Hall 1978, 30).

In Tibet there is a strong tradition of recognizing the paranormal perceptions of children. When a high lama or rinpoche died, the surviving priests of his monastery would go in search of the child who was the lama's reincarnation. Books, shoes, and other personal belongings of the previous lama were laid alongside other similar items having no connection with the lama. Babies and small children were then "tested" to see if they could recognize the lama's possessions (Armstrong 1985, 107). These demonstrations assumed that the reincarnated lama would have paranormal recognition of his earlier possessions.

Christianity also has a long history of accepting the paranormal testimony which comes out of "the mouths of babes." The Albigenses, for example, were a Christian group who flourished in southern France during the twelfth and thirteenth centuries. This sect routinely sought visions and prophecies from their children, and believed that children had a special link to the spiritual worlds.

During the past few centuries there have been hundreds of cases within the Catholic Church of children who see visions of angels and of the Virgin Mary, and who receive instructions or prophecies from celestial visitors. The Church has diligently investigated these cases and surprisingly often issued edicts proclaiming the paranormal perceptions genuine. Although the Church does not necessarily accept the view that many children have paranormal perception, it has gathered abundant data for hundreds of years suggesting that children often perceive phenomena which are not a part of the perceptual world of adults.

One case, investigated by Pope Pius IX but never officially acknowledged, involved visions of two children, Maximin Giraud and Melanie Mathieu, on Mount La Salette in France in 1846. The children were tending cattle when they saw a woman dressed in white and radiating blazing light. The heavenly figure floated toward them and said that the people of that district did not take their religion seriously enough and a famine was going to be the consequence. The figure then slowly dematerialized. Not only did a two-year famine come as prophesied, but a spring of fresh water began to flow at the exact spot where the children spoke to the otherworldly visitor; and the spring was found to have healing properties (Armstrong 1985, 112-13).

A decade later in Lourdes, France, fourteen-year-old Bernadette Soubirous saw a vision of a luminous girl emerging from a cloud of golden light. Bernadette saw and spoke with her on fifteen separate occasions, and during one of these the angelic being told Bernadette about a spring located in the rear of a small cave. That spring, as is well known, is still reported to produce miraculous cures (Young 1977, 116-17).

In many of the cases investigated by the Catholic Church, the heavenly visitor revealed to one or more children is a woman. Sometimes this celestial woman, radiating spiritual light, is identified as an angel, but more often she is believed to be the Virgin Mary. In 1871 two boys saw her in Pontmain, France (Armstrong 1985, 117) and

in the early twentieth century, five boys saw her in Beau-
raring, Belgium. In fact, since 1930 the Church has investigated almost fifty cases involving the appearances of this
"radiant woman" (Armstrong 1985, 118). But by far the
most famous of these occurred in 1917 when three children, ages six, eight, and nine, saw an angelic woman near
Fatima, Portugal. The children believed her to be the
Virgin Mary and, in the course of many visitations, she
predicted a series of coming events for the twentieth century. These were later called by the Church "the Fatima
Prophesies." At least one of the children, Jacinta, later developed other psychic faculties, including the psychic diagnosis of illnesses. The events surrounding the visions of
these children and the sensitivity involved have all since
been officially recognized and "sanctioned" by the Roman
Catholic Church (Armstrong 1985, 118).

Was the secret life of kids a commonly recognized aspect
of growing up in ages past? It is difficult to know for certain just how the ancients viewed children and how widely
recognized their psychic perceptions were. Some biblical
passages might indicate an ancient awareness of their abilities, but these are open to varying interpretations. The
Book of Psalms declares, "O Lord, our Lord...Thou
whose glory above the heaven is chanted by the mouths of
babes and infants..." (Psalms 8:1-2). Surely infants must
perceive some spiritual glories in order to be able to chant
them. But not even in the Catholic tradition is anything
written about a tendency for children to perceive more than
the normal physical, external world. Still there are hints in
the literature suggesting that the special faculties in children were not unknown. The Flemish "Everyman Plays"
contain references to unusual influences of children, and
many folk stories of the Middle Ages refer to children who
perceive fairies, elves, witches, or angels, and of children
who visit alternate realities or spiritual worlds. In the
Grimms brothers' fairy tale "Mother Holle," it is not a
middle-aged or elderly person who accidentally falls into
the magic world at the bottom of the well, but a young
girl. In the Swedish tale "The Old Troll of Big Moun-

tain," it is not a grown-up who perceives and befriends the old troll, but Olle, a boy of five (Olenius 1973, 114-21). Children often play prominent roles in stories about magic and other worlds. Hundreds of such examples could be given, not only from the folk tales of the European tradition but from the New World as well.

The witchcraft trials in Salem offer evidence that the Puritans may well have had a sense that children could perceive non-ordinary realities. During the witchcraft frenzy of 1692 in the Massachusetts Bay Colony, the testimony of several young girls who claimed to perceive visions of other worlds sent dozens of the colony's elders to the gallows. The issue here has nothing to do with the possible reality of witchcraft or the questionable psychic testimony of the girls. It has been persuasively argued that the adolescent and preadolescent girls involved were guilty of mass hysteria, or even that they completely fabricated their trances. The point is, however, that the entire community took their claims seriously, investigated, and were even in awe of the professed paranormal perceptions of the children. No one suggested that children could not have second sight; no one said they could not prophesy; no one said that children could not telepathically communicate with the supposed witches. Instead the children were eagerly and thoughtfully listened to.

The series of events started with Abigail and Elizabeth, ages eleven and nine, and their psychic experiments. During the long, cold winter of 1692, their servant Tituba, a black woman from Barbados, interested them in voodoo stories and spells. She taught the girls to read palms and to prophesy future events. In Chapter 10, I discuss how preadolescents can often open up psychically. In this case Elizabeth started to go into psychic trances, babbling incoherently. Then Abigail and other girls imitated the trances, and started having dramatic convulsions. Dr. Griggs, the town physician, announced that the devil was at work on these girls and asked them to name their tormentors. The first name of a "witch" was then given in trance, and the rest is history. The more attention the girls received, the more dramatic their psychic trances became, each one resulting in more "witches" being exposed.

One wonders if second sight, prophetic dreams, or other paranormal abilities were considered a normal aspect of childhood. Surely the Puritans must have had a precedent in their religious tradition for acceptance of such other-worldly perceptions of children. I personally believe several of the young girls had genuine paranormal experiences, but that their egotism took over and overshadowed their original psychic visions.

There is evidence that in rural America over 150 years later, the psychic abilities of children were still accepted in the folk tradition. In the 1860s, for example, a country doctor from Mineral Wells, Texas, delivered two babies to the Shrum family. Both infants, Jim and Belle, were born with the fetal membrane covering their faces. The doctor declared that they were born with "a veil over their eyes" and that this was a sure sign that they would be gifted with "second sight." True to the doctor's prophecy, both children grew up clairvoyant, particularly having the ability to see events far removed in space (often called "clairvoyance in space"). Their family accepted their paranormal gifts and even bragged about them (Clarke 1983, 90).

The medical establishment during the latter half of the nineteenth century seemed to have the need to recognize and even attempt to explain such cases of "second sight." It is possible that clairvoyance in children and other such abilities were more widely recognized in the scientific community than they are in the present day. Scientists of the past, however, thought of childhood visions as hallucinatory and arising from the children's rapid cerebral growth. Dr. S. H. Clarke summed up what was known about the secret life of kids in the 1870s:

> Many children, especially very young children, possess the power, when they have closed their eyes in the dark, of surrounding themselves, by a simple act of volition, with a panorama of odd sights (Clarke 1878, 212).

Dr. Clarke cited another medical tract, *Confessions* by De-Quincey:

> I know not whether my reader is aware that many children, perhaps most, have a power of painting as it were upon the darkness, all sorts of phantoms; in some that power is simply a mechanical affection of the eye, others have a voluntary or semi-voluntary power to dismiss or summon them; or, as a child once said to me when I questioned him on this matter, "I can tell them to go, and they go; but sometimes they come when I don't tell them to come" (Clarke 1878, 213).

Clarke called such visions "childhood pseudopsia" or false sight, and he had elaborate theories to explain how these visions arose in the childhood consciousness:

> It will be noticed that this form of pseudopsia which may be appropriately called the pseudopsia of childhood, is of two kinds, voluntary, and involuntary, and the latter predominates very largely over the former. The involuntary sort is...produced...by changes in the contents of the globe of the eye, or by automatic cerebro-visual action. The voluntary sort is, of course, independent of any mechanical disturbance of the eyeball, and results chiefly from changes in the cerebral circulation. Both show how easily the delicate nerve centres of children may be disturbed; and...both show that the brain can be made, without great difficulty, to put together the organic cell representatives of pictorial ideas.
>
> It is a matter of surprise that this phantom power of childhood has not excited more interest than it has done, among psychologists and physiologists. Its appearance in childhood, when the nerve centres are delicate, imperfectly developed, mobile and impressible; its disappearance in mature years, when nerve tissues are developed, harder, less mobile, and less impressible; and its reappearance at the very close of life, when, as dissolution approaches, the nerve centres are exceptionally disturbed, often producing visions of the dying; these phenomena are all curious, significant, and worthy of study (Clarke 1878, 215-16).

No matter how baseless is the idea of children's "mobile nerve centres," I am impressed that Dr. Clarke so clearly recognized over a hundred years ago the most common element of the secret life of kids—childhood clairvoyance. And his last paragraph still holds true today. Not only have the medical and psychological communities failed to study this "childhood pseudopsia" in any systematic way, but nearly all their members would no doubt contend that such a condition does not exist.

In the recent history of medicine and psychology, there is one other rather esoteric condition which is sometimes said to account for unusual perceptual patterns of children—childhood synesthesia. Psychologist Arthur Jersild writes that synesthesia is an intersensory experience wherein a "sensation from one sense modality has associated with it images from another modality" (Jersild 1968, 397). Theodore Sarbin, another psychologist, wrote that synesthesia can account for the frequent hallucinations that some children experience:

> Werner and others have written that perception in the young child is primarily syncretic. A stimulus in one sense modality is perceived as belonging to all sense modalities. As he matures, the child's perceptual processes become discrete and, from a practical point of view, more effective (Sarbin 1967, 367).

"Color hearing" is the most frequent form of synesthesia discovered in young children. It involves the perception of some imaginative configuration of color along with a normal, physically detectable sound. Jersild gives examples of this phenomena in children:

> In color hearing an individual reports, for example, that bass tones look blue and high soprano tones look pink. Or the synesthesia may take the form of colors associated with certain names, as when a child of six reports that Mildred, her friend, is blue and Margaret is yellow, the number "17" is pink, and the word "rush" is gray. Tones likewise may accompany words, according to the testimony of those who report this phenomenon (Jersild 1968, 397).

Dr. Theodore Kawoski discovered in 1938 that synesthesiacs tend to see similar patterns of light and color associated with specific sounds. When a certain piece of music is played, for instance, different children with synesthesia will see similar colors and shapes (Kawoski and Odbert 1938, 53).

In my view, the entire concept of synesthesia may merely be an elaborate and fanciful way for psychologists to claim to have understood some organic basis for a condition that actually involves childhood clairvoyance. One familiar with esoteric philosophy can easily understand how the aura of Mildred could be predominantly blue to a child's perception, whereas Margaret's might be mostly yellow. And currents of astral energy have been clairvoyantly seen to structure themselves naturally into specific patterns of color and shape when a certain piece of music is played (Hodson 1979). Such "music forms" would be clearly visible to psychic children and would be a regular part of their expanded perception.

In discussing the historical aspects of the psychic life of kids, one cannot neglect the field of parapsychological research. Ever since the birth of the British Society for Psychical Research in the late nineteenth century, there have been regular studies continuously in progress which concern the paranormal senses. With the advent of J.B. Rhine's work at Duke University, parapsychology has received gradually more serious attention from the established academic community, and even been recognized by the American Psychological Association. Numerous studies have been conducted concerning every one of the distinct psychic faculties I have found associated with children. However, I have not been able to locate any studies in this field earlier than the late 1950s which directly relate to children, and most of these involve the use of traditional "E.S.P." cards, which test telepathy, clairvoyance, and precognition (Van de Castle 1969, 84-103, and FitzHerbert 1961, 81-96).

After ten or twelve years of research, parapsychologists began to recognize that children often seem open to paranormal perceptions. In the last two decades, the evidence has accumulated. Samuel Young's book *Psychic Children* and *Is Your Child Psychic?* by Dr. Alex Tanous and Katherine Donnelly suggest a widespread interest in nonordinary childhood perceptions. Joseph Chilton Pearce, in *Magical Child*, has finally focused attention on the relationship of childhood psychism (which he calls "primary processes") to the normal developmental process. He also effectively relates these issues to contemporary educational trends. Some of his ideas are more fully outlined in Chapter 11.

In succeeding chapters as I examine the various psychic processes I have found among children, I relate them to academic research in parapsychology wherever possible. This research is helpful in providing objective and controlled data. But parapsychologists have not found any clues to the causes of such perceptions in children or the mechanism of their functioning. Nor are their findings well-known or widely accepted. My brother, a clinical psychologist at an eastern university, once told me that no matter how much data is accumulated in the study of E.S.P. or other paranormal phenomena, the vast majority of psychologists will never accept it. Such evidence does not fit their world view, which is essentially materialistic. I think it safe to say that the psychic world of children is today still very much a secret, and it needs to be explored.

5
Telepathy

Probably almost all children have some degree of telepathy, particularly in the form of mental and emotional communication between mother and child (Alter 1979). Of all the paranormal senses, telepathy in childhood has the widest range of variations. Many children show this sensitivity only around close family members and when the atmosphere is charged with particularly strong emotions (love, anticipation, fear, anxiety). Others communicate telepathically with only one particular family member. On the other extreme, many children are so open to the thoughts and feelings of other people that it is almost painful for them to be around others at all. An awareness of this extreme sensitivity in some children is important for those who work with children, and is discussed later.

A close friend of mine, now a psychologist, shared with me her childhood experiences of telepathy and its pervasive effect on her life. Although her experiences are not as fresh as those reported by children, her adult perspective and clear memory enable her to articulate the emotional impact of a childhood of extreme telepathic openness more fully than could a child.

Linda, as I shall call her, can remember the beginnings of these experiences as a very young infant, and these perceptions continued to be an important part of her consciousness through the high school years. (Recent research suggests that it is not unusual to have memories from a very early age, even of birth.) Linda did not exactly read people's minds, but was aware of impulses which seemed to her to be a cross between thoughts and feelings. No words came, yet there was a clarity of meaning behind the received impulses that was more specific than a simple emotional response. As Linda expressed it, she was receptive to "thought-feeling."

Linda said this hypersensitivity was like having her skin peeled off, so that she intensely felt every passing breeze or change in temperature, and extreme or sudden changes in such conditions actually hurt her. Of course these "breezes" were emotional and mental ones. Linda's early life was often painful, especially many of her relationships with other people. Her communication was of a dual nature: she saw how people acted and heard what they said, but at the same time was completely aware of their inner thoughts and feelings. One might think that this telepathic awareness would be interesting and helpful for communication. But for Linda it was a nightmare in which interactions with people became a distressing and confusing jumble of conflicting impressions, resulting in a breakdown of communication and extreme sensory overload. The reason for this, as Linda discovered repeatedly, was that what people say and do often does not match what they actually think and feel.

Her earliest memory was the frightening impression that her own mother, though outwardly nurturing and loving, inwardly rejected Linda and in fact felt antipathy toward her. Linda's mother was a "proper" English lady married to a red-headed, hot-tempered Irishman. After the birth of their first and well-loved daughter, she had hoped her second child would be an adorable blond and blue-eyed "English" boy. Instead, Linda turned out to be a replica of her father in female form—fiery, red-headed, Irish in every way—and the wrong sex! Linda's mother seemed never to get over her bitter disappointment. Every time she said something nice to Linda and reached out to pick her up, Linda shrank because she "felt" her mother's real feelings were of repulsion. This telepathic information was clearer to Linda than any words.

Linda grew up with the distressing lesson that people could not be trusted. They lied. They would say one thing while thinking something completely different.

Fortunately for her, there was one person in her life Linda could trust—her father. Outwardly, he appeared gruff and harsh. He was quick to lose his temper and prone to yell and swear at slight provocation. However, Linda's reality was less this outer view of him and more his inner world of thoughts and feelings. She perceived him as radiating kindness and love. She would be with him whenever she could. He was someone she could fully trust in a harsh world.

However, the harshness of her environment only applied to its human aspects. The world of nature was a source of joy and peace. She tuned out her anxieties, stress, resentments, and fears in social situations by escaping alone to the hills surrounding her home, or to her mother's garden. She was happy around animals, especially her pet cat. In the woods she felt the presence of wild animals and often would walk directly to a tree, for instance, in which a bobcat was hiding. But it was the plant kingdom that gave her the most joy. She seemed to understand plants and could sense a different "message" from each type of flower. Many carefree hours were spent talking to the flowers in her mother's garden.

Hers was a lonely life in many ways. Apart from the animals and flowers, she had few childhood friends. She frequently felt the anger, fear, jealousy, and envy of other children. But with children the dichotomy between thought and action was not as pronounced as with adults. Linda's experience of this more "instinctive, primitive, and amoral" consciousness of children seemed more honest. I should add, parenthetically, that her experience of negativity does not give a balanced picture of the many, positive, pleasant thoughts of these persons. It was just that for Linda the negative side seemed to hold the most power and to affect her most clearly.

She did find one playmate who was "clear." He was slightly retarded, and that fact likely explains why Linda did not feel bombarded by strong thought energy around him. He became a special and safe friend to her.

However, starting school did not bring new friends. In fact, "school was a terrible nightmare" for Linda. Reading the minds of others did not help her in her school work. Her most vivid memories of assignments and tests were of picking up the confusion of other students, and not being able to concentrate or clearly sift out her own knowledge from the "static" she experienced from all directions.

I asked Linda whether she ever found anyone to discuss her difficulties with during these early years. She said that she felt these things just weren't discussed, so she never mentioned her experiences to any adult or child. Throughout her childhood, Linda assumed everybody was as sensitive as she. It baffled her that others seemed to cope with large social groups so effortlessly, when to her the negativity of other people was literally painful. It was not until her high school years that Linda finally learned that other people relied almost exclusively on words for communication. She had always felt that words were unreliable.

Other than learning not to trust people, Linda recalls two other problems in her childhood that stemmed from her uncontrollable telepathic abilities. The first was that she practically never was sure what feelings and thoughts were hers and what came from other people. This is why being alone in the woods was so therapeutic for her. Only in seclusion could she relax and feel comfortable with her own consciousness. In public it was as if the boundary between her own subjective life and the invisible psychic world around her was completely blurred.

Her other difficulty concerned learning the cultural mores and rules of social interaction that seemed so clear to everyone else. Children learn what is appropriate to say and do in public and what is forbidden. Many of these "rules" are never articulated; children learn them by watching the way grown-ups interact socially. With Linda it was difficult to learn how to act "correctly" or "properly" around others because in her world *nobody* acted "correctly." If she observed someone being polite or sweet, very often that person's subjective impulses were not nearly so polite. And Linda was never sure which behavior was known and observed by others.

Linda's story is a clear example of how the functioning of psychic "powers" during childhood can be far from happy or helpful. Some parapsychologists view telepathy as the next step in human communication in the evolution of mankind (Zuisne and Jones 1982, 392). If this is so, let us hope that this telepathy of the future would not render one as helpless socially as it did Linda.

Most cases of telepathy I have evaluated are what might be called "selective telepathy," unlike Linda's "global" sensitivity. Selective telepathy in children, though principally an uncontrolled faculty, does not render the child receptive to the thoughts and feelings of just anyone, but open only to people with whom the child already has a close emotional bond. This bond might be with a school chum, a cousin, a sibling. I recently had a visit from my fifty-eight-year-old cousin, who told me that when she was a child she could read the mind of her younger brother. The two of them would help each other on school exams and communicate secret messages while in the presence of grown-ups.

The most common type of selective telepathy, however, is parent-child telepathy, which has formed the basis for numerous parapsychological studies (e.g. Shrager 1978; Ehrenwald 1971; Mackenzie 1969). For the present purposes, rather than attempt to outline such studies, I offer a few examples of which I have first-hand knowledge.

Many years ago I was called in as a consultant on a case involving Stephen, a highly psychic five-year-old boy who lived in San Francisco. The psychiatrist handling the case had heard of my work and wondered if I would be interested in investigating this child. I was delighted because Stephen turned out to be very unusual and actually had the use of four of the psychic senses. (Therefore, I return to his story several times in later chapters.) For now I shall only introduce him and discuss the frequent incidences of parent-child telepathy in his family.

Stephen lived with his mother and father in a modest apartment in a not-so-good neighborhood. He had been psychic since earliest infancy and was frequently the center of bizarre occurrences, many involving psychokinesis. Although his parents accepted the existence of the psychic world, they nevertheless were distressed and frightened by events that happened around their little boy.

They were concerned primarily about the approach of Stephen's first year at school. They anticipated an awkward school adjustment, and were prepared to hear accounts of odd incidents or troublesome behavior from Stephen's new kindergarten teacher. They felt guilty for allowing such a psychically sensitive child to go "out into the real world" all alone, without the help and advice of someone who understood his "problem." The psychiatrist and I were called in to get to know Stephen and to become familiar with his paranormal gifts, so that if problems did develop with the school, we could act as mediators and suggest ways of handling Stephen. Of course we could never tell school authorities about the real situation with this child and, as it turned out, we never had to. Stephen actually did quite well at school.

One of Stephen's more developed abilities was selective telepathy: parent-child telepathy. He often acted upon or verbalized his mother's or father's unspoken thoughts. For instance, when his mother fixed his lunch, she might be thinking, "In a minute I must go outside and call Stephen." Suddenly the door would burst open and Stephen would race in. "Did you call me just now?" he would ask.

His father reported that Stephen always seemd to know where the father went. No matter what friend he visited or what store he stopped at, Stephen seemed to be aware of it. This psychic "tracer beam" actually annoyed the father, for he felt he never had any privacy. Keeping secrets about birthday or Christmas presents, for instance, was out of the question. A typical example happened when the father decided quite spontaneously to have a beer and a chat with his buddy Joe one day after work. No sooner had Joe poured the beer than the telephone rang. It was Stephen. An astonished father answered the phone and asked how Stephen knew where he was and how in the world he had found Joe's phone number. Stephen, ignoring the questions, simply said, "Daddy, I knew you were there and I just wanted to say hi."

Telepathy between a mother and a very young child is probably so common that most mothers do not even notice it. In a later chapter the notion is presented that infants actually are etherically connected to their mothers in the early years. In a sense, the symbiotic relationship in the womb is maintained psychically (but to a lesser extent) after birth. One young mother, who has a Master's degree in genetics, reported to me that after her son Ron was born, if anyone touched her—even in a friendly and loving way—the baby would scream. During the entire first year of Ron's life, the mother would wake up at various times during the night only to hear Ron start crying maybe one minute later.

She also felt that the baby seemed unusually aware of her needs. On nights when she particularly needed to catch up on sleep, Ron uncharacteristically would sleep undisturbed the entire night. And once when he was one year old, the mother came down with a severe case of flu. She dragged through her household chores until she couldn't continue. Then, again totally unexpectedly, Ron went to sleep for an unheard-of four hours. In this way the mother was able to get a much needed nap—Ron's gift to her.

As Ron grew older, he would constantly voice his mother's unspoken thoughts. He also was intensely aware of any disturbing or unusual emotional states she might be experiencing, whether or not he was physically near her.

A psychiatrist, Berthold Eric Schwarz, wrote a book on the subject of parent-child telepathy which is a fascinating, though somewhat repetitive, account of incidents of telepathy within the doctor's own family (Schwarz 1971). More interesting, I believe, than the 505 telepathic episodes is

Dr. Schwarz's analysis of situations and circumstances that seemed to encourage or hinder telepathic communication within his family.

For one thing, Schwarz found that telepathy with his children, Lisa and Eric, seemed most active when the children were at the ages of three and eight, and least active at the ages of four and six and a half. This indicates that a developmental factor may have been operating. Weather also seemed to play some sort of role, since Schwarz noticed that most of the paranormal incidents he recorded occurred on bright, crisp, and cheerful days, though there also was enhanced telepathy during sudden and drastic changes in weather conditions.

The crucial factors that encouraged or discouraged psychic communication seemed to be emotional. In learning situations, for instance, when Lisa and Eric had an intense desire to emulate their parents, incidents of telepathy increased. Also during times of family excitement or enthusiasm when family members were in particular rapport, there was increased telepathic communication. The Christmas season offered a perfect setting. However, if there was no particular family excitement, telepathy drastically decreased. Family emotions did not have to be positive to encourage telepathy; fear, sorrow, or anger also were effective stimulants. As Dr. Schwarz stated, "Telepathy is bipolar; it is propelled by love and hate, happiness and sorrow" (Schwarz 1971, 57). So it seems that generally a strong emotional need to communicate and an open or receptive frame of mind encourage telepathy.

These examples will give a flavor of this book:

> December 20, 1960, Tuesday 3:30 P.M. Ardis [Dr. Schwarz's wife], while washing dishes, was thinking about some candles she needed for a Christmas centerpiece when Eric came up to her with a birthday candle.

> August 1, 1963, Thursday, 8:20 P.M. I took Eric into the sitting room to tell him I was buying Uncle Floyd's old air conditioner. Before I could say a word about this surprise, he said, "I want a new air conditioner" (Schwarz 1971, 99).

One of the negative effects of telepathy is the passing on of parental fears and anxieties to children. One particularly frightening occurrence is the telepathic nightmare. Linda, previously discussed, provides an example.

Although her childhood psychism largely faded as she approached adulthood, Linda continues to have close psychic rapport with her three children. Although most of the parent-child telepathy in her family involved common incidents such as the children verbalizing or acting out Linda's thoughts, one dramatic episode involved a telepathic nightmare. Linda's sons were two and seven, and she was six months pregnant at the time. She had a frightening dream in which she was a young blond man, probably Dutch, fighting in what appeared to be World War I. In the dream she was lying in a trench as a fighter plane flew overhead firing bullets at her. She was hit several times and died in that trench. Linda awoke in a cold sweat. She was shocked to hear her two-year-old son screaming from his bedroom upstairs, "Airplane, airplane!!" The next day, as Linda was walking her seven year old to the school bus stop, he volunteered that he had a dream the previous night about airplanes. "I was flying in this plane, and I was shooting a machine gun." Beyond being a telepathic dream, of course, this incident might well relate to past life experiences involving this family.

Dr. Schwarz believes this type of non-ordinary communication may play an important role in family dynamics. Indeed, it may even be one way parents pass on information, values, and cautions to their children. Family therapist Bruce Taub-Bynum developed the concept of the "family unconscious," a psychic field that unites members of a family (Taub-Bynum 1984). He cites many instances of unspoken communication in which children know their parents' "secrets," and of siblings and parents picking up attitudes and emotional states from one another. Besides being the most common type of psychic ability in children, parent-child telepathy may also influence children more than we realize.

6
Clairvoyance

There was a time when meadow, grove
   and stream,
The earth and every common sight,
   To me did seem,
Apparelled in celestial light,
The glory and the freshness of a dream;
It is not now as it hath been of yore:—
   Turn wheresoe'er I may,
   By night or day,
The things which I have seen
   I now see no more.
> William Wordsworth
> "Ode: Intimations of Immortality"

Wordsworth certainly was not alone in looking back on his childhood and recalling visions of a world "apparelled in celestial light." Research shows that many children catch glimpses of such a world—seemingly normal healthy children from average homes, who live in an environment intertwined with the invisible realms, so that a great many of their visual perceptions are not shared by the adults around them. These children, like the heroes in Irish fairy tales, continually shift awareness between the solid earth and the unseen realm of Faerie. The wondrous images they bring with them into everyday life profoundly affect their thoughts and behavior. This chapter focuses on children who utilize the fifth psychic sense—clairvoyance.

Such a study, of course, holds particular personal interest, since for me it was clairvoyant children who unlocked the door to the secret world of psychic faculties in childhood. The widespread existence of this fifth sense is evident in the fact that I was so easily able to locate dozens of children to participate in my Master's degree project. I believe that clairvoyance in childhood is almost as commonplace as telepathy. Furthermore, in some ways these two senses can be categorized together. I have been told that clairvoyance and telepathy are the most common of the paranormal senses because they are the most easily "brought through" into physical awareness. In other words, it is possible with little effort for these two astral senses to find their way into physical expression.

According to this notion, the physical brain and nervous system play more of a role in reading the minds of others or in seeing auras than they would in, say, psychokinetic ability. Joseph Chilton Pearce has suggested that a chemical molecule called melanin may be responsible for translating physical and psychic sense data into visual images (Pearce 1985, 10-11). Pearce believes that this molecule, which is found in heavy concentrations in the pineal gland in the brain, may be the link between mind and matter. Whether or not melanin is the biochemical component which helps to transmit telepathic or clairvoyant visual images to the brain, it may well be within the reach of scientists to isolate such a chemical factor.

To relate all the data on clairvoyant children that I have collected over the past fifteen years would take an entire volume in itself. I cannot discuss detailed case histories as in the last chapter. Instead, the discussion is organized according to the types of images the children see and the various conditions necessary for such experiences to occur.

There are three basic types of visions these children perceive. First, they commonly see the "auras" of persons and of other living beings. The aura is either the astral or the etheric vehicle that appears to radiate out from the physical body. The astral and etheric bodies are, of course, organizations of subtle matter which underlie and completely interpenetrate the dense physical body. Although the aura seems to be most clearly observable outside the dimensions of the body, it actually permeates the entire physical form. Children who see the aura describe it as colors which seem to emanate from various parts of the body.

The second type of vision frequently described by children involves organizations of light and color that seem to have little connection with living creatures. These visions fall under the category of "thought forms." Thought forms, according to many accounts (e.g. Leadbeater and Besant 1969 [1925]) are consolidations of superphysical energy generated by thought processes that take on form and color in astral and mental matter. These forms can last from a few minutes to a few months or even years, depending on the intensity of mental force that created them (Jinarajadasa 1967, 138). Clairvoyant children describe myriad colored shapes floating in the space around them. These I refer to as thought forms.

The third type of vision clairvoyant children report needs such a lengthy and detailed discussion that an entire chapter must be devoted to it. I have often found children who report seeing various types of non-physical beings, human and nonhuman. These might be different kinds of animals, deceased relatives, fairies, elves, gnomes, angels, or simply luminescent or transparent human beings ranging from children to elderly adults. Also, there is the invisible playmate. In the next chapter I distinguish true invisible playmates from imaginary companions, and also share accounts of children who see other types of entities as well.

The discussion of children who see auras might as well begin with five-year-old Stephen from San Francisco, who has already been introduced. Stephen not only had an intimate telepathic bond with both parents, but also had a very stable and dependable use of the fifth sense. He saw people's "colors" nearly all the time. This was such a natural part of his perceptual world that he rarely paid much attention to it. When I visited him, for instance, he did not mention seeing my aura until I lit up my pipe. After I took a few puffs, Stephen came over to me, looking intently around my body, and said, "Oh, you shouldn't do that [smoke]. It changes the white light around your body to blue, brown, and black."

Stephen, as so many sensitive children, did not realize that others could not see colors around people. His mother related the incident that helped him understand for the first time that he was the only one in his family who saw such things. One day he was describing the pretty colors in his mother's aura, as he often did, almost in the spirit of a game. Then he turned to his baby brother and sister and described their colors. After a while he innocently turned to his mother and said, "Now you tell me what my colors look like." His mom gently explained that she could not see people's colors.

My findings indicate that Stephen's perception of auras is the exception rather than the rule, for most children whom I call "clairvoyant" see auras only intermittently on

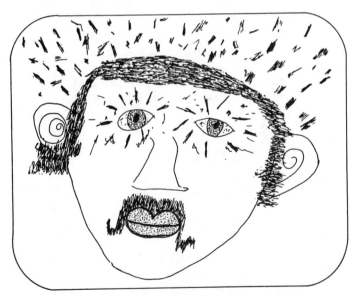

Fig. 1. Eight-year-old Wendy could see auras only when a person was experiencing intense emotion. "This is my teacher. I see his colors only when he gets upset."

special occasions, and the conditions under which their clairvoyance operates is totally beyond their conscious control. One child, for example, whose divorced father had just fallen in love with a woman, told his father, "You're beautiful today." "What do you mean?" the father asked. "Oh, you have pinky twinkles all over you." It seems as though any intensity of emotion—love, hate, anger, joy, enthusiasm—alters the pattern of radiant color in one's aura and makes the colors more vivid. Children may see the aura clearly under such circumstances, even though they normally would not perceive it.

Much of my data on clairvoyance in childhood was obtained by setting up circumstances in which subjects were able to see my aura. I learned from the two boys who had seen my aura while I was meditating that they rarely saw people's "colors"; in fact, they perceived this phenomenon only when an intense emotion was being expressed. But the fact that they were able to see my own aura repeatedly while I was meditating created a perfect, if unusual, methodology which allowed me to begin collecting data. Thus back in 1969 I inaugurated this unique research technique of meditating and recording children's reports of their perceptions into a tape recorder. This method continued to provide useful data throughout the following six years.

Here is a portion of the transcription of a tape in which Drew and Eric described my aura during meditation that first summer:

Eric: Right away we see, Drew and I see a red circle around his neck; it's real light.

Drew: It's starting to make a rainbow; now there's red and pink.

Eric: There's a little bit of blue on top of his eyes, right near his eyebrows.

Eric: And under there, there's orange. Now there's orange around his chest.

Eric: There's a light shade of yellow, right—it's like blended in—but it's the second color. [pause] The rest of the colors just filled in and I'll say a couple and Drew will say a couple. There's green and there's orange and then green again, and I never saw that before. And now there's a reddish purple or somethin' like that—it's the color of the chair he's sitting on. And then there's a light whitish-gray or somethin'.

Drew: And after that I see a purple and then, right now there's a little dot of blue [on the center of the chest].

Drew and Eric seemed to share many of these clairvoyant perceptions, yet occasionally their descriptions were not the same. Also, the boys often had to fish for the correct words to describe the colors they saw. I found this struggle for expression throughout my research. It seems that the superphysical colors clairvoyant children see are not quite the ordinary shades which are associated with the normal "worldly" labels such as "red," "yellow," or "blue."

When I continued my research in a second-grade classroom in California, this same meditation technique offered consistent data and a reliable and repeatable setting for opening up the clairvoyant faculties of children. Here are two more recorded segments of these sessions, both from 1973. The first is with seven-year-old Larry, and the second with Jessie.

Larry: There's a white light going out of his fingers ....I see different colored lights going out of his head ...green light right in the middle of his body....I see blue light going out of his ear.

Jessie [in a different session]: I see a green light around your nose, and a red light around your mouth, and orange around your head....There's some pink light around your ear....I see a color around your stomach now—red.... There's a real, real, real light color around your legs—real light green....There's a blue and green mixed-up color around your chest.

Since these clairvoyant perceptions are part of what I have called the "*secret* life of kids," it might well be asked how I managed to locate enough clairvoyant children to act as subjects in my research. Since these clairvoyant children did not come to me and announce that they were psychic, how did I identify them in the first place? Since I needed as many subjects as I could locate, I interviewed all the children I could. The interviews were quiet discussions held with individual children in a secluded place in the classroom. I had already learned that one must never bring up the subject of unusual perceptions in groups of children.

I was able to evolve an interviewing technique that I believe gave an accurate picture of which kids actually were clairvoyant. I had already noticed that the most common perceptions of these children seemed to be of lights around people's heads and hands. So I would take an unsuspecting child off into a corner and after a few minutes of chatting about unimportant things, I would suddenly ask, "By the way, have you ever seen colored lights around your mom's head?" I would say this in a completely off-hand and nonchalant way, and I could tell immediately if the child knew what I was talking about. The question was so blunt and unexpected that children would not try to find the teacher's "right" answer but would simply say, "No," or "Gee, do you see those colors, too?"

With the child's answer as my starting point, I would go on to more extended interviews. Without asking leading questions, I would try to get children to discuss various aspects of their clairvoyant ability. I allowed the conversation to go in whatever direction the child wanted to take it. Here is an excerpt from an interview in January, 1973, with a seven-year-old already introduced:

Larry: I see spirits and stuff and ghosts fly around, and things go in other people.

J.P.: Things go in other people? What do you mean?

Larry: Like white lights go around and they come out and they go in.

J.P.: Come out where?

Larry: Out of their bodies—in the back and in the front, around your stomach—different colors, like green and red and orange.

J.P.: Do you always see lights coming out of people?

Larry: Sometimes I see them and sometimes I don't.

J.P.: Do you see lights around me right now?

Larry: No.

J.P.: Who have you seen lights around?

Larry: My brothers and my grandma and other people. [I also] see lights around trees and dogs and stuff.

J.P.: Are the lights around trees and dogs and people all the same or are they different?

Larry: They're different. The tree is red and the dogs are orange.

J.P.: Do you think that your mom and dad see these same things, too?

Larry: No.

J.P.: Why not?

Larry: I don't know. I just think they don't.

J.P.: Have you ever seen any light coming out of your own body?

Larry: Yeah, white light...coming out of my belly button....It was like a rope that circled around me.

About this time I interviewed Jessie, another seven-year-old. She and Larry had never spoken to each other about their clairvoyant visions, and the interviews were conducted in strictest privacy.

Jessie: I've seen some ghosts around in my room and colors around people's heads.

J.P.: What colors?

Jessie: Red and blue. And I see white light coming out of people's fingers.

J.P.: Whose heads have you seen these colors around?

Jessie: My mom's and dad's [I also see] dancing flowers and I'll see lights around trees and all that.

J.P.: Say, these lights around trees—do you see them all the time or only at certain times?

Jessie: I see them all the time.

J.P.: You mean you could look out a window now at a tree and you could see color around it?

Jessie: Yeah.

J.P.: O.K., get up and look out that window right now and tell me what you see.

Jessie: Around that big tree over there [indicating a tree completely bare of leaves], there's a big, big green circle around the tree—around where the leaves fall off.

J.P.: What about the trunk, the bottom part of the tree.

Do you see anything there?

Jessie: Uh, huh, a red light.

J.P.: What about the colors around people? Do you see them all the time?

Jessie: Yeah.

J.P.: Do you see colors around me right now?

Jessie: Yeah, green and red around your head, mixed together.

Quinton, a student in a third grade class of mine, had the annoying habit of describing the changing colors and hues of my aura whenever I was upset with the class or when I was frantically trying to maintain classroom order. At such times, my aura didn't seem to reflect the spiritual qualities I imagined I was trying to cultivate in life. He would catch me just after I had scolded someone for an infraction of classroom rules, and would tell me about the red and gray shades that had infused my aura. Or he would tell me about the nasty little lightning bolts that hovered around my eyes when I had to break up a classroom fight or argument. I did have a rough class that year, but I did not appreciate Quinton reminding me of the effect the class seemed to have on me.

When eventually I got around to questioning Quinton about his clairvoyance, during a relaxing silent reading period, he was able to tell me about the pleasant orange and blue hues around my head. It seemed Quinton's clairvoyance had developed following an accident with his bicycle in which he had struck his head and was briefly unconscious. Later he started to see lights and colors around people's bodies. I transferred to another school the following year, so I never found out how Quinton's clairvoyance progressed.

I conducted interviews about paranormal perceptions with my students for a number of years. The children loved being able to share their experiences with an adult. For most of them, I was the first grown-up who was sympathetic to their clairvoyance. Many started to improve, even to excel, in their academic growth as their bond with me deepened. As a result, their parents greatly appreciated my efforts as a teacher.

The similarities of children's descriptions were compelling and significant to my advisors at the university. For example, in the interviews cited, both Larry and Jessie began by telling me they saw ghosts. (I explore what they meant by this in the next chapter.) Also both reported seeing red light around the trunks of trees. That is intriguing. Who would think of seeing red, of all colors, around trees? Yet this was the independent observation of each child.

Other reports were equally intriguing. Stacy, for instance, told me that she saw red torpedo-like projectiles come out of a dog's mouth when he barked. For this reason she was a little fearful of dogs. Stacy also told me that the "lights" she saw around children were more beautiful than those she saw around grown-ups. "Grown-ups usually have dark colors, like brown and black and orange and red around them. Kids' colors are prettier. They are lighter, with purple, pink, green, and yellow."

Few of these sensitive children are as consistently clairvoyant as Jessie, Larry, and Stacy. They see auras and colored images only under specific conditions, and the conditions vary from child to child. Several children have told me that they occasionally saw red, purple, and orange "sparks" or flashes of light coming out of my eyes, forehead, and crown when I was upset or excited. Music also precipitated clairvoyance. One time my second-grade class was singing with a visiting musician. After he led the children in a "New Age" song with the lyrics "Live in love, live in joy," two or three children came to me and said they had seen greenish-yellow light shimmering around the singer's head. One of these kids said it looked like yellow smoke rising from the top of his head. These particular children were not ones who regularly had such visions.

Illness, I believe, can also render the veil between the physical and astral planes thinner and give rise to clairvoyant perception (or other types of psychic response). Recently I visited an eight-year-old boy who was in bed with the flu. Late the previous night, he reported, "I was in bed and mom came in and I saw rainbow colors around her head. It had circles of color like the rainbow, but they

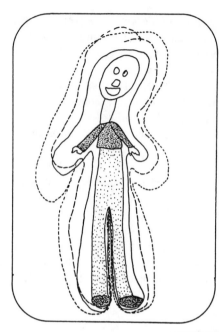

Fig. 2. An aura as seen by six-year-old Joel. "The red, blue, and green colors should be coming out of the body, but I couldn't draw it that way."

Fig. 3. Stacy's vision of a child's aura. "Kids' colors are a lot more pretty than grownups' colors."

weren't in order like the rainbow.'' That same night he saw ''swirling colors'' around his father's head as well. He had never before seen such a phenomenon and had no idea what it meant. When I asked if he had mentioned the vision to his parents, he replied, ''I didn't ask my mom about it because I wanted to keep it a secret.''

Not all these secret visions of swirling colors relate to the energy vortex around human beings. And unlike the rainbow seen by the sick boy, the meaning and significance of some nonordinary phenomena are well understood by the children. One particularly striking incident that illustrates this occurred on a field trip to the local police department with a second-grade class. We stopped at a little cubicle that served as a ''holding'' cell for prisoners waiting to be booked. The children were permitted to walk inside the cell four or five at a time. Stacy, whom I

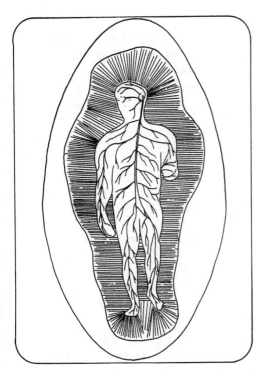

Fig. 4. The etheric double (pale violet-gray) as seen by the clairvoyant C. W. Leadbeater. (C. W. Leadbeater, *Man, Visible and Invisible*, Plate XXIV)

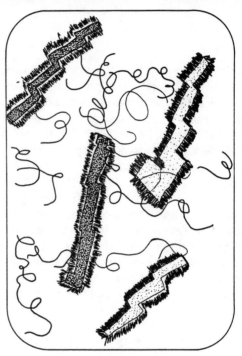

Fig. 5. Stacy's drawing of the black and
red lightning bolts seen in a jail cell.
"They were real BAD!"

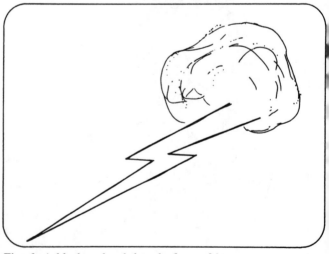

Fig. 6. A black and red thought form of intense rage, as seen
by C. W. Leadbeater (Annie Besant, C. W. Leadbeater,
Thought Forms, Plate 43)

already knew to be clairvoyant, stepped inside for a moment, then came running out, looking distraught. She rushed over to my side and whispered, "Do you want to know what I saw inside that room?" "Not here," I whispered. "Wait till we get back to school and you can draw a picture of it for me." Later she drew a picture of dark, ominous, black and red lightning-bolt configurations that she said were floating all over the inside of that little cell. Yet, she reported, they did not come into the adjoining rooms at all. She said she could not stay inside the cell because she didn't want those things swarming around her head. "They were bad!" she concluded.

In relating this story in seminars over the years, I have always suggested that these shapes and formations were the accumulated and continually reinforced thought forms of anger, hatred, resentment, and fear left over the years by inmates of that cell. In fact, such a living psychic residue is probably a part of the environment in all jails and prisons, and one wonders how rehabilitation of prisoners is possible in such an atmosphere. This incident also suggested to me that there are places not appropriate to take children. Even if they are not actually clairvoyant, children are emotionally sensitive and need to be protected from unpleasant environments.

Probably the perception most widely reported by clairvoyant children is of colors and shapes and forms floating in the air. It is not clear whether these are thought forms or something else. Most often these shapes are not as distinct as the lightning bolts seen by Stacy. Some children see colored lines and squiggles, some see small geometric shapes like diamonds, squares, and triangles. Others see swirling clouds of colored dust, and still others see forms suggesting living, organic things—like Jessie's "dancing flowers." Sometimes these visions are frightening to the children, but more often they carry no particular emotional content. Some children tend to see such patterned shapes of color indoors and others see them more frequently outdoors; many see such things mostly at night, while others see them during the day.

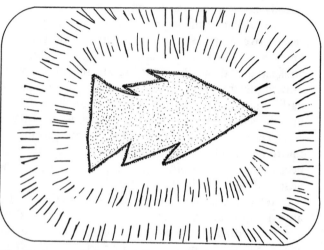

Fig. 7. A very distinct and directed bright yellow thought form that Stacy saw in the middle of the night. "I could see right through it. I had never seen anything outlined like this before."

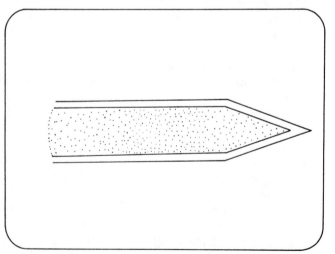

Fig. 8. A yellow and lavendar thought form of devotion to a high ideal, infused with intellect, as seen by C. W. Leadbeater (Annie Besant, C. W. Leadbeater, *Thought Forms*, Plate 43)

Seven-year-old Brynn reported the following:

> Sometimes I see tiny specks of color floating all around by my bedside. They go up in the air by my mom's room and everywhere. They're so tiny and they're mixed up with colors—blue, pink, and violet.

Stacy drew a picture of multicolored, curly lines and said:

> Things float around, things appear and disappear. When I get tired of seeing them, I just close my eyes. I always see these swirls and squiggles and bars-like. When my eyes are closed, I just see colors splattered around.

One wonders about the effect of closing her eyes, as clairvoyant visions reportedly are not seen with the physical eyes.

Another seven-year-old, Karsten, drew a similar picture of colored squiggles and geometric splotches of color, and he explained, "Second after second I see them—sometimes at night, sometimes in the morning, and millions of times in the classroom." Another time on the playground, one nine-year-old named Lorin came to me with an astonished look on his face. "What's wrong?" I asked. "I just saw yellow light darting around the sky in a huge circle," he reported. Later he drew a picture of a huge hoop of flashes of yellow light spinning in the sky. The hoop was taller than any of the surrounding trees.

Although most thought forms, or whatever they are, usually do not seem to be bothersome, difficulties can arise if kids happen to mention these visions to others. I received an interesting letter from a woman, now a student of theosophy, who remembers clearly the awkward experience of being a clairvoyant child.

> I saw everything as made of light/color/motion that is indescribably infinitesimal. Thousands of these dancing colors that are everywhere present could fit on the head of a pin. They would scare me as a child because they swirl in patterns. And, of course, no one else saw them, which caused a lot of trouble. I remember a specific time when alienation set in. I was in the sixth grade when I exclaimed to peers,

"Can't you see these colors moving everywhere?" And
someone said, "You're crazy!" And that was the last time
I talked about it.

Clairvoyant kids often worry that they are freaks or that
something is wrong with them. Children want nothing
more than to fit in with their peer group and be one of the
gang. Psychic abilities in all forms can seriously interfere
with the natural socialization processes of childhood. But I
will postpone this topic until a later chapter.

As with Stacy's vision of the jail cell, reports of clairvoyant phenomena often were instructive. I learned much
about the natural world and its unseen counterpart from listening to kids. Once, for instance, I was dabbling in the
study of the energetic effects of pyramid shapes. The children were finishing an art project one afternoon, and I was
busy fitting together small cardboard pieces of a model of
the Great Pyramid. After I had finished my four-inch pyramid, Stacy wandered by my desk and said, "Oh, that's
pretty." "What's pretty?" I asked. But she had already
walked away, intent on completing her artwork. I went
over to her desk and again asked her what she saw that
was pretty. "Oh," she replied distractedly, "there are
balls of blue light coming out of the top of that thing over
there [the pyramid], and the balls rise up all the way
through the ceiling."

After this unexpected revelation, my pyramid research
became more serious and purposeful. I decided to construct
a large-scale model pyramid, put it on stilts, and make a
little reading corner into which the children could crawl
and sit comfortably on pillows. Two or three children then
independently reported seeing globes of blue light rising
out of the apex of this pyramid, although now the globes
were far larger—approximately two and a half feet in di-
ameter. Brynn said that inside the pyramid were planes of
blue light jutting inward from each of the four corners and
meeting in the center of the structure in a laser-like beam.
"The reading temple," as it came to be called, was always
the most sought-after corner of the classroom.

The discussion of clairvoyant faculties in childhood would not be complete without examination of another aspect of the unseen world that at times can give rise to comforting feelings of joy and at other times to the most terrifying fears. This involves children's relationships to the myriad unseen beings of the inner realms, and is discussed in the next chapter.

7
Inhabitants of the Child's Secret World

She was still living completely in the Garden of Spirits; and though it seemed like an ordinary enough garden, Little Veronica, as I told you, saw it with her inner eyes—the eyes she had brought with her from heaven—and for such eyes as these every garden is a Garden of Spirits, and the whole world is an ocean of life and light. We all once saw the Earth in this way when we were children, but then came the great twilight; our clear vision was dimmed, and now we have forgotten everything. (Kyber 1972, 3)

For those of us whose "clear vision" has dimmed and been forgotten, the "ocean of life and light" clairvoyant children experience is fascinating. In the last chapter I began to paint a portrait of the images and visions that comprise these children's perception of the world around them. To fully understand psychic children, we must first understand their inner world—their garden of spirits. In later chapters I analyze the psychological effects that paranormal perceptions have on them. For now, let us simply journey once more into this "garden of spirits" and discover from the children themselves the wondrous beings who inhabit it.

The most delightful inhabitants of this secret world are the nature spirits. These are the fairies, gnomes, undines, and sylphs portrayed in the folk literature of virtually every country, and observed and corroborated by clairvoyant researchers. According to many, they are members of a parallel stream of evolution who live and work from the astral and etheric levels of consciousness (Jinarajadasa 1967, 25). These creatures are said to differ in size and degree of consciousness and in the role they play in nature's scheme. It is generally agreed, however, that they are connected with the four elemental essences of air, earth, fire, and water, and that their primary role is to assist in building up and maintaining physical forms of nature, such as minerals and plants (Powell 1973 [1927] 179).

The existence of these nature spirits was another of the surprising revelations I received during that first summer at camp. In addition to my aura, young Drew and Eric also reported seeing globes of yellow, red, and blue light drifting from tree to tree in the woods behind our bunkhouse. These globes were transparent, and within them the boys could delineate the outline of tiny figures. Drew related:

> Well, one day when I woke up in the morning, it was real damp and wet, and I saw around twenty-one fairies. I could see the insides [of the globes]. The stomach was fat and the rest of their bodies were real skinny. And one red one, it kept circling all the other fairies, and the blue one kept following it. And I didn't even know what they were doing. . . . The red one looked like a male and the other one looked like a female. It sorta looked like they were dancing, 'cause in the middle, the other ones were going around in circles, and those other two just kept going around them.

Drew himself was not surprised by these astral creatures because he had been seeing them all his life in the woods behind his house in northwest Philadelphia. At camp Drew, Eric, and I used to go on "fairy hunts" to see how many of these nature beings the kids could spot in the woods, and also see how close we could get to them.

The little woodland spirits seemed to be a common part of the life of clairvoyant kids. I rapidly accumulated more and more data on them. My second summer at camp, eight-year-old Kevin reported:

> I saw a fairy one night and it was outside my window. It was about an inch long and it looked green with golden

wings-like. . . . Some of the ones I saw at home are purple
and blue. . . . They fly away as soon as someone comes
toward them.

Another boy, Glen, age seven, whom I met years later
in a second-grade classroom, seemed on friendlier terms
with the fairies, though he admitted he had been scared of
them at age four when he first noticed them. He told me
that almost every night he saw eight or ten "flying lights"
which came into his bedroom and flitted around his indoor
plant:

> I see them just dancing around all over the place and
> around my plant. They're sorta working: the lights help the
> plant grow. [Sometimes] they land on my hand. I watch
> them until they leave. . . at midnight. They go through the
> window and around our backyard plants because we have a
> garden.

One child I met my second summer at camp gave me more
details about fairy life. These descriptions, however,
seemed almost comical coming from six-year-old Johnny, a
tiny kid who talked with a babyish lisp. But, "out of the
mouths of babes". . .

> Fairies are seen all the time. They can be seen night,
> day, and evening. They are white and blue and yellowish.
> They move and they fly; they have wings like butterflies
> only they don't look like them.
> They are shaped like girls only their shoes go up in tip-
> py-toes, and they won't be seen real early in the morning.
> They sometimes sleep with you at night and they protect
> you a lot. They have evil and good powers. The bad fairies
> are dressed in blue and yellow and the good fairies are
> blue and yellow and white. But the only thing about the
> bad fairies is they don't got wings.
> Fairies are seen by different people. People that can see
> good can see them—only certain people can't. Fairies are
> seen in different forests and a lot of them come out at
> night. Some of them you never see anymore.

A friend of mine, a woman about fifty-five who saw
such things as a child, confirmed that there certainly are
"evil fairies." Often as a child, she would wake up sud-

denly at night and see small, ugly, gnome-like creatures standing threateningly by her bedside. Although they frightened her terribly, they never touched her. Looking back on these oft-repeated incidents she now remembers that a confirmed alcoholic lived in their apartment building in the room directly above her bedroom. She wonders now whether the negative influences from his apartment might have attracted the unpleasant creatures she saw.

Gnomes, said to be the specie of nature spirit connected with the earth element, are generally not evil, even though "they don't got wings." One young boy who lived one hundred years ago saw such creatures. He was thoughtful enough to keep a detailed day-to-day diary of his clairvoyant experiences, and this document today makes fascinating reading. It is published in a volume called *The Boy Who Saw True* (Scott 1971 [1953]). This Victorian lad was persecuted by his family for "fibbing" and, like clairvoyant children today quickly learned to keep his secret life to himself. Here's his entry for June 23:

> There is a lovely old tree in Uncle John's garden, and to-day I sat a long time watching a funny old gnome who lives inside it, like one of the gnomes in my fairy-tale book. He has great long thin legs and wears a red cap, though the rest of him is like the color of the trunk of the tree. Sometimes he comes out of his tree and goes prancing about in the grass and looking so funny that I want to gig-gle, but was afraid I might make him offended. When I spoke about the old gnome to Basil, he poked fun at me, and said there were no such things, and I was a little ass to believe such fiddlesticks. I can't make it out, and wish I knew what ails everybody. (Scott 1971, 49)

This last line refers to the fact that this boy had not yet figured out that other people were not able to share the experiences of certain aspects of his perceptual world.

By far the most interesting data I collected on nature spirits was from a seven-year-old girl from New Mexico I met while on vacation in India. We were chatting about clairvoyant children when she suddenly became animated and blurted out, "Well, I can see those things, too." The resulting taped interview yielded some delightful data relating particularly to different species of nature spirits around the world. Here is one segment of that lengthy interview:

Sheri: I see fairies and elves in the woods.

J.P.: What do they look like?

Sheri: Well, which ones, the fairies or the elves?

J.P.: The fairies.

Sheri: The fairies in New Mexico look very pretty. They're dressed in white and have white wings and they mostly have brown hair. They're about four and a half inches tall.

J.P.: What do they do?

Sheri: They like to play games. And they're always near flowers and beautiful plants. That's where I mostly see them. But fairies are up in the high places [i.e. in trees, etc.] and elves are down in the low places—fairies can fly but elves can't.

J.P.: What kind of games do they play?

Sheri: They play like hide and go seek. They peep out and peep in and run across.

J.P.: Do they ever come near you?

Sheri: Well, today I saw an elf on a bush. . . .

J.P.: What colors are the elves that you see?

Sheri: Well in India, they have designed elves. They have pretty designs. But in New Mexico, they have plain colors—like green and red. In India their caps are different: they have several points with little gold balls on the end.

J.P.: What do you mean "they have designs"?

Sheri: On their shirts, their shirts are sort of light, light green with pretty designs on the front—like butterflies and stuff. They have gold shoes with little butterfly designs.

J.P.: Which are bigger, elves or fairies?

Sheri: Fairies. Elves are like only three inches tall. But the elves are fatter than the fairies. And the fairies are mostly girls.

J.P.: Can you see through them?

Sheri: Well, sometimes I can see through the fairies.

J.P.: What work do they do?

Sheri: I've seen them smell flowers. They usually just like to play, smell flowers and sleep. They never eat because they smell flowers.

J.P.: Do you see them more in the city or in the country?

Sheri: The country, because there's more pretty flowers, and they don't like traffic.

J.P.: Are there the same types all over New Mexico?

Sheri: All over New Mexico there are the same kind, because I've seen them in Los Alamos, Albuquerque, and Las Cruces and they're all the same kind.

J.P.: Have you seen any different kinds?

Sheri: Yes, in India; and in New York they're pretty different.

J.P.: What's different about them [in New York]?

Sheri: Well, they don't have any shoes and the elves have red, like, pants-outfits.

J.P.: You usually see fairies only near flowers. Do you think the flowers help them or they help the flowers, or both?

Sheri: They make the flowers prettier and nicer. They look at them and they sort of know the flowers and know what the flowers can do, and they ask the flowers to make them prettier. And by smelling them—the flowers like that—so they get prettier so more elves and fairies will smell them.

This young girl, now a college student, recently contacted me to ask if she could have a copy of this recorded interview. Although she hasn't seen fairies for many years, she has many fond memories of the time when her "eyes of heaven" were open. Sheri was one of the rare children who found some support in the outside world for her unusual experiences. Her mother was sympathetic to her reports, and Sheri also managed to locate one young friend who also was able to see these things. But even that kind of validation did not prevent the natural developmental forces of the human mind from clouding her vision as she matured.

In my experience, perception of such elemental nature

beings seems so common in childhood that one might
wonder if such spirits do not also become the invisible
playmates many children have in their early years. One
friend of mine, now a mother, told me a little gnome
visited her regularly when she was a child. As an only
child, she appreciated the companionship this little creature
offered her over a period of several years. At six when she
went off to school, however, she spoke to one of her new
school friends about her invisible playmate. The friend
said, "Oh, silly, that's not real!" A seed of doubt was
planted in her mind, and when she found her gnome waiting for her at the bus stop near her house, she immediately
asked him, "Are you real?" The gnome turned away and
was never seen again.

Such a story, though in no way proving or disproving
the objective psychic reality of this friendly gnome, certainly illustrates the existence of strong psychological
factors in such cases. Non-physical beings seem to be attracted to children because of the attention kids give them.
Five-year-old Darcy would frequently see a bird-like being
who was his friend and companion for several years. One
day Darcy's mother found him crying. "What's wrong?"
she asked. "My friend is dying," he sobbed. "He told me
he's dying because I'm forgetting to remember him."
Shortly after this incident, Darcy stopped seeing his friend
altogether.

Many psychologists have studied children with imaginary
companions over the years, and it has been documented
that one child in six has such a companion at some point
during his formative years (Hilgard 1970). Psychologists,
of course, believe that these playmates are simply psychological constructs projected by the child's mind into imagined objectivity, and that they serve to help the child cope
with stressful periods of growth and change (Pines 1978).
Some researchers assign such a playmate to normal,
healthy childhood growth (Jalango 1980) and others see it
as a symptom of abnormal and neurotic development
(Rucher 1981).

There is no doubt that an invisible playmate serves a

psychological function in the life of a growing child. However, this in no way precludes the notion that the playmate might also represent a paranormal perception. Food, after all, can serve a variety of psychological functions in the life of a human being; yet no one would question its objective and real existence. On the other hand, it would be unrealistic to assume all imaginary companions have an objective existence on the astral plane and that every child who perceives them is necessarily clairvoyant.

In my own research I have found it useful to delineate three types of childhood companions. The first is the true clairvoyant perception of some entity whose objective existence on the astral plane is brought into the child's awareness. This type I refer to as an "invisible playmate." The second variety is actually a psychological construct created in the child's mind to fulfill some deep-felt emotional need. This type I call an "imaginary companion." The third type is actually a mixture of the two. As seen in the previous chapter, the subjective mind can create objective organizations of energy on the inner spheres known as thought forms. In the process of creating these forms, the subjective mind and the objective world are no longer completely distinct and separate—they are blended and mixed from the perspective of the superphysical planes. A child, therefore, might clairvoyantly see some sort of actual form on the astral plane (maybe even a thought form) and, after projecting his own psychological energy onto that form, interpret it as an invisible playmate, even though the "playmate" may resemble the actual objective, non-physical form in only a rudimentary, almost incidental way.

An analogy of this process might occur while one is walking in the woods at night. Suddenly one sees a deer standing in a thicket a few yards away. But on closer inspection, the "deer" is actually seen to be nothing but an oddly shaped log. Thus, a true objective form has been inwardly transformed into an imaginary, subjective being. An alternative process which might occur is that a child creates a completely imaginary companion that, over time, is impregnated with so much attention and psychic energy that it actually objectifies itself into superphysical exist-ence. In this case, the imaginary companion is transformed into an invisible playmate.

This third variety of companion, though fascinating, is impossible to study or understand unless the researcher himself has a trained clairvoyant ability—something which I lack. But even for one without paranormal sensitivity, it is not difficult to distinguish the true invisible playmate from the imaginary companion. One indication that an in-visible playmate might be "real" is the experience of other supersensible perceptions by the child; if a child perceives an astral entity, he may also be able to perceive an aura—though this is by no means always the case. It is also possible to make an educated guess about a playmate's reality from the child's own description of what the play-mate looks like, its purpose in coming to the child, and what it discusses with the child when they are alone. Often, for instance, a child will get correct information about the future or about some unknown event from such a playmate. If the companion seems to have access to ac-curate knowledge completely beyond the child's ken, then it is very possible that one is dealing with a true invisible playmate.

In my view the best way to verify the objective existence of an imaginary playmate is to have a trained adult clair-voyant corroborate it. Once, for example, the spiritual healer Olga Worrall clearly saw a child's invisible compan-ion—in this case another child—standing next to her (Tan-ous and Donnelly 1979, 27). Another such case occurred to a woman I interviewed in San Francisco. This woman, Mrs. T., discovered her own clairvoyant abilities at age four when she attended her grandmother's funeral in a small town in the Midwest. She saw her grandmother sit up in the coffin, look around at everybody, and then fade completely away. Even more shocking was her realization that nobody else at the funeral saw this event. After that she kept quiet about her visions. Recently she was playing with her eighteen-month-old grandson when she clairvoy-antly saw several "spirits" (as she called them) enter the room. Her grandson quite obviously responded to their presence, looked at them, and proceeded to show them some of his toys. Several times he even giggled as these non-physical beings put their attention on him. Mrs. T., from across the room, observed the entire interaction.

Not all invisible playmates are of the human or near-human variety, however. One woman I met, Rose, had a pooka as a playmate from age four to age nine. A *pooka,* one might recall from Irish folklore, is an entity that appears in animal form, usually as a white horse or a huge black dog. Rose's pooka was a white Arabian horse. Rose was an only child and remembers her childhood as very happy and largely oriented around nature. In fact she met her invisible friend in the garden where they would take long walks together. Though offering Rose warmth, companionship, and even understanding, this pooka was definitely a horse. It did not talk, had no name, and liked to do things such as graze in the fields (although Rose never actually saw it eat). Rose knew this friend was invisible to her family, but it was absolutely real and solid to her. She even remembers petting its flank. Although she usually saw the horse when she was alone, her most vivid recollection of the pooka was on a family trip from Miami to New York City. Her friend followed the car the entire way, sometimes lagging behind, even occasionally out of sight, but usually galloping just behind the car.

Most often the playmates I would consider genuine paranormal phenomena appear not as pookas, but as ordinary-looking children, usually introducing themselves as being dead or angels. One such case came to my attention shortly before I began working on this chapter. Ten-year-old Mason reported that when he was eight a little boy began appearing to him both in school and at home. This boy, Simon, seemed to be younger than Mason, wore a baseball uniform with the numeral 24 on it and a baseball cap, and had freckles and braces. One day Simon entered a small room that served as a library in Mason's school. Mason, alone at the time, was startled by the strange new boy and asked, "Who are you?"

"My name is Simon," the child replied. "I got hit by a truck and died, and now I'm an angel."

"Why are you here?"

"I've come to help you."

Mason accepted Simon's existence and help, and their relationship lasted from October, 1984, to August, 1985. Simon helped Mason in making decisions. Simon did not talk much, and Mason confided that he thought Simon was shy. Mason told the other kids at school about Simon but "they didn't believe me." His mother offered sympathetic acceptance of Simon's presence, but certainly didn't consider his existence a paranormal phenomenon.

Another case involved four-year-old Jenny. I heard about Jenny's invisible playmate from her mother, who was quite worried about her daughter's psychological health. Apparently Jenny had met her invisible friend eight months earlier when she reported that she saw a small girl with dark eyes and hair, a little older than herself. The friend's name was Cece. Jenny had offered her mother quite a detailed description of Cece's appearance and then mentioned nothing more about her until eight months later when she claimed, "Cece is back." The mother was surprised to hear Jenny repeat the identical description of Cece in every detail after such a long interval.

In any event, I agreed to meet with Jenny and evaluate the situation. During the first meeting, I asked Jenny if Cece was present, and she nodded her head and pointed to a spot in the room. She then repeated the details of Cece's appearance and told me that Cece and her mother had died and that Cece was now an angel. I was curious to see if Cece might have access to information which Jenny did not. This would in my mind suggest the objective existence of this invisible little girl. I decided to run a series of experiments which, although not at all rigorous in their methodology, would nevertheless generate data concrete enough to include in my Master's thesis.

A year earlier (in 1972) I had met a fellow parapsychological researcher, Charles Thomas Cayce, now president of the Association for Research and Enlightenment (founded by his grandfather, Edgar Cayce). At that time, Dr. Cayce was investigating a girl with an invisible playmate named Phil. Phil would talk to this girl about God and about life after death and also seemed to have access to concrete information the girl could not possibly know. Dr. Cayce, in order to confirm this, set up a simple experiment in which a colleague would randomly open up a text book and place it face down on a table. Dr. Cayce, in a small room at the other end of the building, would ask the girl if Phil could identify the open page number of this book. Phil would invisibly trace a number on the girl's knee and when checked out, that number would always correspond to the number of the open page of the book down the hall.

Dr. Cayce's research suggested to me a methodology for my own investigation of Jenny's friend, Cece. I asked Jenny if she could send Cece to stand behind me and look over my shoulder. This was done. Then, with Jenny facing me across the room, I took out my driver's license and pointed to a tiny number one. "Ask Cece what I'm pointing to," I told Jenny.

"Cece told me you're pointing to the letter "I." " This response was interesting because it rules out the possibility that Jenny was merely using telepathy to read my thoughts. If telepathy had been used, she would have said "one" instead of "I." But as a visual perception, a "one" can look like an "I." Furthermore, her mother was completely astonished by this response, because, as she later stated, "Jenny hasn't learned any of her letters yet!"

I then asked Jenny to send Cece with me while I walked some distance to the far corner of the room. At that point I whispered almost inaudibly into the empty corner (away from Jenny's direction), "I love you." Returning to Jenny I said, "Now, ask Cece what I whispered over there."

"Cece said, 'I like you,' " Jenny replied. Although certainly this reply could have been a coincidence, it convinced me that my little experiments were successful. I told Jenny's mother that I felt there was ample reason to suspect that Cece might have an objective existence on a spiritual dimension and that Jenny should not be criticized for talking to Cece. Neither should the mother worry about her daughter. The advice seemed good, because the mother told me much later that Cece hung around for a few months and then Jenny never mentioned her again.

Over the years, I have heard two explanations for cases like those of Jenny and Mason. Once it was suggested to me that it is quite common for children who have died, and yet have not fully completed their transition to the astral plane, to want to contact living children who can see them. These earthly children help them temporarily keep their link with the security and familiarity of the physical plane. Perhaps these discarnate children can even etherically materialize themselves to a certain extent to facilitate their communications. These contacts generally are merely for companionship and often all the invisible playmate wants from the living child is someone to play with.

Another theory I have heard is that a "soul" awaiting incarnation on the astral plane will often have a companion in the same transitional state, and they will wait together for an opportunity to acquire a new body on earth. If one reincarnates, the other keeps contact as an invisible playmate to the friend, who is now a young child. It is neither possible nor necessary to find a single theory to explain the presence of invisible playmates. They no doubt can represent a wide range of astral beings with a wide variety of purposes.

Two children interviewed for my project had invisible playmates which differed substantially from the preceding examples. Larry often saw a friend who was "a midget" (in his words) and dressed all in white with white hair and white, eagle-like wings. Larry's friend would just come "to see how I am." They never spoke together or interacted, and Larry did not even know the other's name. Brynn had a playmate shaped like a "big, black dinosaur" that had sparkling lights of all shapes and colors swarming around it. This being would come and talk to her in the evenings when she was in bed.

Though all clairvoyant children may not converse with

invisible playmates, they all see many kinds of creatures—
some frightening, some benevolent—from time to time.
One twelve-year-old boy, David, contacted during my summer camp days, reported:

> One night a little while ago, I walked into the living room
> and sat down, and all of a sudden a whole mess of blue
> spirits came and they were all over our living room. You
> might think I'm crazy or making it up, but I'm not! A
> whole mess of blue spirits were all over our living room;
> and they were just around the lights and on the piano and
> on the stereo, and floating around the ceiling. And there
> was one real big one, and he was alone, like. And they
> were just all over the place—bright blue.

These "spirits" were about one foot tall, he later reported,
and were shaped rather like pictures he had seen of human
embryos, with large enlongated heads and bodies slightly
bent over.

The terms "spirits" and "ghosts" are frequently used
by the children to describe the phenomena they see. I interviewed Larry about this subject in January 1973:

J.P.: You mentioned that you see spirits. How do you
know they're spirits?

Larry: 'Cause they look like them.

J.P.: What do they look like?

Larry: They look like light—they have wings coming out
and stuff.

J.P.: What colors are they?

Larry: White.

J.P.: Can you see faces on them?

Larry: Yes. . . . They're mostly men.

J.P.: Do they fly?

Larry: Yeah.

J.P.: Do they scare you?

Larry: No,. . .because I was seeing things [since] I was
about three years old.

J.P.: You mean you've been seeing things for so long
they just don't bother you anymore?

Larry: Yeah.

Sometimes such beings can be a distraction. Mrs. K.

remembers her clairvoyant childhood quite well, including an incident when she was severely scolded by her teacher for not paying attention to an arithmetic lesson. In point of fact, she was merely distracted by the arrival of three or four tall, luminous figures who began to walk around the desks. Being fascinated by these figures and not at all realizing that she was the only one who saw them, Mrs. K. stared at them intently, and it was then that she received the scolding for not paying attention. Actually she *was* paying attention—only her attention was focused on the events of another world.

A similar visitation occurred in my own second grade classroom in 1978. Every morning the children would gather in a circle to sing songs and to recite poems. We were reciting a poem which began, "The sun with loving light makes bright for me each day," when Lorin said he saw an "angel" outlined in pink and yellow light with large wings and a yellow glow around its head descend through the ceiling into the center of our circle. It stayed until the "sun poem" was finished and then ascended through the roof by means of a shimmering "thread" attached to its back. In this case, of course, Lorin did not receive a scolding for being distracted. He did not, incidently, mention this event to anyone but me.

Another child, seven-year-old Mani, also reported seeing an angel on a field trip to Mt. Diablo, the highest spot in the San Francisco Bay area. Mani said she saw a thirty-foot winged being hovering over a grove of oak trees. It was bright red and she said it looked like a giant "fire fairy." I was particularly intrigued by this vision because local Indian legends tell of a huge red spirit that inhabits Mt. Diablo, and a Spanish padre was reported two hundred years ago to have seen a bright red figure whom he called "the devil"—hence the name "Mt. Diablo." Mani, however, had never heard these stories.

Most of the superphysical entities seen by clairvoyant children are seen, as with Mani's angel, only on special occasions. Clairvoyant children generally do not continuously see the inner realms opened up to them as a

Fig. 9. A entity seen by seven-year-old Stacy in the middle of the night. "It was floating in the air and it had fire up where the face should have been. It didn't talk to me, but it seemed like it was a wizard or something."

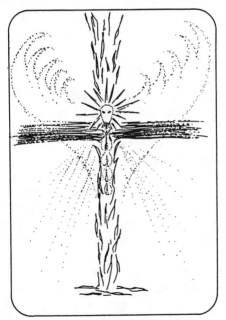

Fig. 10. A great nature spirit or deva overshadowing a harbor, seen by clairvoyant Geoffrey Hodson (*Clairvoyant Investigations*, Plate 8)

glorious celestial panorama, but catch glimpses of this unseen world mixed with their ordinary perceptions. It often takes intense emotion to make a person's aura vividly clear to one of these children, and in a similar way it takes a special set of circumstances to bring an astral being into clairvoyant focus for a child. Sometimes the key is that the entity has a definite purpose for communicating with the child.

One such incident involved a Japanese-American friend who described a paranormal experience she had when she was four. She was picking flowers under a neighbor's oak tree in Menlo Park, California, when suddenly she heard a voice saying, "Don't pick the flowers. There is an animal buried in the earth under that tree." Startled, this young girl looked up to see a tall, elderly gentleman standing by her "with a very kind, kind face." A moment later he vanished. The neighbor lady confirmed to her that her dog had been killed by a car and was buried under that oak tree.

An example of a distressing childhood vision came to my notice some fifteen years ago. I received a letter from a theosophist about a clairvoyant perception his son had at the age of two. It seems the family of three were living in Amsterdam at the time and had just rented a nice second floor apartment in a fairly congested neighborhood. The first night in the new place the toddler, Thomas, was sitting at the dinner table when he started screaming and crying uncontrollably and pointing to the entrance hall by the front door. The almost hysterical screaming continued for some time, always with Thomas's finger pointing to the same spot. Even more disturbing was the fact that this incident repeated itself twice more in as many days.

Finally Thomas's father discussed the matter with the landlord. As a theosophist, he was open to the possibility that a paranormal event or being was witnessed by his son. When he asked the landlord about the entrance hall of his apartment, the landlord's face clouded over, and he asked, "How did you know about that?" Reluctantly, the landlord revealed the tragic story of the previous tenants of that apartment, also a young family of three. Their boy was older than Thomas, almost five. One day the mother was on a shopping excursion and the father was baby sitting. The young boy insisted on going outside to ride his bike. The father gave into his pleadings, but did not immediately accompany him down to the busy street. In a few minutes, the father heard a crash and a scream from the street below. The boy had been hit by a car and killed. The father brought his dead son inside and was overwhelmed with grief and guilt. The feelings became so unbearably intense throughout the afternoon that the father finally decided not to face his wife at all in this incarnation; he hanged himself in the front hall.

When Thomas's father understood that he was dealing with an earthbound spirit, he put his theosophical training into effect and was able to communicate with the deceased man and help him to complete a full and natural transition into the astral world. When that work was accomplished, Thomas never again was frightened in that apartment.

Another incident possibly involving a similarly earthbound spirit was described by a student of mine, Yvonne, who was three and a half years old when her family went on holiday to Santa Barbara. They were visiting the old Spanish mission church there when Yvonne started screaming. She ran through the turnstyle at the rear of the mission, through the garden and the adjoining small chapel, and into the old mission cemetery. In the far corner of the old graveyard, she stopped at a small mausoleum surrounded by a wrought iron fence, and had climbed the gate as far as she could go when her parents finally caught up with her. She was clutching the gate and screaming, "Boy, boy, come back! I want to play with you!" When they pried her fingers loose from the gate, Yvonne ran to the stucco wall of the cemetery and pounded on the closed metal door, still screaming, "Boy, boy, come back!" Her mother turned her around and forcefully took her hand and began to walk back toward the parking lot. Yvonne's tense grip on her mother's hand loosened, and she shook her head as if coming out of a trance. From then on she acted normally.

When asked about the incident later on, however, Yvonne was able to describe in some detail a small, dark-haired boy she had been following. Yvonne's parents later learned that a boy of that description had recently fallen off a cliff near the ocean and died. The boy's body was not buried in the mission cemetery, nor was the site of the accident close to the mission. Nevertheless, it is not difficult to imagine a recently deceased person wanting to bask in the sacred atmosphere of the mission and its surrounding gardens. Yvonne never had another paranormal experience, but for her parents, that one incident was quite enough. Yvonne, incidentally, has Down's syndrome, a condition which may well have rendered her more open and sensitive to the influences of this little boy.

I cannot leave our discussion of apparitions and ghosts without once again returning to our old friend from San Francisco, Stephen. Stephen's two uncles, Vince and Jimmy, died within a couple of months of each other—one from an overdose of heroin, the other from suicide. Stephen's mother reported that for a good two months after these tragic deaths, Stephen periodically saw and spoke to his two uncles. The family would be sitting down for dinner and Stephen would blurt out, "Oh, Uncle Vince is here," and proceed to carry on a conversation with him. Stephen would pass on metaphysical information about after-death states to his parents—information his deceased uncles had given him. One day his mother asked about Vince and Jimmy, and Stephen replied, "Oh, they're gone now." That was the last time he mentioned them.

Long before the deaths of Vince and Jimmy, Stephen from time to time claimed to see invisible beings. Often these innocent remarks upset his mother. One time, for example, she was just returning from a shopping trip and was greeted at the door by Stephen. But he abruptly stepped back a few feet and asked, "Who are those two people you brought back home with you?" And, of course,

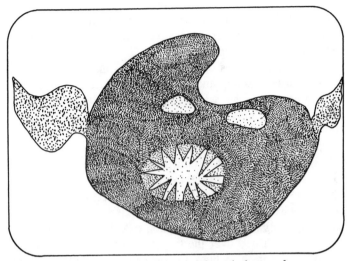

Fig. 11. A frightening bright red elemental

his mother could see only her little boy in the room. Another time his mother was startled when Stephen off-handedly remarked, "You know, we're not the only people who live in this house." He said there were several others living there and that they knew his family well. Of course, according to conventional systems of knowing, Stephen's family constituted the sole inhabitants of the house.

These experiences often have profound effects on the children involved. Unfortunately, the most memorable visions seem to be those which frighten the children. This is not surprising given that an entire genre of Hollywood films is based on the premise that astral demons and ghosts are threatening. Parents often comfort their children when they awaken at night frightened and screaming by telling them, "There's nothing here; you just had a bad dream. It's all in your imagination." I think it is far better for parents to say, "I'm here now, nothing can harm you," and perhaps take the child into bed with them. One never knows what a child might have seen. Even creatures of nightmares may not be imaginary, as there are many astral beings that can be frightening for a young child (Powell

1973 [1927]). To tell a child, "There's no monster here," might be completely contradictory to the child's perceptions and be very confusing.

Not all experiences of invisible beings are disturbing. Some can be calming and peaceful. My wife had an astral companion when she was a child. This particular companion visited her only in one special setting and only when JoAnn was in a certain unusual state of mind. At the age of seven or eight she spent considerable time in a small playhouse her father had built in their back yard. Sometimes she went there in the evening or stayed overnight in the little house. Her friend Laurie often accompanied her, and they would sometimes sit quietly in what might be called a meditative state. A feeling of calm and profound peace would flood over the two girls, and at some point a cylinder of pale blue light six inches long would appear in the middle of the playhouse. Although JoAnn cannot remember seeing an actual figure within the cylinder, she refers to it as her "Tinker Bell," and she knew that its consciousness was female. She said sometimes there were also little sparkles all about the playhouse. The tiny, fairy-like being did not speak, but JoAnn felt she did communicate with her on some deep level. JoAnn, who had been raised Catholic, also associated this entity with the Virgin Mary, although she never thought it actually was the Virgin Mary. After an interval, the cylinder of blue light simply vanished, leaving the girls in an atmosphere of complete and silent calm.

A meditative mood accompanied this clairvoyant perception. Since JoAnn never had any other paranormal experiences, it would seem that different states of consciousness can also have an effect on the secret life of kids.

We have found in most of these cases an ability to both see and hear entities. Clairvoyance is often accompanied by clairaudience. This does not seem surprising in the light of the theory that both these paranormal faculties are part of what I have termed "the fifth psychic sense." In my experience with children, these two generally seem to be linked together, although there are occasionally children who see auras, say, without ever hearing supersensible sounds.

I have also found children who hear unusual things, yet do not seem to be clairvoyant. One eight-year-old boy, for instance, claimed he audibly heard the voice of God "inside my head." Another example is a friend of mine, May, who regularly had clairaudient experiences as a child of four or five. She remembers visiting an aunt who was the town gossip and, incidently, a student of astrology. At the aunt's house May often could hear the voices of several old ladies talking and laughing. It seemed as though there were ten little old ladies having a tea party, yet May was alone in the isolated farmhouse with her mother and aunt. She is convinced, from her present spiritual perspective on life, that for some reason discarnate beings were attracted to her aunt's house and liked to "hang out" there.

By far the most vivid childhood recollections of this particular young woman, however, are of events from her previous lifetimes on earth. In the next chapter I consider instances of children who experience this second psychic sense, remembering past lives. I return to the subject of clairvoyant children later as I examine the cause of childhood psychism and the practical implications of these abilities in the daily lives of such children.

8
Memories and Visions from the Past

Our birth is but a sleep and a forgetting:
The soul that rises with us, our life's Star,
Hath had elsewhere its setting,
And cometh from afar:
Not in entire forgetfulness,
And not in utter nakedness,
But trailing clouds of glory do we come....
> Wordsworth, "Ode: Intimations
> of Immortality"

The above lines from Wordsworth's "Ode" beautifully introduce an entirely different aspect of childhood psychism. These "clouds of glory" which the poet claims all children trail behind them may crystallize a completely different type of vision from that discussed in the previous two chapters. Rather than colorful hidden realms in space, children who possess the second psychic sense catch glimpses of worlds within worlds, hidden from ordinary view behind the veil of time. The second sense is the ability to thumb through the pages of one's own life history, to inwardly explore one's past lives.

In my own life reincarnation has always been at the root of spiritual philosophy. It was the concept of reincarnation which first began to awaken inner spiritual panoramas for me at age eighteen, views that I had not discovered in my traditional Methodist upbringing. I remember many late night discussions with high school chums on the capricious nature of the Christian view of a single lifetime on earth which abruptly catapults one into an afterlife of eternal happiness or suffering. Surely a universe meticulously governed by laws as have been uncovered in the fields of astrophysics and chemistry could not be sustained by such an illogical cosmic policy. The turning point in my own quest was when I attended a lecture by the well-known theosophist, Geoffrey Hodson. I shall always carry with me a particular statement by Hodson: "Without reincarnation, life is a hopeless riddle."

Children almost never share the feeling that life is a hopeless riddle. Elisabeth Kübler-Ross, in her work with dying children, found that even in facing their mortal end, children tend to approach life with cheerfulness, hope, and an uncanny spiritual fortitude. Although they seldom verbalize their understanding of the purpose of life, children often seem to approach stresses and strains with a mysterious inner knowing.

Sometimes that inner knowing includes the notion of reincarnation—although to children, reincarnation is not experienced as a mental concept, but simply as the way things are. Often unbelieving parents feel distress when this occurs. The topic of reincarnation came up unexpectedly, for instance, in the family of my brother's girlfriend, people who were strict Roman Catholics. My father had just died, and my brother was taking leave of his sweetheart to join my family in mourning. The three-year-old sister of his girlfriend asked why Tom was so sad. "Oh, his father just died," her big sister replied.

"But, you don't have to be sad," said the child turning to Tom. "Your father will be born again in another body soon."

Another incident occurred on a visit to a Montessori school when I was speaking privately to a six year old whose father had recently died. Another little girl rushed over to us and blurted out, "You know, sometimes it takes God as many as ten years to build another body for you after you die." I was startled by her outburst and asked if someone she knew, perhaps her mom or dad, had told her that.

"Oh, no," she replied, "my mommy doesn't even believe in God."

"Well then, how do you know what you just said is true?" I asked.

"Oh, I just know."

Some children are not only aware of the concept of reincarnation, but actually remember past lives, as has been carefully documented by Dr. Ian Stevenson (1974). In many ways, however, children remembering isolated segments of particular lifetimes cannot actually be said to possess the second psychic sense. Adults who have the full use of this faculty not only tune into their own lifetimes, but also can do extensive "readings" into the past lives of other people. Edgar Cayce is one of the best known of those who possess this ability. Our definition of the term "psychic" involves the ability to perceive sense data or impressions from completely non-material sources. Therefore, children who have genuine "far memories" are undoubtedly operating in a psychic realm—the impressions they register from a past life did not originate in their present nervous system and brain. So even though their abilities are not fully articulated second sense faculties and are usually not under conscious control, I have categorized far memories under the general heading of the second psychic sense.

To further complicate the issue, far memory in children seems to occur in a wide variety of forms. Some have recurring dreams of past lives; some catch flashes of other times and places mixed with present life memories; and others simply have unusually strong positive or negative reactions to people, situations, or particular objects. Of course the most dramatic type of far memory is that in which children recall the exact details of a single, usually recent, past life. Dr. Ian Stevenson, psychiatrist at the University of Virginia, has investigated over two thousand cases of such childhood memories, which he feels are "suggestive of reincarnation." Although others have worked in this field (Cook 1983), Stevenson's work is the most extensive. He has used the most meticulous research methods possible. Here he describes the evaluation of a typical research case:

> A typical case of this type begins when a small child, usually between the ages of two and four, starts to tell his parents, and anyone who will listen, that he remembers living another life before his birth....A child claiming to remember a previous life usually asks to be taken to the place where he says he lived during that life....If the child has furnished enough details...the search for the family of the person he has been talking about is nearly always successful....The child is then usually found to have been accurate in about ninety percent of the statements he has been making about the deceased person whose life he claims to remember. (Stevenson 1977, 307-308).

To give the reader a flavor of Stevenson's work and a sense of how detailed and compelling far memory experiences can be in the life of a child, one of these "typical" cases will be summarized.

Jimmy Svenson lived in Alaska and was half Norwegian and half Tlinget Indian. In 1954 when he was two years old, Jimmy started talking of a previous life when he had been his mother's brother and had lived in a town a hundred miles away. For the next three years he talked a great deal about this other life. He insisted his name was John (the uncle's name) and not Jimmy, and reported details about his uncle's house, dog, and general lifestyle. He said, for instance, that he used to drink wine all the time, and the family well knew that the deceased John drank heavily. At age six Jimmy said to his mother's other brother, Hans, "I'm not your nephew, I'm your brother." At six and a half he was taken to John's village of Klukwan where he proved to be completely familiar with the village and surrounding fishing areas. During their visit to the village, he told his family that he had been fatally shot in the stomach by the skipper of a fishing boat.

In fact, John was on furlough from the army and had gone out in a small fishing boat with two women. Two hours later the boat was found on shore with the plug in the bilge hole missing. The bodies of the two women were found, but John's body was never recovered. John's brother Hans believed that John had been murdered by the jealous lover of one of the women, and it was even rumored that there had been a witness to the murder. But nothing was ever proved.

Two years after John's disappearance, a baby boy was born to John's sister, and was given the name John, but the father later insisted the name be changed to James John Svenson. Little Jimmy had four round birthmarks on his stomach which looked like healed gunshot wounds. (In some cultures it is believed that scars from one life often show up as birthmarks in another life.) By the age of nine, Jimmy had stopped talking about his previous life and the topic seemed to have been forgotten. (Stevenson 1974, 225-31).

Although such cases are fascinating, they certainly are not common. Nor are they typical of the kind of second sense activity I have observed in young children. Even so, Dr. Stevenson and his colleagues have found hundreds of such cases "suggestive of reincarnation."

One factor influencing past life memories apparently is the cause of death in the prior life. Researcher Emily Cook and others have found that a high percentage of children who describe previous lives report violent deaths (Cook 1983). Phobias relating to violent death also frequently show up in the child's present life. Perhaps the sanskaras (mental and emotional impressions) created by a violent physical death carry so much psychic energy that they are precipitated into activity (in this case, memory) in the next earthly life. This would be especially true, it seems to me, if the reincarnation occurred quickly.

The cases of far memory I have come across are not nearly so spectacular or dramatic, although the cause of death in the previous life is often a factor. One four year old I met in Chicago, Joshi, frequently seemed to relive a violent car accident from a previous life. At odd times throughout his young life, Joshi would pretend he was driving a car. While steering, he would talk to himself and describe his "driving." Then suddenly an expression of horror and pain would distort his features. He would shield his face from an imagined impact and scream, "and then there was an accident and the car was all smashed up!!" He would crumple up in a ball and moan. Then he would completely relax, take a deep breath and say (out loud) to himself, "and then I was in the Dead." As if remembering others might be watching, he would then look around, make contact, cheerfully pat his own chest, and say, "And now Joshi is in here!" This kind of trance-like memory would replay itself in exactly the same way every few weeks. Joshi's parents believed in reincarnation, so they were not distressed. Unfortunately, I lost touch with the parents and do not know if the episodes stopped as Joshi matured.

Often such a trance-like consciousness seems to accompany childhood far memories. It is almost as if these children have been momentarily catapulted into another time and place, and until they regain their present life composure, they are not quite sure which life they're living. One three year old, April, used to get a blank look on her face and shout, "I'm a man, I'm a man!" Then she would look around in confusion, shake her head, and say almost dejectedly, "No, I'm April."

Children often can confuse elements from different lifetimes. A friend who is also a teacher had an unusual early childhood in which impulses from past lives spilled over into her present. Her parents had no idea what to make of their strange daughter. At the age of three, my friend compulsively began doing advanced and complex yoga postures. Her body seemed able to do this naturally and effortlessly. And she would never sit down at the dinner table in any position but a full lotus. Her parents were quite distressed about this at first, but when they realized that the contortions did their daughter no harm, they became proud of her and invited neighbors and friends to see her extraordinary movements.

I also experienced elements from past lives mixing with my present during my early years. All during my childhood I had a vivid, though confused, memory which I am now convinced had its source in a past life. I would remember a complex of tents where I used to live and sleep. They were very cozy and to my child's mind, very "neat." They were brightly colored, mostly striped, and filled with soft pillows. From the time of my earliest memory till I was nine, ten, or eleven, I searched for these tents. They somehow represented home to me; they were where I lived, where I belonged. The only trouble was that I didn't know where to find them.

I used to play at my cousin Ginny's house. We made "forts" out of card tables covered with blankets, and I associated these play forts with my tent homes. So I decided those tents must be in Ginny's house and would search from room to room. I was frustrated when I could not track them down. I spoke to my mother about them, and she told me that I must have had some sort of a dream. But I knew they were not part of a dream. I brooded over the tents for years. I now believe they must have been part of a dim recollection of some gypsy life in Romania or of a Bedouin life in Morocco. Reincarnation was not discussed with me in childhood, so no explanation was offered for the mental and emotional confusion caused by the apparent memories of a different life.

Sometimes the memories of previous lives are more clear and are understood to be just that—far memories. One young daughter of a student of esotericism in Miami grew up speaking fluent French before she learned English. There were no French speakers among her family or neighbors. Furthermore, she would refer to previous lifetimes in a completely natural and nonchalant way. At age two while watching her mother dress for a party, she remarked, "Oh, I used to have a dress like that when I was big."

Another little girl hated hearing the organ music in church every Sunday. One day she explained to her mother, "The last time I remember hearing music like that, I was lying in a box."

Sometimes it takes an altered state of consciousness to focus these impressions in a child's mind. I have not yet discussed my friend May, whose clairaudient experiences concluded the last chapter. She remembered many past lives as a child, but had to be in a hypnogogic state of consciousness (between sleeping and waking) to pull through those memories. Between the ages of three and six, May was invited every afternoon by her mom to take a nap. Although nap time for most girls this age is a time of torture (after all who wants to sleep when there's so much playing to be done), for May the nap was a time for inner journeying.

May would lie in her bed with eyes closed and would soon be intensely aware of her bodily sensations. Then there would be a feeling of heaviness in her body, often accompanied by thirst. She would feel a tingling in her throat and chest and then a "lifting of consciousness." From her present spiritual orientation, May explains this "lifting" as the rising of her astral body about halfway out of the dense body. In this hypnogogic state, visions would open up before her closed eyes, offering glimpses of scenes from other times and other places. Though her parents did not believe in reincarnation, May knew even then that the central character in these visions was herself in other lives. She looked forward to nap time because of these visions, even though some were not pleasant. They included experiences of violent death in other lives, and each death memory was repeated many times.

When I interviewed her, May discussed the two past lives that materialized most clearly for her as a child, and which have remained vivid to her as an adult as well. In one scene, viewed countless times, she appeared to be a male American Indian. She saw this Indian, apparently on a hunting expedition, fall backwards and crack his head against a large boulder. The fall was fatal and concluded the episode. In the second vision, May was a woman living in a tribal society in a desert region. The memory suggested a period of some 200 years ago. She had committed some unpardonable sin and was condemned to death by the tribal council. In her vision May saw herself being taken into the desert and buried alive.

One might think that remembering such an experience would be traumatic for a five year old; yet the detached attitude May had concerning these memories was encouraged by the fact that she felt none of the pain, fear, or horror that doubtless accompanied the original experience. Also, for someone who knows from personal recollection that reincarnation is a fact of existence, death would perhaps not be so frightening.

Although the truth of reincarnation was obvious to May, she never spoke of such matters to her parents or friends. Her only memory of mentioning such things as a child was when she went to first grade and met a boy she somehow knew she had known in a past life. She told him they had been friends when they had lived before in another land, but the other six year old had no idea what she was talking about. They did become fast friends, however.

When May was fourteen, yoga classes brought about a rare psychic awakening which transformed her uncontrolled, random childhood psychic experiences into expanded paranormal abilities fully under her conscious control. She then became affiliated for a time with the Church of Religious Science and actually did healings and psychic readings for other people.

Another example of a child with this second psychic sense was related to me by my cousin Mary Ellen, whose father (my uncle) was a Methodist missionary. Mary Ellen was raised on the Blackfoot Indian Reservation in Browning, Montana. Her best friend in those early years was a young Blackfoot boy, who told her about an incident which had occurred while his family was on an excursion to Canada. They were traveling on a country road in a horse-drawn wagon when the boy who was seven or eight years old, shouted, "Stop! You have to stop here!" His parents were baffled since they were in unfamiliar territory. The boy jumped out of the wagon and headed in a definite direction.

"Where are you going?" his father called after him.

"I have to get something."

"But you've never been here before."

"Oh yes I have!" he shouted back. Then he ran to a specific tree, searched for a while, and returned with a carved figure he had found wedged in a crook of the tree's main branches. The boy explained to his parents that he had hidden this object on that particular tree in his other life. This boy had never spoken of reincarnation before, and one can be sure he didn't pick up such "heathen" beliefs from my missionary uncle. But apparently the sight of this tree powerfully stimulated some past sanskaras, and before he knew it his past-life experience had become a present-life memory—actually a compelling obsession. The mere presence of once familiar surroundings brought memories flooding back to him.

My cousin was able to examine the carved figure, which obviously had been crafted by a member of an Indian tribe, but not the Blackfoot. This story deeply impressed Mary Ellen as a seven-year-old, and reincarnation has been an accepted part of her world view for the fifty years since then.

Memories from past lives, I believe, are in a latent or semi-latent state in a sheath of consciousness not far removed from a child's waking mind. This concept is examined in detail in Chapters 11 and 12. René Querido, director of the Rudolf Steiner College in California and a lecturer on child development told me recently that he believes past life impressions are held in a latent state in the mind in an area above and behind the physical head. Owing to the loose and still-developing connection between the young child's etheric body and physical body, these past life memories, he said, can "leak" into the child's waking consciousness. Usually, however, such memories need a strong emotional "trigger" to erupt into consciousness, and even then they generally arise only as vague emotional or mental preoccupations and not as distinctly clear memory images.

I would venture to guess that such preoccupations occur

to many children. One eleven year old, Alex, for example, became obsessed with swords. He saved his allowance and did odd jobs until he had enough money to buy a huge, carved broadsword from Toledo, Spain. For months Alex carried the sword and participated in mock combats. For two years he even slept with the sword by his side. Were long-forgotten memories being triggered by this sword? Was he unconsciously reliving a life as a warrior when he had to keep his sword by his side for protection, even while he slept? Many odd childish fetishes and obsessions make more sense if understood as psychic leaks from earlier lives.

Three main factors can trigger such a preoccupation with a past life recollection, however vague it may be. The first of these factors has already been illustrated. A particular situation or environment can bring far memories to the surface, as it did with the Indian boy. Similarly, I remember traveling as a boy in Egypt with my grandmother. In the Valley of the Kings in Luxor, I was at home. I knew nothing of reincarnation, but I knew I never wanted to leave there. I had no visions nor clear recollections from the past, but I was aware of an overpowering feeling of familiarity, love, and "homeness" for that geographical area.

The second type of trigger does not require exotic locales. A child can become obsessed with a certain historical period through exposure to the era in literature or films. Or a specific object, like the sword, can abruptly call the sanskaras from the past into expression. In my own childhood at age nine, I saw a movie with Kirk Douglas called *The Vikings*. As with the Egyptian experience, I had the sense I was seeing something extraordinarily familiar. The film called forth feelings that were very deep, yet seemingly foreign to my nine-year-old consciousness. I became obsessed with Viking life, Norse mythology, and that particular film, which I must have seen a dozen times. No one can convince me that I have not had some richly fulfilling lives in Scandinavia during Viking times. Yet I never really remembered such lives. The Viking impressions arose as an emotional longing for another time and place, and I frequently had brooding daydreams about what it must have been like to live in ninth century Norway. If such experiences were staples in my own "unpsychic" childhood, I think it's very likely that emotional breezes from past lives sweep through the minds and hearts of many other children.

The third psychic trigger for far memory is another person. All children are attracted to certain people and repulsed by others, such as that favorite aunt or the cousin who scares the child, the one he never wants to be alone with. Although sensitive children certainly can pick up telepathic or psychometric cues from people which could account for strong attractions or repulsions, instant feelings for other people also may arise from sanskaras from the past. I believe children are extraordinarily receptive to such feelings about others and that their ties of love or antipathy should be honored. A child should never be forced to kiss a particular aunt he's afraid of. That fear may be well founded; it may be caused by a powerful, lingering impression from a past life, and should be respected.

When past life impressions do not come in waking consciousness, there is yet another way this second sense can manifest—through dreams. Researchers into reincarnation claim that anyone can have dreams which contain images and impressions from previous lives. One researcher told me that dreams which are in full color are more likely to contain imagery from earlier existences. In any event, due to psychological factors to be addressed later, there is no doubt that children are even more likely to dream of their past than are adults. An example of such a dream can be recalled from Chapter 5, where telepathic Linda dreamed of dying in a trench in World War I, while in another room of the house, her seven-year-old son, was simultaneously dreaming that he was a fighter pilot shooting at enemy troops hiding in trenches. His dream also seemed to be set in World War I. Linda has always believed that her son was in fact responsible for her death in her last life, and that the karma generated during that life and others had again drawn them together.

Although all speculation about past life impressions in dream images is pure conjecture, I believe there are two clear indications which suggest that a child's dream might stem from a previous existence. The first is when the dream is set in a historical period completely foreign to the child's present life (Dreaming of exploring the New World the night after seeing "Christopher Columbus" on T.V. would surely not indicate a paranormal experience). The other indication is the recurrence of the same dream. This is a particularly important element. When there is unfinished business from a previous life, the sanskaras involved may be subconsciously active and carry a certain charge of emotional energy. The recurrent dream could be one way to release this energy in a more or less helpful and purposeful manner. Just as clear past life memories may be generated from violent or untimely deaths, such factors may also impel the recurring dream.

The most fascinating case I know of a child's recurring dream which apparently replayed the events of a past lifetime is the extraordinary epic dream of eleven-year-old John. It unfolded over several consecutive nights and always picked up where it had left off the previous night—kind of an astral "mini-series." John remembers dreaming the dream first when he was seven, and at the time I interviewed him (in 1972) he could recall dreaming the entire story at least thirty or forty times.

John believed that his dream was set in the mid-nineteenth century in a country that might have been Spain. In the dream he lived in a harbor town and got involved with the new clipper ship trade. Rather than try to paraphrase and summarize, I will let John describe it:

> In the beginning of my dream, I'm about three or four years old—I was able to talk but not very much. I met this old man that worked on the ships and I was friends with him for a long time, and he told me about the ships.
> And then I was older and we lived right next to a ship yard, and I woke up around six o'clock and I'd get dressed real fast and I'd run outside and I'd watch the ships go out. It was always foggy and jungly where we lived. And I re-

member some of the ships brought back slaves and stuff and sold them. They brought back girls and they were doing dances inside these wooden cages, and they were selling them.

I had this friend. I can't remember any name, but my name is sort of like Francis or something like that—sort of like a girl's name. I remember my friends, but I can't remember how my mother looked. My dad must have been dead. All I remember about my mother is that she's fat and she always went around going to the markets. I can remember my mom went out and bought stuff and we had our own little garden in the back.

[As a child] I remember peeking in through these windows [at the local tavern] and watching the sailors who are drunk throw knives to see who was the best shot. I remember later on I was real good at knife throwing too. And I was good at sword fighting—but not big swords—I couldn't have no big, fat swords. I used those round, skinny types. I remember I bought a saber and I showed my mom. I got it at an auction-like (Transcription from taped interview, 1972).

John drew several illustrations for me of the settings in his dream. One picture shows the house where he and his mother lived. It was white stucco with a thatched roof and had a second floor entrance with rounded doors and windows. The fact that John could sit down and draw such detailed pictures indicates the vivid quality of his epic dream.

John told me the story would always reach some sort of nightly conclusion as he woke up. Then it would pick up the next night exactly where it had left off. This process would continue until the entire saga had unfolded, usually taking a full week. Each time the dream was replayed, it was an exact rerun, with nothing left out and nothing added. Later in the dream he became first a cabin boy on a clipper ship, and then a first mate. In the concluding episode, John was captain of his own ship. John's narrative continues:

I was the captain of a small vessel. It wasn't very big—it didn't have very many cannons. I had dark, black hair and was around twenty or twenty-one [or older]. I had long sideburns and I had a funny looking white shirt with puffy

Fig. 12. The house where John lived in his recurring dream.

Fig. 13. The sinking of John's clipper ship in which he was drowned.

sleeves. I had long pants and a pair of black boots and a belt with a sword and everything.

My boat was launched in 1845. That's when it was launched, I guess, because it had an "1845" [carved] on each side of the boat in the front.

Anyway, we got a letter from the king and went out with three other ships. And we had to go through a part [of the sea] with two cliffs on each side. I dreamed that when we were going through there we were all firing cannons. We were battling people [on the cliffs] with uniforms and tin hats and stuff—I don't know who they were. [In the battle] all our ships got sunk, and I remember I went inside and everybody was bailing out of the boat because it was sinking. And I remember I went inside my cabin to get something and a cannonball landed near the door and I got stuck in there. . . . I had chills in my stomach and I was slamming on the door and the water [inside the cabin] was getting higher and higher and I couldn't get the door open. And I remember being under water and my throat was all yucky and I just drowned I guess.

. . . I guess I died, but I woke up, sort of, in my dream I woke up, and I was on land and I was sort of like clear plastic, like a ghost. I never found out what I really was.

I was on land and no one could see me. I'd go out and walk around and there was this lady in a white dress who got out of a carriage, and she sat down in the garden next to me. She couldn't see me. And I used to stick my hand up, and I'd be up on the top of the apple tree and get an apple and start eating it. And I'd be talking to myself. That's about the end of the dream. And then it'd start all over again.

Interestingly, John did not tell his parents about this dream. They were well aware of his obsession with clipper ships, however. He could sit by the hours drawing detailed pictures of various types of sailing vessels. This interest carried over into school as well, and as his teacher, I often had a hard time getting him to put aside his clipper ship books or drawings to make room on his desk for his math book. But the dream itself was part of his secret life. The only way I found out about it was that, as part of my university study, I asked him if he had ever had any unusual experiences or dreams. The topic of reincarnation never came up between us. It had never occurred to John that the dream actually represented a previous lifetime. The notion of reincarnation was foreign to his Christian upbringing. He knew without a doubt, however, that the character in the dream was himself, even though his appearance was totally different. He did confide that the lifetime in the dream "sure was a lot more funner" than his present life.

Whether they are recurring dreams like John's or isolated recollections of past lives during waking consciousness, it seems clear to me that such experiences are far more common in childhood than in adulthood. Perhaps it would be well to offer some preliminary thoughts on how and why this might be true.

The Buddha was reputed to have said that a human being is nothing but a bundle of thoughts. I recall an old Lebanese Druze friend who would recite that quote when explaining the nature of the higher mind. This "bundle," he would say, is vast, containing sanskaras which have originated in countless epochs and cycles of human and even pre-human history. These impressions from the past are responsible for the molding of one's present human body and have virtually pre-ordained one's everyday life of thoughts, feelings, and actions. An adult, however, deals in life with only a tiny "sub-bundle" of these sanskaras. The immense array of remaining coded bundles of thought-energy is effectively screened off from waking consciousness.

To understand psychic children, one must realize that for them this screening process does not seem to work effectively. They easily register sense data from the surrounding subtle environment and also, apparently, as readily tune in to impressions from their own "higher" mind—from their "master bundle" which originated in past lifetimes. Observing children carefully gives hints of how these impressions are expressed in their lives. Kids' habits in work, play, or artistic endeavors, and their off-handed comments and actions, reveal habit patterns that cannot be adequately explained from the limited perspective of a single lifetime.

I would hazard a guess that this second psychic sense is among the most common of all paranormal faculties in childhood. Its expression may vary greatly from child to child and the resulting far memories may come out in subtle ways, perhaps so subtle that they are not even recognized as stemming from past lives. But if one would like proof of the theory of reincarnation, let me suggest observing kids closely, for the fabulous "clouds of glory" from their remote past are easily revealed.

9
Some Rare Abilities

After almost thirty-five years, it remains one of Lorenzo's most vivid recollections. It was a psychic experience, but not one of the common varieties discussed so far. Lorenzo, even at age seven or eight, knew it was unusual. His mother insisted that it was not a real experience, that it was all his imagination. But Lorenzo at eight years old knew it was real.

He had been playing by himself in his bedroom when his toys suddenly faded from view, and he felt as though a cone-shaped mechanism was projected out of his forehead. He was startled, but not frightened. Bit by bit, an image crystallized at the end of the cone. It was as if a tiny movie were being projected on a screen five inches in front of him, but the projector and the film were inside his head and poking out through his forehead. What he saw was a fire, with the image as clear as if Lorenzo were right there watching it burn. The flames roared high and licked the walls of a large office building, one that he did not recognize. No sound was attached to the vision, no sirens, no screams, no crashing walls. Then it stopped. The cone vanished and the movie was over.

The next morning at breakfast, Lorenzo saw his father reading the newspaper. On the front page Lorenzo saw a picture of the same fire he had "seen" over fifteen hours earlier!

All through his childhood, Lorenzo was able to see auras and other non-ordinary visions. But he told me his childhood clairvoyance did not involve the cone-like projector in his forehead. It seemed to Lorenzo that he saw auras with his eyes, but this seeming glimpse into the future was completely different. Although he cannot now remember any other prophetic visions, he never forgot that one.

In my research I have found reports of childhoood paranormal experiences like Lorenzo's, but they are not common. I have never encountered some of these abilities in my own extensive work with children. In this section, therefore, I rely heavily on data gathered by other researchers. The faculties reviewed here are the ability to perceive future events (the third sense); psychometry (the sixth sense); psychic diagnosing (the fourth sense); and astral travel and healing ability (two other fifth-sense faculties).

Precognition is probably the most controversial of these senses. The value of knowing future events has been hotly debated for centuries, and many people literally define "psychic" as the ability to predict the future. Information about these abilities comes largely through tabloid newspapers, and the annual predictions by "leading psychics," who forecast which president will be assassinated and what film star divorced, show that this psychic sense is extremely unreliable. But whether or not precognition is helpful or accurate, the fact is that many kids do experience it.

This ability can take several forms and work through several different sensory mechanisms. Children who are particularly open to psychic impressions can pick up hints of the future as easily as other types of paranormal sense data. From the perspective of the inner dimensions of consciousness, time is a relative concept. Events on earth manifest as eruptions of inner activities. Causes on the inner planes precipitate effects on the physical level. Thus the *future* of earth is already a network of complex forces which can be perceived as the *present* in the inner realms of consciousness. The forces involved, however, are so complex that even the pronounced ability to perceive them does not guarantee their accurate interpretation in terms of actual future events. Impressions of "the future" can apparently leak through from the astral plane into a child's consciousness, and these leaks can occur in a surprising variety of ways.

The most subtle form this psychic sense can take is vague feelings of what's going to happen around one. My cousin, Mary Ellen, frequently had such feelings as a child growing up in Browning, Montana. She told me she never considered it a psychic ability because she didn't pick up distinct impressions of the future which would have enabled her to make predictions. Rather, she just "had a sense" of what would happen to her.

She remembers one incident that illustrates how this precognition operated. Each year on the Blackfoot Reservation there would be an exciting event called the "Blackfoot Stampede." This was a track and field day in which everyone on the reservation—young and old—was invited to participate in a series of races. Ribbons were awarded to the winners. When Mary Ellen was around ten, she remembers knowing or sensing exactly which young man would win each race. She told no one except her brother about her predictions. Every contestant she felt would win actually did win. Although the episode seems rather startling to Mary Ellen today, at the time she paid little attention to it. She assumed that everyone had such feelings but kept them to themselves.

Another child with strong feelings about some future events has already been introduced—young Stephen from San Francisco. When Stephen was four, his mother became pregnant. When she was about one and a half months pregnant, Stephen asked her, "What are you going to name my baby brother and sister?" His mother immediately assumed Stephen didn't understand how the birthing of babies works. She explained, "No, Stephen, you'll have either a baby brother or a baby sister. You won't have both."

"But what are you going to name my baby brother and sister?" Stephen persistently repeated.

His mother gave the incident no more thought until six months later when the doctor informed her that she would have twins. It was no surprise to learn a little later that the twins were a boy and a girl.

Actually, Stephen may not have been using a precognitive ability. Perhaps he had seen the twins on a super-physical plane ready to take birth, and was reporting a clairvoyant perception. Other phenomena with Stephen were equally hard to categorize. Once, for instance, I was playing a card game with him called "concentration" or "remember," in which the players try to choose pairs from a face-down array of cards. Stephen was no fun to play with, because he effortlessly chose pair after pair. This too may have had something to do with precognition, but it also makes sense to conclude that he matched pairs of cards by using an X-ray type of clairvoyance (see Leadbeater 1971 [1903] 45-46).

One of the most unusual prophetic abilities I have found is that of a seventh-grader, Jenny Ann, whom I met in a school where I taught. As far back as she can remember— at least since she was five—Jenny Ann would see into the future with great regularity. At least once a week an image would form in front of her face so that she could closely observe it. The image would always reveal an event that Jenny would experience in her life within the next two or three days. Jenny described this precognitive image:

> It's just a picture—a clear, full color picture. It's not fuzzy or anything, and it lasts only for a split second. It's usually a picture of someone doing something. The events I see are not big things, just little things. But I see it happening right in front of my face. Then a few days later, I see the same event happening in real life. Sometimes I'll see a place where I've never been before, and then later I'll see the place in real life.

There was no particular inner feeling that warned her when this was about to occur and no astral glow. The phenomenon could take place at any time. Jenny told me she could be at her desk doing school work when an image would suddenly crystallize, typically of ordinary little things.

One day, for example, Jenny Ann saw an image of a

friend from her gymnastics class trying a new routine on the parallel bars but slipping and falling. The girl was not hurt, but was unable to complete the movement. A few days later in gymnastics class, Jenny reported, she saw this girl fall in the middle of the same routine.

Now, at age twelve, these paranormal experiences occur only occasionally, perhaps once every two months. I asked Jenny how she felt about the experience fading away:

> I don't really want it to go away, but it does seem to be fading. I don't want it to stop because it's neat to see these things.

As neat as the experiences are, however, in all the years of her childhood, she mentioned the phenomenon only a few times to her sister. Her parents never knew, nor did any of her school friends. When asked why, Jenny replied, "It's no big deal. I don't think it's worth talking about, and I don't even think about it that much."

Another woman, Vivian, considered her precognitive feelings as a child useless. She was frustrated that she would sense things about to happen, yet could do nothing to interfere with the outcome. Vivian asked, "Why was I given that information about future events if I could never do anything about it?" Her most vivid recollection was a quick visionary flash, similar to Jenny's, of some high school friends near an overturned car, crawling around on the road after an accident. Several days later, she was driving on a winding, mountainous road when she suddenly knew her vision was going to merge into reality. "Oh, my God," she screamed to her friend next to her, "right around this next corner...!" Sure enough, the overturned car was there, the boys were there—one crawling from beneath a bush—exactly as in her vision. This experience so terrified the fifteen-year-old Vivian that she prayed to God to shut down this psychic faculty. She wanted nothing to do with it. The prayer was answered.

Very often this precognitive ability reveals significant or traumatic events to the child who possesses it. Often death or catastrophe is the theme, and if, as Vivian felt, the child who foresees such an event can do nothing to alter it, perhaps the perception comes as a warning from the child's higher mind so that the shock of the actual event will be less disturbing. The younger sister of a good friend of mine used to get startling warnings of impending deaths. When she was eight years old her father was entertaining some of his friends when this girl suddenly saw a vague, shadowy outline of a skull just over the head of one of the guests. Two weeks later that same man died very unexpectedly. She saw the ethereal skull over the heads of three other people during the next few years, and each of these other people died within three weeks of her vision. As she approached puberty, this precognitive ability began to scare her more and more, and so she willed for the death visions to stop. And they did. In Chapter 13 I share an interview with the late healer Olga Worrall, in which she describes the difficulties she experienced in her family when she tried to warn her mother that her young brother was going to die.

Sam Young, journalist and a former editor for *Saturday Evening Post* and *Look* magazine, tells of a similar case, that of young Clara. One day when she was eight, or possibly younger, she announced to her parents that a young cousin, Mitch, was going to die. Since Mitch lived in a town some thirty miles away, the family was not aware of any health problems. Clara recalls:

> I said I wanted to see him. When I was asked why, I said he was going to die. They [her parents] said no, Mitch was not going to die, he was perfectly healthy. Only a couple of days later, my grandfather saw Mitch's father in town and was told that Mitch was very sick. Soon after we learned Mitch died. When I went to the funeral, even the children kept away from me because they had heard I'd known of the death ahead of time (Young 1977, 157).

Probably the most common technique of tuning in to impressions of future events is through dreams. Since time on the astral plane does not exactly correspond with physical time, and since dreams have traditionally been linked with out-of-body astral experiences, it seems logical that dream life could be connected with this third psychic sense. Although such prophetic dreams may involve commonplace events such as those Jenny Ann described, they are more likely to be connected with dramatic catastrophes. In my research I have come across both types.

An example of a mundane precognitive dream involves eleven-year-old Ryan, who dreamed of a snake crossing the street. His father, who was working in the yard, saw the snake and caught it, then gave it to Ryan. That was the end of the dream. About a week later, his dad actually did see a gopher snake slithering across the street, caught it, and gave it to Ryan, who still keeps it as a pet.

Charmian, now grown and with children of her own, remembers two types of childhood dreams: one the vague, ethereal, disorganized dream common among children, the other intensely vivid and clear, always in full color, which seemed as real as waking life. This latter type sometimes turned out to be precognitive. When she was eight, Charmian dreamed of a city on fire. People were running about in a panic, and Charmian wanted desperately to help them. She had a complete recollection of the dream in the morning, as well as a lingering longing to help the unfortunate victims of the blaze. Downstairs at breakfast, she snuggled up to her father and told him she had "a scary dream." Then Charmian saw bold headlines on her father newspaper: "WHOLE CITY UP IN FLAMES."

She also remembers a similar dream which involved helping flood victims by a large river. In this dream she actually was able to help the people. In the morning the paper read, "MISSISSIPPI FLOODS IN LOUISIANA." Neither of these dreams involved Charmian's home town, or even her home state. No one in her family lived in the city that caught fire or in the flooded area. Was she perhaps actually doing astral work which involved helping the victims of a major calamity?

Another precognitive experience came in the form of an astral visitor Charmian perceived clairvoyantly. She was eight at the time and was lying down for a nap when "a lovely lady appeared by my bed. She had violet eyes and

long brown curls in her hair. She smiled sweetly at me."
Charmian had never seen the woman before, and though
she seemed completely solid and normal and "real," the
experience frightened the young girl, who called for her
mother. The lady began fading away, disintegrating in
patches, much like a cloud of smoke. By the time the
mother arrived in the bedroom, the lady had vanished.
Charmian explained to her mother what had happened and
tried to describe the lovely visitor. The description seemed
familiar to the girl's mother, and she showed Charmian
five or six photos. Charmian was able to identify the
woman as the subject of one of the photos. This was a
friend of the mother's named Nell Peterson. About this
time the door bell rang and a telegram was delivered. It
was a message from Mr. Peterson that his wife, Nell, had
died suddenly. Charmian's mother then understood. "Nell
always had wanted to meet you," she told her daughter.
"I guess now she has."

Another paranormal faculty frequently found in children
is psychometry, sometimes called clairsentience. This is the
ability to sense non-physical impressions of an object
through touch—generally through the hands and fingers.
Although it is well documented in the lives of many children, I have never encountered this faculty myself. The
following examples of this sixth sense do not carry the
stamp of personal corroboration as do most of the rest of
the data in this book.

Some children who use this sense can learn the history
of objects merely by touching them. For others, psychometry manifests as an ability to "see" with the fingers—
"dermal-vision." Such children "read" with their hands
or identify colors, shapes, or pictures by touching them.
This is an ability that can easily be tested, and the testing
conditions are simple and easily replicated.

Sam Young discussed a child with psychometric ability.
This example illustrates the ability to react to and identify
sanskaras of physical objects. When the child involved,
Linda, was six or seven, she was taken on a school field
trip to a museum. In a room full of sixteenth-century

French antiques, she spontaneously began to talk about the different pieces to her classmates. Linda explained who made each vase or chair, to whom it had been sold, when it arrived in the museum, etc. She only stopped when she saw the shocked look on the faces of her teacher and the museum guide (Young 1977, 13).

Another case that came to my attention concerned seven-year-old Tina. One day Tina was looking through her mother's jewelry box when she noticed a set of red rosary beads. She pulled them out of the box and held them for a while; then she ran to her mother and said, "These were grandma's beads. She always kept them with her because she loved them so much." Then she told her mother exactly how, when, and where grandma had died. The astonished mother confirmed everything, but since the grandmother had died before Tina was born, she was mystified by Tina's sudden knowledge.

For someone who can use this paranormal sense, however, such knowledge is not beyond one's ken. The explanation might be that every experience a human being has creates psychic impressions, sanskaras (see Meher Baba 1967, 54-64). The residue of these impressions is deposited on objects the person touches, wears, or uses during that experience. The red rosary beads held a psychic record of the grandmother's death. After all, her hands were ceaselessly telling the beads even at the actual moment of her passing. Tina "read" this vivid psychic record through the sense of touch.

In recent years several journal articles have reported on children with dermal-vision, the second type of psychometry, in the People's Republic of China. One article by Tao Kiang describes three experiments with ten and eleven year olds who were able accurately and consistently to identify colors, symbols, and Chinese characters contained within a sealed box. The researcher concluded that all of the four children studied had reliable use of what he termed "sighted hands." (Kiang 1982, 304-08).

I recently learned of another case of dermal-vision, involving a young woman, Whitney, who related her experiences of some years in the past. She agreed to allow the story to be published here only if I changed her name and disguised some of the details of the case. Whitney has such unpleasant memories of this period in her childhood that she does not care to associate with people interested in such matters. This is the story of a child who was exploited and harassed because she was "different."

Whitney learned of her psychometric abilities at the age of eleven. While playing at a friend's house, the friend's mother, who dabbled with E.S.P. experiments, asked the two girls if they would cover their eyes, run their fingers over a page of a magazine, and see if they could tell what was on the page. The friend had no success at all, but Whitney found she could read almost the entire page with her fingers.

Her parents were not believers in such powers, but could not argue with Whitney's demonstrable ability. Word got out in their small town in western Canada, and soon Whitney's story hit the front page of the local newspaper. Then followed a session on a radio talk show, and even a T.V. appearance. Whitney at first enjoyed the notoriety her psychic talent brought, but it didn't take long for the fun to turn into a nightmare. People started calling her day and night from all across the country to be healed or to seek tips on which horse to bet on. Many others doubted her ability and tried to expose her. At school her status slipped from being a celebrity to being somewhat of a freak. In the face of the mounting stresses of her new life, she withdrew from school activities and became aloof from her friends.

Finally some well-meaning parapsychologists convinced her to participate in a series of E.S.P. tests. They were able to document her abilities and help her cope with them. When she was twelve, they suggested she become involved with hospital work, because they had discovered that her "sighted" hands also carried a healing charge. During the next couple of years, however, Whitney became disenchanted with psychic work. "I just got disgusted with everyone doubting and criticizing me. I didn't want my friends to think I was strange, [so] I decided to turn it off completely.''

This ''turning it off'' seemed almost effortless, and now, thirteen years later, Whitney has no conscious trace of her paranormal faculties. Her few years as a psychic child have been filed away deep within and are no longer discussed. Her childhood ''secret life'' that, for a time, became so terribly public has become her own private memory. Even her husband of several years does not know of her childhood journey into the psychic world, and Whitney sees no reason to bring up the subject. ''Right now,'' she said, ''I just have no interest in psychic abilities. And at this point I can't see being interested in them again. I don't think [the abilities] helped or hurt me. It was just an experience. But I think it was too much, too fast.''

Other books (e.g. Tanous, Young, Pearce) generally point to the desirable aspects of such psychic talents and encourage their exploration and expansion in children. Whitney's case, and many of the other examples cited, call into serious question this point of view. A good number of adults I interviewed for this book told me they consciously tried as children to close down their paranormal faculties, and usually succeeded. Are these abilities desirable, and should they be encouraged in children? These are significant questions wih no easy answers. In Chapter 15 I explore such issues in detail and offer my own conclusions.

Whitney's case reminds me of another example of the sixth psychic sense. Sam Lentine also had the ability as a child to sense things through touch and to heal. For Sam, however, the difference lay in the fact that he was born blind. Sam's blindness somehow intensified his other senses and extended them well into the psychic realm. As a young child he learned how to ride a bicycle and to play ball. He could sense psychically where the sidewalk was for his bike, or where the ball was and when to hold up his hands to catch it. He could also tell whether or not a person was healthy. As Sam explained recently in a magazine article, "I could tell that something didn't "look" right or feel right around a person. I didn't know what an aura was—but I could sense it" (Myers 1983, 76-81).

In later years, after taking college level anatomy courses, he was able to use his psychometric ability for accurate diagnosing. Now he is working full time as a health professional and hopes to start a holistic healing clinic of his own. It would be interesting to study further the paranormal abilities of children born blind or deaf. I have no data on this subject myself, but it would seem reasonable that handicapped children might have fascinating secret lives.

In the introduction to the seven psychic senses, I mentioned that the fourth sense, true psychic diagnosing, is said to be the most rare of all paranormal faculties. Although Sam Lentine may possess this ability, it seems more likely that he diagnoses by means of psychometric sensitivity to diseased tissue. The only case of a child with the fourth sense I have come across is discussed by Sam Young. Linda Martel died in 1961 at the age of five. But in her five short years she became well known in Europe for her ability to diagnose illnesses and to heal with the touch of her hand. Linda had the true fourth sense, in addition to her healing hands (a fifth sense ability). She was able to diagnose an illness instantly without touching or making contact with a patient in any way. In fact, she could even diagnose by looking at a photo—knowing at a glance what the person's illness was and how it needed to be treated. Years after Linda's death, people still claimed to be healed by standing near her grave or by touching a piece of her clothing (Young 1977, 50-52).

The final paranormal ability I wish to discuss in this potpourri of anecdotes is astral travel. I believe that astral travel—or out-of-body experience—is part of the fifth psychic sense, which also includes clairvoyance. Astral travel and clairvoyance seem so different, but apparently the physical structures needed to register impressions of the astral plane while one is out of the body are similar to those structures needed to register astral impressions while one is in the body. These abilities are not necessarily developed in tandem, though presumably anyone with one should be able to cultivate the other.

Occult researchers have long agreed that the process of going to sleep is a form of unconscious astral travel. When one falls asleep, the astral body apparently dissociates from the physical and hovers above it. This dissociation is usually an unconscious action. Normally consciousness involves interaction of the astral body with the physical brain and nervous functions. For many children, however, it is possible to maintain clear consciousness even while dissociated from the physical brain system. These children feel themselves leaving their physical bodies and floating around their bedrooms. With any group of children of virtually any age, all one has to ask is, "Have any of you ever felt yourself floating over your bed at night?" and there will be an astonishing number of positive responses.

Knowing I would be working on this chapter, yesterday I asked a group of six children, six and seven years old, this basic question. One small black girl responded with her own experience:

> ...I felt like I was going up somewhere. It felt funny. I didn't get scared, but I didn't feel like I was sleeping—I felt like I was awake! It felt like my stomach was going up. I was trying to come down but it just kept on raising me higher and higher. I kept on going up and up and up until I felt like I was in space.

She said the experience of lifting out of her body happened frequently between the ages of three and five, but recently had stopped. I asked her why that might be and she wisely replied, "I guess I'm getting too old for it."

Other children, though not consciously lifting out of their bodies, often wake up with strong dream images of floating or flying around. When I was five or six, I remember frequently having dreams in which I could fly. One day I woke up from an afternoon nap with such a vivid sensation of being able to fly, I immediately ran out to the yard, took a running leap, and tried my best to lift off the ground. My childhood consciousness was tremendously perplexed by the density of my body—I simply could not fly. But I knew deep down that somehow, somewhere I *could* fly! I had done it before, and I knew precisely what it felt like. At that time I could not clearly distinguish the gross world from the subtle world of my dreams. My brother, Tom, had an even harder time. He once was so convinced he could fly that he jumped off the roof. Fortunately, he grabbed a power line on the way to the ground and my grandfather rescued him.

Since conscious out-of-body experiences are so common, they have long been a favorite focus for parapsychological research. In one such study (Twemlow et al., 1982) the researchers examined children of twelve and older who reported such sensations. But rather than review such findings, I will offer a case which not only shows how such a psychic talent can be experienced, but also illustrates a whole range of psychological ramifications which can surround the childhood use of this faculty.

This account involves Linda, the telepathic girl discussed in Chapter 5. As a child, Linda had an unhappy home life. Her mother and sister deeply resented her and made her life unpleasant and difficult. Before the age of about three, Linda lived near Oceanside, California, and had plenty of playmates, but then her family moved to the other side of the Los Angeles basin, and in that new neighborhood she had no other children to play with. The pressure of her mother's and her sister's negativity began to affect her, and this is when she started her astral travel. One of the ways she learned to cope with the unpleasantness around home was simply to leave her body and go to a place where things were more happy. Linda told me, "It was the only way to escape the energy of my mother that was actually hurtful to me. To be alive [survive] in this world, I had to learn to get away."

For several years, Linda did not understand that she left her body. Most of her astral adventuring took place at night or during nap time. As Linda put it, "I would go to bed and I would spin out of my body.... Then I could go where I wanted."

It wasn't until Linda was in kindergarten that she began to realize that this "spinning out" was actually her method of leaving her body. As a very young child, she thought it was the room spinning or her bed spinning, and then suddenly she would be free. But at about age five she started learning how the process worked: this sort of spinning sensation would begin, and her entire body would seem to be twirling in a counter-clockwise direction, even while her physical body was lying still on the bed. The spinning would go faster and faster until suddenly she found herself catapulted completely out of her body—which was now visibly lying on the bed below her.

Her descriptions of her travels as a child are fascinating. For the first couple of mintues after "spinning out," Linda would find herself in a dark, murky world that she now believes to be one of the lowest astral subplanes. She said it was thick like molasses without being sticky. She could not see very well in this dark region, but she did sense the presence of certain creatures that she did not want any closer conscious contact with. Linda told me it was as if one came up through a hole in the bottom of a lake, and in order to reach the fresh, clear water, you had to go through the layer of mud and muck and weeds at the bottom. Early on, Linda learned how to zip through this dense layer and into the "light." It was not until puberty that the dark murkiness started to exert a hold on her.

Once in the light, she left her California neighborhood far behind and spent "hours" in natural surroundings, usually mountains or meadows. She had a favorite meadow where she climbed a big tree. She was often joined by a myriad of butterflies, birds, and insects. The area was also inhabited by several kinds of fairies and earth-gnomes. The gnomes were her friends and she trusted them, even though they never communicated with her in any conventional way. She almost never saw people in that world—in fact that was really the whole idea. When she became older, she learned how to fence in her secret meadow psychically, so that no people could discover it by mistake. After all, it was people who seemed to make her life miserable, and as a child she felt safe in her meadow partly because nobody was around.

At other times Linda would be more adventurous and travel to exotic places. Although solitary flying may have been possible, Linda's mode of transportation, as she recalls, involved riding some sort of wind current. She wonders if she actually rode on the back of some huge air spirit; and yet, if it were an entity of some sort, she had no communication with it. Linda says it was like being the heroine in the Norwegian fairy tale "East of the Sun and West of the Moon," a girl who rode the North Wind. On these journeys, she would often go to high mountain areas. The terrain she visited seemed solid and real, not ethereal, nor did it glow with otherworldly light. All during her journeys she remembers a cord, a shimmering silver-gray cord, which stretched out of her back from between the shoulder blades. When it was time for her to wake up, this cord would zip her back into her body, which lay where she left it, in her bed in California.

Linda did not have to be lying in bed for her journeys to occur. Another environment that needed escaping was school. "At school," she told me, "I would particularly take off. School was a terrible place." Because her attention, however, might be required at any time, Linda was not able to escape completely from the area of the school and go to her meadow. She had to remain partly at her desk. She explains, "There were ways I had of leaving, where I would kind of leave but I would keep enough of me in my body and I would stay near enough to listen to both worlds—the physical and the astral. If the teacher asked me a question, I would sometimes be able to hear her and to respond."

At puberty the simplicity and ease of her astral travel began to alter. The astral muck, which never seemed to affect her as a youngster, started exerting an inner pull on her. When she was around twelve, the troubles really started. One day she spun out of her body in the usual way, went to her meadow for a while, and then started the physical re-entry process. But for the first time that silverish cord did not snap her back into her body. The "descent" slowed down to a snail's pace, and she felt the lower astral thickness was actually sticking to her, and the snail metaphor seemed literal. Linda describes the feeling: "I felt like I was on the back of a huge [room size] snail and I could not do the spinning to get back into my physical body. I could hardly muck my way back. And when I found that I wasn't getting back in, I started to panic. It was as if I couldn't breathe—I was suffocating. When I finally did get back in [my body], I ended up feeling sick." When Linda panicked in the returning process, she also perceived several "nasty," amorphous, dark entities in the gloomy, thick atmosphere. She was terrified of them, but they never seemed interested in her.

The difficulty in returning to her body continued and repeated itself in every inner journey she had from then on. She always ended feeling terribly sick and nauseous. Finally, at the age of thirteen, just the preliminary spinning to leave the body would bring on this ill feeling, and the anticipation of all the problems she would have in returning to her body so frightened her that she simply stopped the spinning and went to sleep in the ordinary way. And that was the last time Linda allowed herself to project astrally.

Astonishingly, she said our interview was the first time she had talked openly about this secret aspect of her childhood. I said, "You mean you never mentioned this to any of your playmates or friends or to your mom?" "No," she replied. "I learned as a very young child that anything I told my mother I really liked, she would take away from me. This traveling was something special to me, and I thought she could take it away from me. So I didn't tell her about it—I didn't tell anyone...until now."

For this child, psychic ability really had a functional and even therapeutic value. It protected her from an unsafe and unpleasant home environment. And for Linda, the lesson was learned early in life that for her real happiness, safety, and security came from the inner realms of consciousness and not so much from the physical world. This childhood realization may have been the first step down a spiritual path of study, discipline, and awakening that Linda still pursues some thirty years later.

10
When the Subjective Becomes Objective

Knives flying through the air, unusual accidents, children waking up with lacerations and mysterious burns—all these are phenomena which deal with a darker side of childhood psychism. Not all psychic sensitivity in children is as innocent as the anecdotes in the last several chapters might indicate.

Normal sensory perception seems to deal with more or less passive reception of sensory aspects of the world around one. In psychic perception the range of sense data available is not limited to the energies and matter of the physical dimension. Vision, for instance, is a primarily receptive phenomenon, and one cannot say that it is dark or dangerous or evil to be able to see. Similarly, clairvoyant vision is predominantly a passive ability, though one's will power can be trained to focus it. It is hard to imagine how clairvoyance could be dangerously misused, though there are many examples of people who have become egotistical because they considered their clairvoyance "special" and "advanced."

The accounts in this chapter, however, concern a psychic faculty that can be misused because it is not passive and receptive. It is an active and energetic faculty that may or may not be under the conscious control of the will, and it can, therefore, be very dangerous. I have called it the seventh psychic sense.

Imagine giving a four-year-old child a pack of matches and a handful of firecrackers or a loaded revolver. If there were a serious accident, one could not say the child was guilty of wrongdoing. He is innocent because he does not understand the terrible power and force of his "toys." Yet, guilty or not, the energy is there, ready to be released, and the child has the power at his fingertips to release it.

Similarly the child who possesses the seventh sense, sometimes called "psychokinesis" or PK, can act (either with or without his conscious control) as a channel for tremendous psychic forces. The firecrackers and revolvers are nothing compared with the power available to such a child. Poltergeist phenomena aptly illustrate how children can unconsciously act as channels for awesome unseen forces. Whether or not it is possible to discover how this inner force is channeled, one can understand that this type of paranormal sensitivity falls into a completely different category from the other psychic talents. Spiritual teachers have recognized this difference and consistently cautioned students against using this talent because of the dangers of abuse (see Meher Baba 1973, 231-32). History is full of examples of those who possessed, or tried to possess, this seventh sense: Eliphas Levi, Grigori Rasputin, Comte di Cagliostro, even Charles Manson, the notorious "cult" murderer of recent times.

But wait! Is it possible to discuss psychic ability in children and the homicidal psychosis of Charles Manson in the same breath? I admit that I have never met a child who tried psychically to murder someone, but I have encountered some frightening results of conscious or unconscious use of this power.

A friend of mine told me about a shy eleven year old named Jack whom he knew in South Carolina. Jack transferred to a new school in the middle of the school year and was immediately confronted by bullies bent on taunting the "new kid." There seemed to be nothing Jack could do about it. Over a two-week span the incidents escalated, always initiated by the same small gang of boys egged on by a forceful leader, and Jack, along with a few other unfortunates, were the targets of their abuse. Jack wasn't a fighter, so all he could think to do was to tell his parents and his teacher, and that had not helped.

One day after school, Jack was severely beaten by the boys and went home with bruises, cuts, and a bloody nose. This latest abuse was the last straw. Before he fell asleep, all Jack could think about was how much he hated the ringleader, and he visualized all the terrible things he would like to do to punish this boy. Finally he fell into a fitful, though dreamless, sleep.

The next day at school Jack noticed that the bully was not in class. Later he learned that in the early hours of that morning, the bully's mother had been awakened by screams and cries from her son's room. She rushed into his bedroom and was horrified to find his sheets stained with blood. All over his body were tiny, oozing lacerations, which appeared as though they had been made by some small surgical instrument. On his face were open blisters that made him look as if he had been severely burned. The doctor who was called searched for clues as to how these injuries had been inflicted. The official conclusion was that the boy must have been sleep-walking, though no evidence was found as to where he had been or how he had cut himself. When Jack heard the story, however, he felt sure that he had somehow been the cause of the boy's injuries. Far from feeling justified or satisfied, Jack was overcome with remorse.

Was this a case of coincidence, or the workings of the seventh psychic sense, psychokinetic power? Psychokinesis has been defined as the capacity of the mind to affect changes in physical matter. Through concentrated thought force, had Jack, without realizing it, been able to give his hatred of this particular boy a horribly concrete materialization? This incident sounds like voodoo, although Jack did not actually intend to injure his victim.

Ocassionally, children are aware of this power. A friend of mine, who now works with children, was himself psychic as a child. Fascinated by magic, he performed innocent, childish rituals. But the consequences of one of his rituals was not so innocent. A boy on his block (in England) had been teasing him mercilessly. After weeks of humiliation, my friend had decided to focus one of his rituals on the other boy. He sat under his favorite tree and concentrated on hurting his adversary, although he did not specify any particular form this injury should take. After more than an hour, he concluded his ritual and went off to play. That afternoon the other boy fell and broke his leg in several places. The break was so severe that it did not completely heal for well over a year.

A California psychologist who has worked with many psychic children told me in a recent interview that he believes that many so-called accidents of children are really not accidents at all, but the result of strong and focused psychic forces. When a child is being picked on by another, he automatically concentrates force onto his tormentor. Since a child's mental life is so closely tied to strong emotional currents in the astral plane, this raw, emotional force, when consciously or unconsciously focused by a resentful child, can affect physical phenomena, even causing injuries. This seventh psychic sense can be used even more easily to affect someone else's mind. For example, a child victim of a psychic attack might get dizzy or confused, say, when climbing a tree, and fall. Seventh sense abilities, however, need not be mischievous and harmful. Thomas Armstrong (1985) reports that children can often be instrumental in healing. Also, affecting the minds of others is not necessarily harmful but can be of help.

Children sometimes can have an uncanny effect on the instinctual, astral minds of animals. My cousin told me about an eight- or nine-year-old boy in the jungles of Equador who seemed to have a close affinity with poisonous creatures, particularly one type of deadly snake. He had received media attention because he could walk into the jungle and locate the nesting spot of this type of snake, and could pick up and handle the snake without being bitten. He demonstrated his unusual ability by posing for photos while playing with a five-inch scorpion, while more than a dozen scorpions crawled over his body.

In the East, the affinity of a child with deadly snakes is

taken to be a sign of spiritual advancement. Stories are told of various masters, such as Ramakrishna or Meher Baba, who played with cobras or vipers as children (Anzar 1974, 6). But such a feat does not necessarily signify spiritual advancement, for it can also be accomplished by using the seventh psychic sense. Through its functioning one can superimpose one's own mental state over the mental or emotional impulses of another human being or animal—a kind of telepathic hypnosis. This is why this sense is often called "mind control."

Another friend, Sonja, used this mind control to levitate. When she was five or six, this ability was a game to her. She would lie in her bed, focus her mind, and rise three or four feet into the air. It was nothing special to her at the time, though it was a closely guarded secret. Looking back over the experience now, Sonja is astonished at what an unusual child she must have been. Later I review an interview with this fascinating woman, who has retained many of her psychic gifts as an adult.

One could not have a complete discussion of this seventh sense without mentioning a phenomenon much less spectacular than levitation or handling poisonous snakes. This is "spoon bending," the ability to bend metal objects with the mind, first popularized by the Israeli psychic, Uri Geller, who became the subject of much parapsychological research. Although one would think that metal bending would offer extremely concrete laboratory evidence for the existence of PK, controversy surrounds such research. For one thing, researchers such as Annamaria Bononcini and Aldo Martelli have found that children who profess PK power often have great difficulty in producing phenomena on command in a laboratory setting (Bononcini and Martelli 1983, 117-125). For another, these "paranormal metal benders," as these children are called in another article (Hasted and Robertson 1980), are often accused of fraud. Stage magicians refute metal bending evidence by demonstrating that such phenomena is easy to fake by using the techniques of show business magic (see Nicol 1979, 16-21).

Nevertheless, many parapsychologists pursue this research, even dabbling with spoon bending themselves. The parapsychology department at J.F. Kennedy University in California occasionally sponsors "PK parties" at which interested adults try their hand at paranormal metal bending. Although some of these adults get good results, the success rate seems to be far higher with children.

Sometimes merely showing them how awakens this ability in children. One woman in San Francisco, who is interested in a wide range of spiritual issues, took her daughters to a workshop given by the well-known lecturer Marcel Vogel. During the workshop, Mr. Vogel suggested to the children present that they could bend spoons and other metal objects if they simply followed a certain procedural sequence. The kids were told how to hold a spoon in their hands, close their eyes, and gently rub the spoon. Then they were supposed to concentrate on "making the spoon feel like butter." Finally they were to visualize it bending.

For four-year-old Rose and six-year-old Adriana, the spoon meditation produced instant and striking results. They could easily bend virtually any piece of metal they could hold. Rose and Adriana were excited about their new-found psychokinesis, but their mother was even more thrilled. She would ask the girls to "perform" for every guest in their home. The kids dutifully bent forks and spoons and keys, but they did not like "showing off" their new power. After three days, both children told their mother they were tired of the game and didn't want to bend metal any more. The mother was sensitive to her daughters' needs and did not press them. After the intensive three days of PK phenomena, not only did the girls stop practicing this power, but they never mentioned it again. After one year, the mother asked Rose and Adriana to try again to bend spoons. The girls went through the steps very carefully, but nothing happened; they no longer had the ability.

Why would psychokinesis come and go so dramatically? If these girls had a psychic ability one year, why would it be gone the next? This seventh sense, more than any of the others, seems to have a strong psychological component. Since in many cases it involves an act of will to alter the physical metal—mind over matter—the state of the child's mind has a powerful effect on the phenomenon. Also, it should be remembered that if everyone has all seven of the psychic senses unconsciously on the astral level, as previously suggested, then the crucial issue is registering impressions on the physical nervous and glandular systems. In the case of these two girls, when they first produced the phenomenon, they were excited and extremely motivated to achieve results. A year later they were no longer interested in spoon bending, and did not care whether they could do it. This psychological shift evidently had an effect on their psychokinetic ability.

Evidence shows that this paranormal faculty is connected in childhood to suggestibility and motivation, and large groups of kids have demonstrated the ability to spontaneously bend metal with the mind after simply being given the suggestion that they could do it. The best known instance of this was initiated in 1973 with the appearance of Uri Geller on the B.B.C. After demonstrating fork and spoon bending, Geller asked his English television audience to try to duplicate his demonstration themselves. The experiment was wildly successful as over 1,500 people reported to the B.B.C. that they had indeed been able to bend metal. The most relevant bit of data for our present purposes is that almost all of these 1,500 people were children between the ages of seven and fourteen, with the average age being nine.

Geller went on to invite the public of Germany, Sweden, South Africa, and Japan to try spoon bending as well, and the results were almost as dramatic as in England. Again most of those who responded to the challenge were children. This unusual epidemic of childhood psychism became known as the "Geller Effect" (Pearce 1977, 189-200).

In the United States, efforts were immediately made by the psychological establishment to debunk Geller. But researchers in England and Japan were already testing some of the children who claimed to be paranormal metal benders. In the Japanese studies, one eleven year old was found to be able to throw a piece of metal in the air and have it twist and bend in odd ways before it reached the ground (Pearce 1977, 194-95).

Joseph Chilton Pearce discussed childhood psychokinesis extensively in *Magical Child,* and to a lesser extent in *Magical Child Matures.* He believes that the PK phenomenon is related to a structure inherent in everyone's mind-brain system (Pearce 1985, 81), but that the ability is not exhibited unless the surrounding cultural environment accommodates its existence and allows it to be exercised. Children, Pearce explains, during their elementary years are in the process of "roughing in" their ideas of how the universe operates by accommodating and organizing their concrete sensory experiences of the surrounding world. This emerging world view, however, is still very malleable, and if their experience demonstrates that people can bend spoons with their minds, then they are suggestible enough to adapt their minds and world view to this newly-discovered sensory reality. This total acceptance of its reality appears in itself to unlock the door to the actual experience of psychokinetic power.

Of course, such a view does not adequately describe the complexities of psychic awareness in children. I've met many children who strongly believe in the reality of such power, yet cannot seem to experience it themselves. On the other hand, many others who are told repeatedly that the psychic world is false, nevertheless are the involuntary recipients of a daily smorgasbord of paranormal perceptions.

In addition to the bending of silverware, another aspect of psychokinesis is the influencing of watches. The mechanism of normal wind up watches seems sensitive to the effects of energy fields. It is not uncommon, for example, for some people to discover that if they wear a wind-up watch, it will not keep the correct time. I myself can buy a new watch, and within one month it will simply stop running. I have noticed this phenomenon since high school days, and I have wrecked perhaps a dozen watches before finally discovering that battery-powered watches do not go haywire when strapped to my wrist. I have concluded that the mechanism of a watch is somehow sensitive enough to respond to particular patterns of etheric energy in the aura. Over the years, I have heard of others who also cannot wear wind-up watches, apparently for the same reason.

Geller discovered his psychokinetic abilities as a child of six when one day in school he observed his new wrist watch behaving strangely. At first the watch simply never showed the correct time, but later it went wild. "One day," he related, "I was looking at the watch when, right before my eyes, the hands started spinning like mad. I really saw them running. Then they stopped at some hour completely different from the correct time. I think that was the first time I realized this thing was being caused by me, that there was something I was doing, or something about me, that made it happen" (Young 1977, 43-44).

Researchers in parapsychology have found that the ability to affect watches is fairly common among children, and that children can actually be trained to do it. In another interesting bit of research out of China, four scientists set out to attempt to measure the psychokinetic force used to move watch hands. They studied a twelve-year-old girl who could move the hands of a watch by passing her hands over it. They also succeeded in training five other children to do this. Then they monitored each experiment with an oscilloscope and camera to rule out the possibility of fraud. The researchers were able to measure an electrical force of more than 100 milliwatts emanating from the subjects. Through a series of measurable, individual pulses, this psychic force was able to affect the gear wheels of the watch. (Nianlin et al 1983, 25-30).

I think it is more interesting and significant to understand how such psychokinetic abilities manifest in the daily life of a child, than it is to study how such abilities can be measured in a laboratory. When it is present, mind control is not an insignificant element in a child's life. It can exert a profound psychological effect on the child. Indeed, it can influence a child's sense of identity and be a powerful force affecting family relations and family dynamics. This can be illustrated by sharing anecdotes about five-year-old Stephen, who was discussed earlier. Stephen not only was telepathic and clairvoyant, but also had psychokinetic abilities, and these were by far the most troublesome of his psychic gifts. Strange, unexplained things continually occurred around Stephen. His parents knew that Stephen was somehow responsible, consciously or unconsciously, for these unusual happenings.

For example, one night the entire family was awakened by the loud blaring of the radio downstairs in the living room. Stephen was already awake, but had not been downstairs. His father went down and was astonished to find that he was not able to shut the radio off. Not only was the switch not in the "on" position, but the radio was not even plugged in. Then suddenly it went off by itself, and Stephen went to sleep.

Sometimes the phenomena occurring around Stephen frightened his mother. Occasionally, when he would come into a room, a picture would drop off the wall or a vase would wobble on the coffee table. Once when Stephen entered the kitchen for lunch, a sharp knife on the counter flipped up in the air, spun around twice, and landed on the floor. Stephen's mother scolded him that time and said one of them could have been hurt. But Stephen said he didn't do it on purpose; it just "happened."

Flying knives and pictures dropping off the wall suggest another category of psychism: poltergeists. Poltergeists (German for "mischievous spirits" or "noisy ghosts") in many cases can be considered a byproduct of seventh sense activity. Poltergeists generally involve the spontaneous movement of objects in a house (usually in a harmless way) and have often been linked to the presence of an adolescent. Stephen's case, however, suggests that the presence of a teenager is not a requirement. In fact, most cases I have personally come across do not fit the "normal" pattern of poltergeists. This leads me to believe that the causes of such phenomena—whether books falling off shelves, lamps crashing into walls, or sudden banging or explosive sounds—are varied.

These causes, from my perspective, can be threefold. First of all, as the name itself implies, poltergeists may in fact be astral entities bent on raising havoc. I have been told that some poltergeists actually are human or non-human spirits (non-physical entities) which are somehow caught in a limbo state between the astral and physical worlds. They are attracted to the intense emotional energies of pubescent teenagers and attempt to drain off that energy to propel themselves into a better, or more stable, state. This process is haphazard, and the emotional energy (from the astral level) can be randomly discharged, causing the often violent moving of objects. Tom Armstrong seems to agree. "Children," Armstrong says, "seem to be tuning in to a subtler level of energy and attracting entities that really are 'out there' in some way" (Armstrong 1985, 123).

The other two causes of this paranormal activity have more to do with the child's own psychic sensitivity, and less to do with outside entities. As the term "mind control" implies, a child with the seventh sense in full operation would have no problem causing the noisy commotion associated with poltergeists all by himself. In most of the cases I have encountered, however, the children involved seem to be unconscious participants in the phenomena; their psychokinesis could well be involuntary. This unconscious use of PK would make it appear superficially as though some outside entity or force is involved, when actually it is the child who causes the disturbances. The third possible cause of poltergeists is that the strong astral forces naturally surrounding and channeled through an adolescent could produce such random phenomena without the teenager actually being psychic at all.

There may be a fourth possibility as well. Poltergeists could be caused by a combination of any of these three circumstances I have mentioned. In fact if all three conditions were present—entities needing emotional energy, a child with PK, and excess astral force due to puberty—polter-geists would very likely be present as well.

An example might be helpful at this point. I was thumb-ing through an old journal from 1931 and happened on an article about a German peasant girl, Hannah Zupp. At age five, Hannah was subject to what appeared to be epileptic fits. The unusual aspect of the fits, however, was that

> ...following each fit there would be strange manifestations in various parts of the house; china dishes would fly about, chairs and tables move of their own accord, books and or-naments would come crashing to the ground (*Meher Mes-sage* 1931, 77).

These poltergeist disturbances seemed in no way to involve Hannah's conscious mind, but were unmistakably related to sudden changes in her nervous system and general bodily condition. Gradually the fits and accompanying poltergeist disturbances lessened over the next six years. Finally, when Hannah was eleven, the "epilepsy" and the polter-geists completely disappeared.

Although the Zupp family imagined that their lives would now return to normal, three years later when Han-nah was fourteen, they had new evidence that their daughter was indeed not an ordinary child. Over a three-month period Hannah's outward appearance changed so completely that she seemed transformed into a different person. Even more mysterious were the trances that began at the same time. Almost every night, Hannah would sleep-walk into the family parlor and produce remarkable works of art, both in pencil and in watercolor. Though she had previously dabbled in art, this prior training in no way could account for the "extremely beautiful landscapes and seascapes" she produced nightly while in trance. She re-membered nothing of these somnambulistic activities. She also suddenly acquired the ability to speak fluent French, Russian and Greek while in trances (*Meher Message* 1931, 78).

When the child is between the ages of twelve and four-teen, as will be shown in the next few chapters, new layers of consciousness open up. These must work through the astral level. It would seem that for Hannah these newly awakened astral forces apparently not only altered her physical appearance, but made available to her knowledge and artistic talent from a previous incarnation (although of course she might have been channeling, which would indicate the awakening of other sanskaras). Although it is simpler to bring such prior impressions through an entranced surface mind, Hannah nevertheless would need a direct psychic link to her astral senses to accomplish it. In Hannah's case, therefore, it might be said that the emergence of new pubescent astral capabilities awakened in her a paranormal faculty.

Normally these astral forces in an adolescent are not nearly as civilized as they were with Hannah. Resentment, anger, rebellion against authority, and jealousy can be components of the adolescent's process of groping for a stabilized ego structure and identity, and poltergeists can sometimes emerge from this process.

Dr. William G. Roll, a psychologist, studied 116 cases of poltergeists from 1972 to 1974, and discovered a number of patterns and consistencies. Despite the fact that both previously cited examples occurred with five year olds, Roll found poltergeists to be definitely most often associated with puberty. The median age turned out to be 13.5 years. In his study he referred to these adolescents as "RSPK agents," that is, agents of "recurrent, spontaneous psychokinesis." More than half of them had either physical or psychological problems—22 actually were prone to seizures, convulsions, fainting spells, or dissociation.

Even the ones without overt psychological problems commonly shared one particular characteristic with all the others: all seemed to have strong conflicts with authority figures—parents, teachers, or employers. Outwardly, many of the RSPK agents appeared to have mild dispositions and non-aggressive personalities. But psychological tests revealed repressed anger and a tendency to deny the existing conflicts in their lives. Many of these children also lived in physical or psychological settings where it was almost impossible to express their anger directly. Roll concluded, "One may theorize that the inner conflict of such subjects finds an indirect avenue through the poltergeist phenomena" (Zuisne and Jones 1982, 413).

Roll's opportunities to study and observe poltergeists in action yielded some intriguing findings. He noticed that objects sent flying across the room during a poltergeist incident followed bizarre, unpredictable patterns. "They follow zigzag and other trajectories that physics fails to predict for falling objects, and they carefully avoid causing injury to the observers" (Zuisne and Jones 1982, 414). This latter characteristic is perhaps the reason poltergeists are referred to as "mischievous" spirits rather than "malignant" spirits. Roll also investigated incidents in which small objects such as stones appeared actually to pass right through walls and other solid objects and into and out of closed rooms (Zuisne and Jones 1982, 414).

Two parapsychologists in Bologna, Italy, also had good luck studying poltergeists and other psychokinetic phenomena. Four subjects, all adolescents, were given psychological tests of various kinds, and all were found to exhibit marked suppressed aggression, which, it was hypothesized, could be finding an outlet in the PK phenomena. Three of the subjects showed evidence of "organic psychosis," which perhaps was traceable to lesions in the brain. The boy involved with the most dramatic of the poltergeist activity proved to be somewhat emotionally and intellectually retarded, which was exacerbated by severe family problems. His parents deserted him, he spent years in an institution, and when he finally was adopted, he developed a strange and ambivalent relationship with his adopted mother. Apparently, one of the results of all this was the appearance for over six months of poltergeists (Bononcine and Martelli 1983, 117-25).

For the parapsychologists, the problem is not the observation of poltergeists or other PK phenomena but finding a scientific explanation. It is not enough to claim that objects move because of an adolescent's projected aggression and hostility toward authority figures, and claiming it is all related to lesions in the brain is inadequate as well. Dr. Roll acknowledged that the most difficult problem facing parapsychologists is that of explaining how in psychokinetic phenomena of all kinds the "subjective becomes the objective" (Zuisne and Jones 1982, 414).

For the esoteric student such an explanation is not nearly so elusive. For one thing, the esoteric view perceives the astral and etheric dimensions of life activity as realms in which the distinction between the subjective and the objective are lost, or at least blurred. As discussed earlier, a person's subjective thoughts become objective impulses of energy on the astral plane—thought forms. It seems plausible that the incredible force of confused and distressing adolescent passions and desires could create thought forms powerful enough to affect changes in physical matter and even move physical objects. Indeed even a person's aura can sometimes be intense enough to alter physical matter. Some of the phenomena which occurred around five-year-old Stephen could have been caused simply by the discharge of etheric force from an extremely vital aura.

Of course, one cannot rule out the possible role of unseen entities. After all, "poltergeist" does translate as "noisy spirit." One possibility is that the elemental spirits of nature—the fairies, elves, and gnomes that many psychic children see—may well be the "noisy ghosts" that we are searching for. Arthur Powell, who researched and collated material on astral entities and astral phenomena from forty well-known treatises, gave some illuminating insights into the elemental kingdom that suggest its inhabitants might be tied into the mischievous activities of poltergeists. Powell stated that these nature spirits have occasional contact with humans, but this contact is not always of a positive nature. They tend to be "tricky and mischievous," and their basic distrust of people leads them to play pranks or frighten people. These pranks, though they can be extremely annoying, are generally not harmful or malicious (Powell 1973 [1927], 183). For instance, Powell says, it is often nature spirits who masquerade as deceased relatives at spiritualist seances. They can produce the "spirit lights," the raps, the moving objects and even materializations—all in the spirit of a playful joke (Powell 181-82).

Their playfulness makes nature spirits particularly attracted to children (Powell 183). In Chapter 7 of this book, I related anecdotes of children's contact with this elemental kingdom. Nature spirits are said to have great rapport with so-called "dead" children in the astral world. But more importantly, they have frequent contact with living kids as well. Somehow it is easy for me to imagine a band of these mischievous creatures basking in the emotional turbulence of an adolescent's aura, getting so "pumped up" by this energy that they zip around his house making all sorts of strange noises and knocking over lamps, pictures, and vases in the process. Of course, such thoughts are merely interesting speculation and should not be taken as any kind of definite answer to the question of what causes poltergeist disturbances.

It does seem a shame that so many parapsychologists feel that their science must build up knowledge and understanding of hidden forces of nature from ground zero. In my view, a much broader understanding of these issues could arise if the scientific research of the parapsychologists could be illuminated by the theories that have been offered for thousands of years by those who have studied and experienced the inner non-material dimensions of life—some of the same realms that the parapsychologists would like to measure objectively. Indeed, it is almost ridiculous to think that these researchers must stop dead in their tracks with questions such as, "How can the subjective become the objective?"

In a way this volume represents my own small attempt to pull together the fields of parapsychology and esoteric philosophy. I have offered several chapters of carefully researched incidents of children's psychic experiences. Most of these have come from my own journals and notebooks, and I have known and personally interviewed most of the children discussed. But research data such as this is only the beginning of an attempt to understand psychic sensitivity in children. Now that the data has been presented and my stories have been told, it is necessary to turn to a more theoretical perspective. The remainder of this book will examine theories which seek to explain how and why children perceive so many interesting things that are completely veiled from adults. I'll attempt to identify the exact nature of this perceptual veil that seems eventually to descend over children's senses, and explain exactly how and when it makes its appearance. The raw data of parapsychology can be illuminated by philosophical theory. The secret life of kids can be explained.

11
Why are Children Psychic?— A Look at Evolution

Ever since I met that first clairvoyant child in 1969, I have been eager to discover the underlying causes for this childhood condition. I remember seven-year-old Brynn, a participant in my original university research project, who was clairvoyant. In addition to seeing people's auras, she befriended a most unusual reptile-like entity that frequently visited her at night. Brynn was eager to discuss her "secret life" because I was the first adult who took her visions seriously. I was able to help her simply by lending my ear, and she certainly was a big help to me in my work at the time.

Years passed, and one day I happened to see Brynn at a shopping center. She was by then a thirteen-year-old junior high school student. When I asked Brynn if she still saw the colors around people, she looked quizzical, and turned her gaze upward as though searching the deepest recesses of her mind. Finally she turned to me and said very seriously, "No, I guess I don't. I haven't thought about it for years. The last time I can remember seeing something like that...gee, I guess I was nine or ten."

Brynn's clairvoyant faculties had faded away so gradually that she had not even been aware of the process. When she was thirteen they survived only as a memory. Why did this girl, who years earlier had identified acupuncture points on my body as flares of yellow fire, lose her abilities? Why was she now interested only in boys and rock-

and-roll music? Why do childhood psychic faculties disappear as children grow up?

My first explorations into the causes for the appearance and disappearance of childhood psychism led to ancient history and prehistory. I discovered a mysterious phrase that seemed to me to reveal secrets of child psychology and processes of developmental growth seemingly ignored by academia. This phrase was "ontogeny recapitulates phylogeny."

"Ontogeny," from the Greek *ontos* (being) and *genes,* (producing or beginnings) is the personal history of an individual living organism. "Phylogeny" is also from the Greek. *Phylo* means "race" or "specie," so *phylogeny* de-

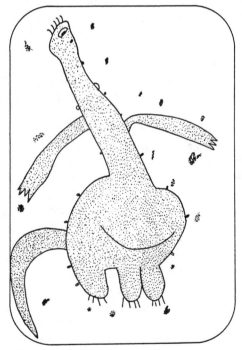

Fig. 14. The dinosaur-like entity that came to visit Brynn every night for six months.

notes the evolutionary development of an entire species. The aphorism "Ontogeny recapitulates phylogeny" means that during development a child actually re-experiences and reviews psychological and physiological states which the human race as a whole progressed through in earlier epochs.

That is an astounding principle, yet is still not the whole picture. If we take the embryological period as the genesis of the unborn child and trace development from conception, we discover that prior to birth the human being actually recapitulates the entire development of life forms from their earliest beginnings on this earth. A human being begins as a primitive, single-celled organism in the womb, and progresses through all the forms of various species (Nilsson 1977, 50). At one point the human embryo is indistinguishable from the embryo of a fish, displaying the structure of gills, although these never become functional (Pearce 1985, 10). At another point the embryo looks like that of a reptile and later like a chicken. Still later it develops a vestigial tail. Only after the eighth week does the human embryo acquire truly human form (Nilsson 1977, 71).

After birth, recapitulation limits itself to phases of human development down through the ages, and this is where we find clues to the causes of childhood psychism. In the earlier embryological phase, science has verified the idea of recapitulation; the vestigial gills and tail have been photographed and the similarity of the undeveloped embryo to prehuman life forms is clear and irrefutable. But the concept of the child recapping the physiological and psychological phases of early man is a notion that does not lend itself to such verification. Paleontologists and anthropologists have only rudimentary guesses about the functioning of the nervous system and brain of early man, and prehistoric consciousness has hardly been mentioned in the literature. After all, how can one know about ancient man's consciousness? There are clues to the early perceptions of man through the study of early scriptural writings such as the Vedas and the Old Testament. In the Old

Testament, for example, the sky is never referred to as being blue—in fact the color blue is never mentioned at all. Perhaps during that phase of human evolution the cool end of the color spectrum was not part of man's perceptual reality. But modern science did not reveal enough data to help my research.

Fortunately, the data relied upon in this book is not limited to the confines of traditional science, but takes into account the realm of occult science. However, the reader should consider the following thoughts as provisional and useful only insofar as they help to account for the data I have gathered concerning early, developmental functioning of psychic abilities in children. Data obtained by occult means must remain speculative and open for modification.

In Western occult literature the "modern" concept of ontogeny recapitulating phylogeny has been discussed for at least a century. H.P. Blavatsky stated:

> The human fetus follows now in its transformations all the forms that the physical frame of man had assumed throughout the three Kalpas (Rounds) during the tentative efforts at plastic formation around the monad by senseless, because imperfect, matter, in her blind wanderings. In the present age, the physical embryo is a plant, a reptile, an animal, before it finally becomes man (Blavatsky [1888], 1963, 1:84).

After the fetus "becomes man" and is born into the world, it begins to recapitulate aspects of consciousness and physiological development known in earlier epochs. If this premise is accepted, then it follows that one can learn about aspects of the development of consciousness in prehistorical ages from a study of the developmental phases of childhood. Conversely, one can learn about children by understanding how modern, logic-centered mentality developed gradually in the course of the evolution of human consciousness. The best way to research this latter notion is to turn again to the esoteric literature. Most literature about prehistorical epochs and the development of early man came to light through paranormal means. In much the same way that a child can remember an earlier lifetime on earth, occult researchers can investigate earlier epochs. The results of this research shed important light on the topic of psychic children (Steiner 1959, 38-41).

The most important notion here is that man in earlier ages did not perceive the world in the same way that modern man does; and other aspects of human consciousness, such as thinking, feeling, desiring and willing, were equally different. For one thing, occult researchers assert that early man possessed a certain degree of clairvoyance, although quite dull and dream-like and not self-conscious (Steiner 1959 [1939], 114).

Dr. Rudolf Steiner, founder of the Anthroposophical Society, discussed the psychological aspects of these ancient human beings in some of his writings. According to Steiner, early man first developed a "will-oriented" consciousness, focused purely on the sensory strength of his action in the world, with little emotional or mental investment in his deeds. In later epochs, emotional and instinctive energies came to the fore and became the central aspects of human consciousness. Still later the intellectual faculties were awakened and the emotional life became less conscious and more dreamlike. It is easy to see how such stages of development could be correlated to different periods of childhood growth. Steiner described in a more detailed manner the consciousness of an early race of man called "Lemurian":

> By and large, MEMORY was not yet developed among this race. While men could have IDEAS of things and events, these ideas did not remain in the memory....But their ideas had a quite different strength from those of later men. Through this strength they acted upon their environment. Other men, animals, plants, and even lifeless objects could feel this action and could be influenced purely by ideas. Thus the Lemurian could communicate with his fellow-men without needing a language. This communication consisted in a kind of "thought reading" (Steiner 1959, 72).

Dr. Steiner goes on to say that these people deeply understood the plant and animal kingdoms through this telepathic inner communication, and they had, in addition, a very developed use of the faculty of will. The goal in life of a Lemurian was to develop a vivid imagination, which Steiner asserts was actually a clairvoyant ability to perceive mental and emotional images (Steiner 1959, 75).

It is easy to think of these characteristics as those of a two- or three-year-old child. Such a child is wilful, impulsive, and focused on building the powers of imagination. The best preschool education, therefore, is one in which the child can learn by doing—by using the will, the power that channels hands, legs, and physical senses. The Montessori educational approach, for example, is developed out of this understanding. The teacher does not teach by telling children something and expecting them to remember, but demonstrates to children how to do a task and invites them to imitate the action. For learning educational tasks, the Montessori preschool teacher relies on the ''muscular memory'' of the child's limbs rather than mental memory. On the other hand, good preschools also allow children plenty of time to play. In play children use their wills to awaken imagination. Images from the child's daily life enliven and activate real play.

So theoretically, the preschool child's consciousness might be compared to that of the ancient race of man often called ''Lemurian.'' But what about the telepathic ability to commune with plants, animals, and other human beings that was said to have been a part of the Lemurian perceptual apparatus? Those who have studied childhood telepathy report that telepathy is strongest in very young children, and particularly so between children and their parents. I have reviewed much of this data in Chapter 5. Joe Pearce stated that a child's first bond is with the mother (and later other family members), and the next bonding is with the earth itself. These bonds with the mother and then Mother Earth are so close that they sometimes result in a kind of inner communion between child and mother or nature. One four-year-old expressed this to me. We were playing in the sand by Lake Michigan when he turned to me and asked,

"Why does the outside here [outdoors] seem like it's inside my home?" The Lemurian rapport with nature could not have been better expressed.

The next phase of prehistorical development mentioned by occult researchers is the race of Atlanteans. Again I wish to share Steiner's views, though Steiner had no special monopoly on this information; many other occult researchers have obtained equally interesting data and partially corroborate what he said about early man. Neither should Steiner's work be taken too literally because in such research, error is not only possible, but probable. According to Steiner:

> If we go back to the first period of Atlantean humanity, we find a mental capacity quite different from ours. Logical reason, the power of arithmetical combining, on which everything rests that is produced today, was totally absent among the first Atlanteans. On the other hand, they had a highly developed MEMORY. This memory was one of their most prominent mental faculties...Nowadays man thinks in concepts; the Atlantean thought in images. When an image appeared in his soul, he remembered a great many similar images which he had already experienced. He directed his judgments accordingly....The faithful memory did not allow anything to develop which was even remotely similar to the rapidity of our present-day progress. One did what one had always "seen" before. One did not invent; one remembered (Steiner 1959, 42-43).

The faculty of logical thinking was beginning to develop at the end of the Atlantean epoch, but it was not until the next race of man (the Aryan or fifth root race) that this mental force fully matured (Steiner 1959, 56). I am purposely avoiding discussion of prehistorical dates for these early races because such dates are highly controversial and, in any event, the timing is largely irrelevant to our present discussion.

Since the individual power of thought had not matured during this period, the Atlanteans, according to Dr. Steiner, always followed leaders whose own development and abilities far exceeded those of the common man (Steiner 1959, 60). They venerated these leaders as almost divine messengers.

Psychic sensitivity accompanied these mental and emotional characteristics. As mentioned, these people had a highly developed memory, a power Steiner connects to an attunement to deep forces of nature. "Memory is closer to the deeper natural being of man than reason" (Steiner 1959, 44). Because of this, human beings then were more attuned to the nature elemental beings than modern man, and they could control what Steiner called the "life force." They were able to "put the germinal energy of organisms into the service of their technology" (Steiner 1959, 45).

All of these aspects of consciousness remind one of the modern child during the late preschool and early elementary years. All one need do is to tell a story to a five- or six-year-old to see how wrapped up the child is with the inner, image-making powers of consciousness, and memory at that age seems phenomenal. Especially before the birth of logical reasoning at about age seven, children want their favorite stories repeated again and again, and they will correct the teller if any details are changed. They often seem to remember every word accurately.

Even after age seven, the child relies on the power of memory, rather than logical thinking, and the child at six, seven, or eight has a very special relationship with authority. The words of the teacher at school are taken as truth, and the teacher is frequently quoted, imitated, and indeed almost worshipped.

The Atlantean connection with earth forces also can be paralleled in the life of a growing child. As discussed, control of life force or psychokinesis can easily be awakened in a child of this age, as with the eight and nine year olds who could use such psychic force to bend spoons in the Uri Geller experiments.

Joseph Chilton Pearce developed some interesting theories about the connection of such childhood psychic talents with the forces of the earth:

> These talents are biological, part of nature's built-in system for communication and rapport with the earth, part of our bonds with that matrix, part of the emerging system for survival...almost surely stage-specific in their unfolding,

and no more fragile or rare than general intelligence (Pearce 1980, 149).

Pearce called these paranormal faculties "primary perceptions" because they arise from an ancient ability to bond with the earth—an ability children share with primitive peoples and with animals (Pearce 1985, 70-71). Although children in a sense are born with primary perceptions, these perceptions do not start to unfold as true psychic faculties until the child is around age four, because "to the very early child, primary perceptions would be indistinguishable from any other experience" (Pearce 1980, 157).

> In the early years, primary perceptions are almost surely part of the general cognitive fabric of the child's reality. Not until some division of labor among brain functions has begun and the effects of selective inattention have encroached will primary perceptions be distinguished by the child as something other than his ordinary five sensory functions (Pearce 1980, 151).

In the child of four there occurs an important brain growth spurt which intensifies his sense of self in relation to and, for the first time, opposed to the world. Once the child's mind begins to separate itself from the earth, which in a sense was previously an undifferentiated part of the self, it is necessary to re-establish links of communication with the earth. These links, according to Pearce, are the natural, childhood psychic abilities.

> Primary perceptions are designed to establish links between self and world, and they utilize sound biological procedures in the brain. Primary perceptions furnish a way of drawing on nature's body of knowledge and of being informed by this general field of awareness as needed for well-being (Pearce 1980, 160).

Pearce offers his own theories, within this model, as to why different psychic faculties unfold:

> Psychokinesis is quite rare before age seven but is frequently found after that age. The reason is clear: Psycho-

kinesis is a creative interaction with the earth, ordinarily stage-specific to the shifts in logic and matrix taking place then.

On the other hand, primary perceptions such as ESP [i.e., telepathy] are simply matters of information selectively drawn from the flow of things through the individual primary process in one's brain and communicated through ordinary conceptual patterning. No creative interaction or acting back on the earth matrix is involved, and so almost surely different brain functions would be employed than in psychokinesis. ESP is simple reception from the primary process, designed to enhance well-being and security and to give information over a wide range (Pearce 1980, 152).

In his later book, *Magical Child Matures,* Pearce gave several examples of how this type of childhood perception, which he has renamed "intuition," is shared with primitive peoples such as Eskimos, early American Indians, and Australian Aborigines (Pearce 1985, 68-71).

Patterns of life of primitive peoples often seem to parallel what archaeologists know about prehistoric peoples. So the fact that children share these "primary perceptions" with earlier peoples is a further indication that these psychic processes are vestigial or atavistic. These two words are often used to characterize paranormal perceptual abilities of children because they indicate that such sensitivities are remnants of earlier phases of human growth. In fact, these vestigial abilities may be remnants of different and earlier modes of biological functioning, as Pearce suggested.

Some esoteric writers speak about physiological processes that function similarly in children, modern primitive peoples, and early man. These biological aspects of consciousness reportedly work quite differently in modern adults. According to these notions, before the present evolution of the intellectual, logical mind, consciousness did not manifest so much through the cerebro-spinal nervous system, but functioned more through the autonomic nervous system. With the evolution of what might be called "brain consciousness," the autonomic functions that previously had been part of conscious awareness "went to sleep," so to speak. And that is our current state of affairs.

In addition, in these former times the astral body was less evolved and developed and could not effectively transmit consciousness from the mental planes into the physical system. This more vaguely or loosely organized astral sheath of ancient man, however, was extremely sensitive to sensory impacts from the astral plane. According to the clairvoyant and theosophical writer Annie Besant, these astral vibrations were able to register on the large, nucleated ganglionic cells of the physical autonomic nervous system due to the aggregated concentration of both astral and etheric matter at the autonomic nerve centers (Besant 1967 [1904], 145). As a result of this interrelation between the unevolved astral sheath and the autonomous nervous system, early man was able to see and to sense superphysical reality along with physical sensations. In fact, according to Dr. Besant, these human beings could scarcely distinguish between the psychic world and the physical world:

> So long as the sympathetic system is acting as the dominant apparatus of consciousness, so long will the origin, astral or physical, of impacts remain as the same to consciousness (Besant 1967, 145).

Dr. Besant ties all this into ancient races, discussed earlier in this chapter:

> The Lemurians and early Atlanteans were almost more conscious astrally than they were physically. Astral impacts, throwing the whole astral sheath into waves, came through the sense-centers of the astral to the sympathetic centers in the physical body, and they were vividly aware of them. Their lives were dominated by sensations and passions more than by intellect, and the special apparatus of the astral sheath, the sympathetic system, was then the dominant mechanism of consciousness. As the cerebro-spinal system became elaborated, and more and more assumed its peculiar position as the chief apparatus of consciousness on the physical plane, the attention of consciousness was fixed

> more and more on the external physical world, and its
> aspect of activity, as the concrete mind, was brought into
> greater and greater prominence. The sympathetic system
> became subordinate and...hence a lessening of astral con-
> sciousness and an increase of intelligence (Besant 1967,
> 147-48).

This "lower" form of psychism or primitive psychism, as
it is sometimes called, survives today in people of simpler
cultures, in many children, and in some mediumistic
psychics. Its impulses are characterized as vague, unfo-
cused, and beyond the conscious control of the subject.
C.W. Leadbeater observed early in this century that more
"primitive" people often possess sporadic etheric vision.
But this clairvoyance corresponded to "nervous disturbances...almost entirely in the sympathetic system, and beyond the man's control" (Leadbeater 1971 [1903] 22).
Besant adds that among modern-day Aborigines consciousness is more localized in the cerebro-spinal nervous
system than was the case with their Atlantean ancestors,
and therefore they can easily distinguish physical sense
impressions from astral ones. The latter are still strong,
however (Besant 1967 [1904], 146-47).

It is fairly obvious that a young child shares this primitive or ancient hypersensitivity to the autonomic nervous
system, both physically and psychologically. It is well
known that changes in digestion or diet easily affect a
child's state of mind. In children younger than age seven
or so, the sense of self seems to depend upon the stomach,
which is controlled by the autonomic system. Preschool
children with their distended bellies often draw pictures of
people in which arms extend out of stomachs instead of
shoulders, and if a three year old says "me," he will point
to his stomach instead of to his heart, as adults will. All
this indicates that the child's consciousness works through
the autonomic system more than an adult's. Rudolf Steiner
noticed this very different direction in a youngster's consciousness:

> It is characteristic of the child that it not only experi-
> ences the external world less consciously than grown-up

people, but also that its experiences are much more intimately bound up with metabolic changes. If a child sees colors, their impressions strongly affect its metabolic processes. The child takes in outer sense impressions right down into its metabolism. It is no mere metaphor to speak of a child digesting its sense impressions, for its digestion responds to all its outer experiences.

In later years man leaves the digestive, metabolic processes more to themselves. He experiences the external world more independently of them....His response to his surroundings is not accompanied by the same lively activity of glandular secretion as in the case of the child (Steiner 1986, 56).

Differences in glandular secretions were also discussed by Max Heindel, the founder of the Rosicrucian Fellowship. He observed that this lower type of psychism, common to children and early man, has to do with the direction the psychic force moves in the astral sense centers, and with the physical glands which this force activates:

In the far past when man was in touch with the "inner" worlds, these organs [the pituitary body and pineal gland] were his means of ingress thereto, and they will again serve that purpose at a later stage. They were connected with the involuntary or sympathetic nervous system. [In] the latter part of the Lemurian and early Atlantean Epochs...man then saw the inner worlds. [Psychic] pictures presented themselves quite independent of his will. The sense centers of his dense body were spinning around counter-clockwise...as the sense centers of "mediums" do to this day. In most people these sense centers are inactive, but true development will set them spinning clockwise (Heindel 1953, 23-24).

Heindel stated elsewhere that the clairvoyance of children has the same involuntary or receptive quality as that of the medium (Heindel 1928, 5).

The literature frequently mentions the early role of the pituitary and especially the pineal gland in the functioning of this involuntary, primitive type of psychism. Recent research has shown that one of the main functions of that enigmatic organ, the pineal gland, is to produce the molecule melanin. Melanin is not only involved with the general linking of consciousness to matter, but is more specifically involved with the perception of light. Melanin can translate sound waves into light and transform electrical impulses into light waves (Pearce 1985, 10). It is no wonder this gland is often referred to as the "third eye." As is the case so often nowadays, modern science is beginning to validate the teachings of the Ancient Wisdom.

Manly P. Hall, the founder and president of the Philosophical Research Society, relates the early activity of the pineal body to the activity of paranormal senses in children:

> It is said that children, recapitulating their previous periods of evolution, have a limited use of the third eye [the pineal body] up to their seventh year, at which time the skull bones grow together. This accounts for the semi-clairvoyant condition of children, who are far more sensitive than adults along psychic lines (Hall 1957, p. 11).

In order to understand the functioning of the psychic senses in children, it is important to grasp the distinction between the so-called lower, primitive, atavistic, involuntary type of psychism discussed in this chapter and other "higher" or voluntary faculties. Children, along with ancient man and modern people who live in close association with the forces of earth, possess this atavistic type of sensitivity. "Higher" psychic ability functions in a completely different way, and is usually fully under the person's voluntary control. This capability exists either as an adult talent or has arisen as a byproduct of spiritual practices such as yoga or meditation.

Even a study of the pineal gland gives evidence of the two major types of psychic functioning. Dr. Besant suggested that the pineal and pituitary glands had quite different functions in earlier epochs than they do now. Since these were connected with early psychic sensitivity, it is not surprising that they formerly had a close tie with the autonomic nervous system.

There are two bodies in the brain especially connected with the sympathetic system in their inception, although now forming part of the cerebro-spinal—the pineal gland and the pituitary body. They illustrate the way in which a part of the body may function in one manner at an early stage, may then lose its special use and function little, if at all, and at a later stage of evolution may again be stimulated by a higher kind of life, which will give it a new use and function at a higher stage of evolution...

As...man advanced from the Lemurian into the Atlantean Race, the third eye ceased to function, the brain developed round it, and it became the appendage now called the pineal gland. As a Lemurian, [man] had been psychic, the sympathetic system largely being affected by the surgings of the undeveloped astral body. As an Atlantean, he gradually lost his psychic powers, as the sympathetic system became subordinate and the cerebro-spinal grew stronger....

As evolution goes on...the pineal gland becomes connected with one of the chakras in the astral body, and through that with the mental body, and seves as a physical organ for the transmission of thought from one brain to another (Besant 1967, 198-201).

So, according to Besant, the pineal gland was connected with ancient psychism through the autonomic nervous system, and then went more or less dormant in its activity. At a later stage in development, it will again reactivate in conjunction with voluntary psychism, completely related to chakra function through the cerebro-spinal nervous system.

In conclusion, I must emphasize an important point: Children possess an ancient, vestigial form of psychism that has very little relation to the mature and consciously directed psychism of someone like C.W. Leadbeater or H.P. Blavatsky. This point is little understood. I have met many people who wish to help children develop their psychic abilities and who even give them elaborate exercises to do with this end in mind. If the premise in this chapter is correct, it is quite obvious why these atavistic psychic abilities should not be encouraged or expanded. They are an evolutionary throw-back, merely a short recapitulation of earlier, less advanced stages.

However, the concept of ontogeny recapitulating phylogeny does not by itself fully clarify these atavistic psychic powers of children. There are many fascinating mechanisms of consciousness in operation that can be understood only in the context of an encompassing spiritual view of the entire process of child development, as discussed in the next chapter.

12
Why are Children Psychic?—
Some Mechanisms

When I was a child I spoke like a child,
I thought like a child, I reasoned like a child;
When I became a man, I gave up childish ways.
1 Corinthians 13:11

Some people nostalgically remember their childhood as a more innocent and carefree time. Others neurotically cling to childish mannerisms or habits which adversely affect their work, their marriage, or their relationship to the world. Such people eventually need to seek psychiatric help, because the way of psychological health is to grow up, to go beyond the habit patterns of childhood.

As children grow up, every aspect of their lives is gradually transformed until maturity is reached. Ways of thinking, patterns of emotionality, and even the structure and shape of the physical body change dramatically by the time the child reaches his majority, between eighteen and twenty-one.

The primitive, atavistic psychic abilities often found in young children also change as the child matures. In most cases, these psychic abilities completely vanish without leaving a trace, and rarely resurface in adult consciousness. Many people feel that it is somehow unfair that they should lose their natural childhood sensitivities. Along with the eighteenth century philosopher Jean Rousseau, they feel that children should keep in tune with the nature forces of the earth and should be encouraged to retain their natural psychic gifts—atavistic or not—and so they search for ways of expanding these sensibilities.

The fading of these childhood abilities, however, is an entirely natural, inevitable, and helpful aspect of development. I agree with St. Paul that the mature human being should put aside "childish ways," including childhood psychic powers. But to understand the relationship between the psychological principles of child development and vestigial, inner sensibilities, we must venture beyond the bounds of traditional developmental theories and return to the esoteric psychology introduced earlier. Before plunging into such explanations, however, I would like to share an analogy developed for lecture purposes to create a simple picture of how children use and then lose their "normal" psychic sense awareness.

The younger a child is, the more focused he is on the objective, external, sensory world. As he matures, his mind, his ego, becomes more prominent, and layers of subjective mental and emotional energy are opened up for him. The more subjective his inner focus, the less he is aware of psychic impressions—because the psychic is really part of the external, sensory environment.

Picture, if you will, a woman driving home from a day at work. On this particular day, this person's mind is free of stress; the day went well, she is happy. Nothing special is on her mind. She has no specific plans for the evening, no worries about the future, and feels just plain good. Since her mind is uncluttered and carefree, she notices a new store that just opened on Elm Street, and the new batch of condominiums that are being built on Seventh Avenue. She sees the row of apple trees that have just burst into bloom and spots a friend walking along the road. In short, she is almost hypersensitive to the external environment because there are no inner concerns.

On another day, however, it is a different story. She has had a bad day at the office. She was late to an important conference and her client was upset. Her secretary has come down with the flu and will be out for several days, though tomorrow she is really needed to help prepare a presentation to the boss. Furthermore, the new neighbors are coming for dinner, and she has to stop for some groceries on the way home. And to top it off, the air conditioner in her car has broken down in the middle of this hot, homeward commute.

What a change from the previous day! On this day she notices no new buildings, trees in bloom, or pedestrians on the sidewalk. In fact, she is so preoccupied with internal struggles and worries, she twice almost causes serious accidents. Rather than being truly focused on the environment and the road ahead, she seems to be driving on automatic pilot, while her mind is spinning with thoughts and worries.

From a developmental point of view, the image of someone driving home from work with a carefree attitude is analogous to the child before the age of seven or eight. The preschool child is a sensory being, totally focused on the surrounding environment due to the fact that a mature subjective mentality has not yet awakened. Such children are often so hypersensitive to the environment that their senses penetrate a fuller range of that environment and also register etheric and astral impacts.

As the child matures, sanskaras build the subjective mind. The developing ego causes increased absorption in subjective thoughts and feelings. The more there are inner thoughts and feelings, the less aware the child is of the external environment—both physical and superphysical. As with the driver on that second day, the child of eight or nine tunes out much of the objective sense data that had earlier so occupied him. Joseph Pearce has pointed out the child's "selective inattention" to the external supersensible world quickly seems to deaden psychic awareness.

Such an analogy makes the process sound simpler than it is. The esoteric understanding of why a child is psychic and why this eventually fades away is based on a description of how the child and his ego-mind incarnate from higher spheres. This process, as I will describe it, is culled and integrated from the writings of a number of clairvoyant researchers. The validity of this vision relies on the accuracy of the individual formulations of these writers, and this is difficult to judge. The researchers seem largely to agree, although they tend to emphasize different aspects of child development. Taken together, their views seem to offer a comprehensive picture of the incarnating being we call the child.

Since the formulation presented here cannot be found in any literature, it is difficult to give individual credit for specific aspects of this view of child development. Credit is acknowledged where possible, but my presentation is a blend of the work of various writers. Research into the superphysical realms, it should be remembered, is undertaken by those who have some direct or indirect access to observable states of energy and matter on the inner planes of consciousness. Two such researchers are Sri Aurobindo and his companion referred to as "the Mother," and another is Max Heindel. The theosophical husband and wife team Dr. Laurence and Phoebe Bendit wrote an illuminating and helpful book, *The Etheric Body of Man*, which outlines the crucial role of the etheric body in the growth and health of children. However, it is the many lectures on child development by Dr. Rudolf Steiner that provide the primary impetus for my investigations. So I am most indebted to him and his work with the Waldorf Education movement.

To follow the discussion here, it might be useful for the reader first to review the vocabulary of esoteric terms in Chapter 3.

The story begins when the timing is appropriate for an individual human atma to reincarnate on the physical plane. The process proceeds gradually and in stages. First a subgroup of the myriad individual sanskaras—those coded units of light which form the causal body of man—separate and "descend" into partial expression in the more energized field of the kama-manas. This group of sanskaras will form the backdrop of the individual's personality in the coming lifetime, though at any single point in that lifetime the majority of them will exist only at a subconscious or unconscious level. But that sanskaric cluster within the kama-manas represents the germinal roots of all thoughts, feelings, words, and deeds slated for potential expression within the context of the specific karma of the coming incarnation.

As these sanskaras gather and organize energy within the structure and pattern of the kama-manas, desire is born. When latent sanskaras are infused with energy, the result is desire—the desire for expression, for manifestation in earthly life, the field in which the sanskaras were originally generated. Sanskaras provide impetus behind the repetition of previous actions, feelings, or thoughts. Since these actions, feelings, and thoughts represent blends of subtle energy which arose from physical expression in the physical world, the "desire" or tendency of the sanskaras is for expression in the physical sphere. The energy generated at this level, therefore, is the impulse of incarnation, the living force which impels an individual into the coming life.

In the meantime, the future parents, according to the dictates of karma, have prepared the fertilized egg within the protective womb of the mother. At this time the atma makes its initial contact with the zygote, sending a beam of light through all the planes of consciousness, ending in a spinning etheric disc. This disc sets up an individual pattern of energy, magnetically attracting forces from all realms of existence to build up the future vehicles for the incarnating child (Bendit and Bendit 1977, 45). This spiritual beam of living energy is what in some esoteric systems is called "the heart." It is a structure that will continue to form the core of the individual's being throughout that incarnation on earth. In a sense this "heart" is the connecting channel between the causal body, the kama-manas, and the physical body. It is a sort of elevator of consciousness along which higher, spiritual forces can be transmitted into lower levels, and through which one's earthly consciousness can become aware of higher forces through spiritual progress.

As the physical body grows within the womb of the mother, etheric matter is simultaneously gathered and organized into the matrix of a new etheric body, and astral matter is similarly coalesced in a new astral vehicle. Since the sanskaric forces dictating these growth processes are "descending" from the levels of the causal and kama-manasic bodies, they are first materialized in astral matter, and then transmitted to the etheric and physical counterparts. These three, the astral, etheric, and physical, work as a unit; they are the vehicles of incarnation—they represent the personality or ego working within the domain of matter. However, although they work in close harmony with each other, their patterns of growth are different and their functions within the consciousness of a human being are very specialized.

The physical body is able to take on its individual characteristics because of the sanskaric forces transmitted through the astral and etheric vehicles. It undergoes the most concentrated and rapid growth in the early years of a child's life. The mature functioning of the astral and etheric bodies represents the more subjective aspects of mentality, and these subtler bodies are developed later in a child's life, even as these aspects of consciousness were developed later in the evolution of human consciousness. The physical body, which was brought to perfection earliest in the history of humanity, is the vehicle most easily available for the incarnating child to influence and use (Heindel 1928, 6-7). So when the physical body is released from the protective womb of the mother, most of the forces working through the astral and etheric planes are focused into processes of physical growth.

During the first seven years of a child's life, the astral and etheric vehicles are not yet "born" as separately functioning components of consciousness. Steiner stated that these vehicles are still protected within womb-like envelopes during the early years:

> Even as man is surrounded, until the moment of birth, by the physical envelope of the mother-body, so until the time of the change of teeth—until about the seventh year—he is surrounded by an etheric envelope and by an astral envelope. It is only during the change of teeth that the etheric envelope liberates the etheric body. And an astral envelope

remains until the time of puberty, when the astral or sentient body also becomes free on all sides, even as the physical body became free at physical birth and the etheric body at the change of teeth (Steiner 1965 [1909], 22).

During early childhood, it has been reported, these two superphysical vehicles are far larger than the physical body of the child and are loosely structured, especially in the region of the head. It seems certain that the layers of the sanskaras which correspond to astral and etheric levels have not yet come into focus for the child. Sanskaras, obviously, do not exist independently in each sphere. Rather, each individual sanskara is made up of membranes of coded light corresponding to the different levels of consciousness (Mackie and Duce 1981, 6). The radiant core of each sanskara is found at the level of the causal body. The densest layer of a sanskara is in etheric levels, although the elongated, double-helix of the genetically coded DNA molecule may be said to be the physical shadow of a sanskara.

The child is trying to incarnate into the physical world and take over, so to speak, his inherited physical body. This work is concentrated on the purely physical aspects of life during the first seven years or so, and focused largely through autonomic processes. Therefore, the child has little subjective mentality, and even his emotional life, so impulsive and easily aroused, really has no depth. What feelings there are seem superficial and come and go rapidly. Even memory, in which the etheric is essential, does not really begin to find full expression before ages four to seven. Adults rarely remember anything from their childhood before age four, and often not before age six or seven.

So the lack of a subjective life before age seven relates to the fact that sanskaras do not find specific expression through astral and etheric mechanisms during this phase, and these vehicles are as yet still "unborn" or incomplete. The freedom from impressions—the natural "purity"—of the etheric and astral vehicles, coupled with their cloud-like, loose structure, indicates the reasons a child can so easily tune into non-ordinary perceptions from other worlds. Objective astral impressions—visions, smells, sensations, thought forms floating by—are all easily reflected and impressed on the child's clear, unpolluted astral body, much as images of sky, clouds, and trees are reflected in a calm lake. This is similar to the case of the driver of the car who had no subjective thoughts bothering her but was free to be ultra-sensitive to the environment.

These passing astral impressions reflected in the child's astral and etheric bodies are easily transmitted into physical consciousness through the unusually energized autonomic nerve centers. These centers are the immature chakras. The Bendits reiterated this view: "the etheric field of every child is for some years entirely open, and hence vulnerable to the atmosphere in which it has to live" (Bendit and Bendit 1977, 56). These authors also suggest that the lower form of psychism common to children, animals, and earlier races of man works mainly through the undeveloped solar plexus chakra and relies on the "passive permeability, or direct flow of impulses through the fourth level [of ether]" (Bendit and Bendit 1977, 113). This "fourth level," to be discussed, has to do with screening the subjective and psychic impressions, which arise from activity in the higher bodies, from waking consciousness. Phoebe Bendit described the undeveloped chakras of a young child:

> In a baby, where consciousness is slight and simple, the chakras show only as slight depressions on the outer surface of the health aura. From the center of this cup a thin stalk runs to the spinal cord or to the particular nerve center to which the chakra corresponds....In the baby, which is psychically wide open to its environment, there is no adequate covering to the depressed cup. In the mature chakra, working healthily, there is a membrane of etheric material which covers the mouth of the cornucopia-like organ and serves as a filter for impressions from the psychic world, and does not allow everything to pass through into physical consciousness (Bendit and Bendit 1977, 35).

Annie Besant described the dreamy consciousness often seen in children. It is helpful to conceive of such children as not completely incarnated or "down to earth." After all, the child existed in the astral realm prior to physical birth, so it seems natural to bring into physical life a sensory residue from this other world. Or, to use Wordsworth's poetic expression, it is completely natural to imagine that the child, descending to earth from the higher spheres, might pull through to the physical a few of those astral "clouds of glory" which are trailing behind. However, such astral "glory" isn't really very helpful. The goal of the incarnate child is to learn to tune into physical reality, a process which usually necessitates blocking off astral impressions. Here is how Dr. Besant posed the issue:

> Up to this age [seven] the consciousness of the Thinker [soul] is more upon the astral than upon the physical, and this is often evidenced by the play of psychic faculties in young children. They see invisible comrades and fairy landscapes, hear voices inaudible to their elders, catch charming and delicate fancies from the astral world. These phenomena generally vanish as the Thinker begins to work effectively through the physical vehicle, and the dreamy child becomes the commonplace boy or girl, oftentimes much to the relief of bewildered parents, ignorant of the causes of their child's "queerness.". . . .
> If parents could see their children's brains, vibrating under an inextricable mingling of physical and astral impacts, which the children themselves are quite incapable of separating, and receiving sometimes a thrill. . . from the higher regions, giving a vision of ethereal beauty. . . they would be more patient with. . . the confused prattlings of the little ones (Besant 1967 [1904], 18).

Another interesting component to the mechanism of childhood psychism relates to the bond between parent and child. It is said that the child does not fully separate from the mother at birth, but that an etheric link between them is maintained, usually for the first four years. This special psychic closeness and connection results in a channel of life force flowing between mother and child (Bendit and Bendit 1977, 56). This channel is not broken by health problems, emotional states, or physical separation. One might even say that the child lives within the mother's aura. This magnetic tie explains the unusually intimate and deep sense of knowing most mothers have for their young ones. Joseph Pearce discusses how Ugandan mothers know exactly when elimination is needed for their babies. This, of course, is fortunate because Ugandan babies wear no diapers, so this intuitive, psychic knowing on the mothers' part prevents a lot of cleaning up (Pearce 1980, 58).

Most importantly, however, this etheric bond explains accounts of parent-child telepathy such as those related in Chapter 5. The mother's strong moods, desires, and emotional states are automatically communicated to a young child, even if the mother is at work and the child in a day care facility miles away. Not every child will be conscious of such maternal moods, yet this reality places tremendous responsibility on the mother to live up to the highest ideals of parenthood. Fathers, too, participate in this bond; the difference is that a mother's psychic link was established during the nine months of pregnancy, whereas a father's must be created and maintained through loving attention to the child. The father rarely is as tuned in as the mother.

When the child is about age four, this link is snapped as the etheric body prepares for "birth" and becomes more independent. This psychic disconnection explains night fears and other anxieties observed in children at this age. The child becomes afraid of the dark, does not want to lie alone in bed, and begs to have the bedroom door left open and night light on.

Before the unfolding of the rational cognitive mind, children live in a flowing sea of emotions that are always changing. A small child is obviously more emotional than rational. As the Bendits have observed, "The early years are energized primarily by feeling, and this increases the sensitivity of the solar plexus, which is often uncontrollably responsive to both external and unconscious internal stimuli; hence the fears and tendency to emotional tantrums at this age" (Bendit and Bendit 1977, 65).

Often children of four and five say and do things that seem "off the wall" and outrageous. Most children are psychically sensitive before the awakening of the rational mind, and these children are merely responding to currents of adult emotionality in their homes. The open astral membrane of a child's consciousness allows emotional states of the adults to be picked up and reflected in the child's words and actions. The child could not explain a particular action or outburst, because it is an unconscious physical modeling of the adults' psychic state.

Although such sensitivity may continue throughout childhood, when the child is six or seven a significant change takes place. This is the birth of the intellect, the process of logical thinking, which Jean Piaget called "concrete mental operations." Most often the child's openness to the nonphysical environment begins to close off. To understand exactly how this occurs, it is necessary to examine the structure and functions of a psychological mechanism of consciousness called the "etheric body."

Most writers on the unseen aspects of child development agree that a significant change takes place in the vital or etheric field of the child at age six or seven. Max Heindel put it this way:

> By the seventh year the vital body of the child has reached a perfection sufficient to allow it to receive impacts from the outside world. It sheds its protective covering of ether and commences its free life (Heindel 1928, 12).

Steiner claimed that the etheric body is "born" at age seven. It is released from its etheric womb and is freed to meet etheric forces directly and independently, both in their physical aspects and in the etheric environment itself (Steiner 1965, 22).

When a child is born, matter used in structuring its immature physical, etheric, and astral bodies (the three sheaths of consciousness connected with mental, emotional, and sensorial life on earth) is inherited or borrowed from the mother's and father's corresponding layers of matter. During phases of childhood growth, the child's innermost mind endeavors to incarnate fully and take over these lower vehicles, so that it can consciously express its personal destiny in manifested life. The sanskaric forces of the child's individuality must grow and also transform the essentially inherited characteristics of the astral, etheric, and physical bodies he is born with. This process proceeds gradually in stages and is not fully completed until the age of eighteen or nineteen.

At around age seven, the etheric and astral energies that were formerly needed for purely physical growth are freed to enliven new depths in the child's subjective life of thinking and feeling. While certain layers of the etheric field remain closely tied to processes and functions in the physical body, other levels become "freed" for subjective functions. Of these Steiner said, "When the etheric body is separated off [at seven], then what formerly worked in the physical body now works in the realm of soul" (Steiner 1965, 24). A split occurs in the functioning of the layers of this vehicle. Christof Lindenau, a student of Steiner's discusses this split:

> During childhood a portion of the etheric body releases itself from its activity in the physical body and is henceforth at the disposal of the activity of the soul. . . . It is precisely through this liberated part of the etheric body that man is by nature predisposed to become a cultural being. . . . It is not simply a question of a partial freeing of the etheric body FROM something, i.e. from the life of the body, but also a freeing FOR something: for the life of the soul itself within the processes of thought, feeling, and volition. Just as this life of the soul requires the foundation of the physical body for its healthy development, so also does it require the foundation which the etheric body offers it by placing a portion of its forces at the soul's disposal (Buckemuehl 1985, 208-9).

Because of this split in etheric functioning, the psychic child often suddenly loses his psychism.

Etheric matter can be regarded as the most subtle component of the physical world, comprised of the formative forces of life underlying all physical processes, organic and inorganic. However, the etheric forces are most observable in their activity in living, organic tissue. It is usually reported in esoteric treatises that the physical plane consists of solid states, liquid states, gaseous states, and matter in four etheric states. However, Phoebe Bendit, in her clairvoyant investigation of etheric states, delineated seven major ethers (Bendit and Bendit 1977, 29-31). Three of these are connected with solid, liquid, and gaseous physical matter and are the formative, living, growth forces behind physical phenomena. The three most subtle of the ethers are associated with subjective experience—the forces behind logical thinking, memory, and emotional life. I have heard these "higher" ethers referred to as "brain force," as they represent the living vitality and higher impulse of consciousness that enliven the thinking and feeling components of physical brain activity. The middle etheric level, or the fourth state, Mrs. Bendit calls the bridge. It is the link between mind and matter, between the subjective, inner consciousness and physical, cellular functions.

The etheric field as a whole, functions as the bridge mechanism between the activities of the superphysical components of the ego-mind and the physical body:

> The vital aura is, in effect, the bridge mechanism between the objective physical world and the individual within. No subjective experience can reach the physical brain without it, no impact from the outer world can reach the mind except by means of it (Bendit and Bendit 1977, 24).

The focus of this bridging mechanism is at this middle etheric level, which is often called the etheric web or the etheric screen.

Sanskaras working from the kama-manas gradually penetrate into the etheric field and surround themselves with etheric matter during the first seven years of life. These etheric sanskaras form lines of force which articulate with the nerve currents of the physical body. When a child is seven, these two networks of energy join and begin to work as one. The vague etheric cloud seen by clairvoyants around a young child's physical form now tightens around these emerging, highly individual sanskaric patterns, and the entire etheric configuration begins to conform and mold itself according to the contours of the child's physical structure.

Because the ego's individual sanskaric network becomes the etheric body only at this age, in the East it is said that a child is not karmically responsible for his individual actions until age seven. Sanskaras create and guide karmic relations, and it is not until these sanskaras are rooted in the etheric level that karma can be processed. This is not to say that the circumstances of a child's early life are not affected by karma. The results of previous karma can and do manifest in the child, but new karmic forces cannot be generated, as a rule, before age seven.

The Bendits discussed the etheric maturity reached at age seven in a somewhat different way:

> If development is normal and has taken place under good conditions, about the age of seven the child enters into possession of a fully formed, if not fully developed, etheric organism in which all the levels of energy will be functioning basically in the way they will function for the rest of its life (Bendit and Bendit 1977, 60).

The network of sanskaric fibers reveals itself most clearly to clairvoyant vision in the web that grows over the child's chakras:

> Usually around seven, the chakras change. . . . They develop a fine mesh of etheric energies like a membrane, over the open end. This membrane or web has a special function, in that it filters out the impacts from the psychic world and limits what enters physical consciousness. In this way it not only shuts out invasion from the objective physical world but also from the personal unconscious or subjective psychic world of the individual himself (Bendit and Bendit 1977, 59).

This web and the fourth level of the etheric body act as the bridge of consciousness for the child, but they also serve to create a division or separation in the consciousness as well. Previous to the web's growth, or "tightening," there is a certain unitary consciousness. Sensory impressions, thoughts, feelings, and psychic sensitivity are all blended together into a scarcely distinguishable whole. The child thinks with his fingers, feels with his stomach, picks up paranormal impressions through the sensitivity of practically every part of his anatomy. But when the etheric web tightens and the sanskaras start to function through the medium of the etheric body, and, as Steiner said, the ego begins to "descend," entirely new levels of thought and feeling begin to open up in the child's consciousness. There is a dramatic splitting of conscious awareness between the objective life of the senses and the subjective life of the mind and heart. The mental and emotional processes, which previously had flowed into and mingled with the actual chemistry of physical life, are now blocked at the etheric web. Hypersensitivity to metabolic activity and the workings of the autonomic nervous system dull, and eventually consciousness withdraws completely from this level. The etheric counterpart of sanskaras focuses consciousness for the first time on purely subjective activities.

The more the child's thought processes create a full and rich subjective life, the more unresponsive the child becomes to paranormal impacts from the psychic environment. The subjective world becomes so divided from sensory life that the etheric matrix gradually prevents superphysical impressions from passing through to awareness at all. This is like the movie camera focused on a distant view, then suddenly refocused on a person in the immediate foreground. When the camera is refocused, the background, formerly so clear, becomes a blur. Similarly, a child's subjective experience of sanskaras comes into mental focus, and this very refocusing of consciousness causes the psychic environment to blur. The Bendits said that as a child incarnates more fully into his physical body, he becomes more completely involved with physical life, and the psychic world is crowded from awareness. The psychic becomes the victim of selective inattention:

> ...it is the exception rather than the rule that [psychic impressions] penetrate the barrier of the etheric field and so make themselves known to physical waking consciousness. This is in part due to unresponsiveness in the fourth etheric

level, but it is also due to the fact that we are so busily occupied with physical action, and with the enormous crowd
of physical impressions which are constantly assailing our
senses. We therefore pay little attention to the subtler and,
usually, rather muted stream of extrasensory impacts which
underlie them (Bendit and Bendit 1977, 112).

The child's early psychism works through the primitive
medium of autonomic processes in the abdomen and the
solar plexus chakra. With the growth of subjective awareness, consciousness leaves the abdomen, ascending eventually to the region of the head, where adult consciousness
seems to reside. Higher or voluntary psychism functions
generally through the etheric brain and through the chakras
in the head (Bendit and Bendit 1977, 113), so that involuntary childhood psychism has little relationship to the awakening of mature psychic awareness.

As a footnote to this discussion, it is interesting to realize that the etheric screen at the middle etheric level brings
about the mature ability to form mental images or pictures
in the mind. This fourth etheric link "acts as a screen on
which (a) physical sense percepts register and are perceived by the indwelling mind." In addition, "(b) the con-
tents of the mind itself are thrown [onto the screen],
through which they may become known to physical waking
consciousness" (Bendit and Bendit 1977, 98). Steiner reported that the mentality of children between ages seven
and fourteen is characterized by an imaginative picture-
making ability. An understanding of this picture consciousness is highly significant in all pedagogical work at the elementary school level. It is actually this etheric screen that
allows pictures imprinted on the sensory mechanism to be
transmitted to the mind, and conversely to transmit pictures
from the mind to brain consciousness. This further explains
why so many adults have no clear memory of their childhood before the age of six or seven.

The next change in consciousness in the growing child
which is relevant to understanding childhood psychism occurs at puberty. It is related to the ability of the physical
body to reflect forces of the astral organization, which rep-

resents the mature ego or personality in incarnation. These astral forces affect the process of the circulatory system, stimulate the endocrine glands, and work right into the growth of the bony structure of the body (Steiner 1972 [1928], 83-86). The child's ego at puberty fully incarnates into his body, even into the body's mineral substance. These processes actually start around age nine when the pressure of the astral body begins to push in on the edges of the still growing etheric body, and the elastic surface of the latter stiffens somewhat. The child loses some mental and emotional flexibility and begins to express strongly his own individual opinions. This is also a time when the child who has held on to a little of his clairvoyant or telepathic sensitivity is apt to lose it.

The transformations within the youngster at puberty, however, are far more dramatic and exciting. Occult researchers say that at this time the astral body is "born"—released from a protective envelope of astral matter and freed to express itself as an independent vehicle of consciousness of the ego in incarnation (Steiner 1965, 22). This means that sanskaric forces (from kama-manas) which operate through astral matter (or the astral layer of the sanskaras) become mature and are accommodated by the lower etheric and physical structures. When this occurs, there is a vast expansion of mental, emotional, and physical life. The adolescent becomes capable of abstract reasoning, adult desires, and mature sexual functioning of the physical body. When the protective astral womb is removed, the astral body not only becomes a fully expressed aspect of conscious life, but also is free to directly contact environmental astral forces (Steiner 1965, 23).

Even though these outside forces are generally experienced only on a subjective mental level, they nevertheless can be quite disturbing. The astral plane is a world of opposites—pleasure/pain, love/hate, joy/sorrow. Intense contact with these potent forces can throw the adolescent off balance at times. Max Heindel described this difficult phase:

> That is the time when the feelings and passions are beginning to exercise their power upon the young man or

woman, as the womb of desire stuff which formerly protected the nascent desire body is removed. When the
desires and the emotions are unleashed, the child enters
upon the most dangerous period of its life, the time of hot
youth from fourteen to twenty-one, for then the desire body
is rampant and the mind has not yet come to birth to act as
a brake (Heindel 1928, 18).

According to Steiner, before the child is twelve or thirteen,
the "unborn" astral body is not articulated or lined up
with the physical form, and it extends well above the head.
At puberty the astral actually descends through the head,
electrifying the pituitary gland, which in turn stimulates the
entire endocrine system. In addition, the chakras deepen
and extend fully into astral matter. There is also increased
activity in the cerebral spinal nervous system as a result of
brain stimulation, and the child's mental life expands into
what Jean Piaget called "formal mental operations."

Phoebe Bendit observed that as astral influx enlivens the
chakra system, the balance among the centers can be drastically upset, and psychic disturbances can result:

> ...with the psychic and the physical changes, the chakras
> are also disturbed, and remain so until the new pattern of
> both mind and body is established and stabilized....It can
> be said that during the period corresponding to most rapid
> physical growth, they are apt to be thrown out of balance,
> to become unstable and over reactive and, to some extent,
> vulnerable in the same way as are those of a very small
> child....At this time of life, new currents, both from the
> subtler, psycho-spiritual levels and others from the chemi-
> cal, come into play and have to become readjusted around
> the central fourth [etheric level] before poise and stability
> are regained (Bendit and Bendit 1977, 68).

In my experience, a child is apt to become either more
or less psychic at puberty, but rarely is the status quo
maintained. Since the ego is more solidly incarnated and
there is a tremendous expansion of the subjective life of
thoughts and feelings, often the last vestiges of psychic
ability are lost. The brooding teenage boy and the social
teenage girl become so preoccupied with their newly found
selfhood that the psychic hyperawareness of the world
around them fades. However, since their egos are finding

full expression, innate religious or occult interests stemming from past lives often begin to crystallize at this time. But these new spiritual interests have nothing to do with earlier paranormal awareness.

The powerful astral energies seemingly can do more than throw the chakras out of balance. Occasionally, astral forces discharge into the psychic environment, creating poltergeist phenomena. Various types of astral beings, usually of a subhuman variety, can be attracted, and the unbalanced chakras of the adolescent may allow him to perceive these entities on astral or etheric levels. One can easily see why adolescents are often interested in seances, ouija boards, or magic. However, dabbling in such astral games can have disastrous consequences, throwing off the teenager's emotional balance even more, or attracting unpleasant poltergeist-like entities. However, as seen in Chapter 9, these poltergeist disturbances are usually of short duration.

When the chakras reach a state of mutual poise with normal adult functioning, psychic awareness again closes down, unless there is a predisposition to such awareness from earlier lifetimes. In that case, such a psychic talent may well manifest during the teenage years. I have met one or two people who opened up permanent adult psychic ability at around the age of thirteen or fourteen. This higher type of psychism, however, would work through the cerebral spinal system and function under full, conscious control.

Sometimes adult psychic ability appears between ages eighteen and twenty-one, a time when kama-manas fully descends and integrates with the three lower vehicles of ego expression. Although kama-manas is not really a component of conscious awareness, sanskaras waiting for expression on that level of existence do filter through to astral consciousness and awaken new propensities, talents, and interests. The view is often stated in theosophical literature that it is at this age that the incarnating ego is ready to take on its life's work, to find its destiny in the world. Psychological damage can be done when a parent or a school system tracks a child into a career before his inner propensities have clearly unfolded.

During childhood, the youngster moves from a life of more objective, sensory awareness to more subjective awareness; from a life of more concrete mentality to a life of more abstract mentality; from a life of egolessness and a feeling of unity with all life to the separate, independent feeling that comes from full ego awareness.

These processes all have to do with the subtle units of life energy, the sanskaras, gradually working their way more fully into expression through physical, etheric, and astral levels of materialized mind. The physical, etheric, and astral bodies function as a unit in the mature adult, expressing specialized aspects of the mind in earthly incarnation. The higher mind, in essence, is itself a bundle of sanskaras, and these are gradually released into expression in the materialized personality. Guided always from the essential mind at the causal and kama-manasic levels of being, the growth and articulation of the physical, etheric, and astral bodies take place in successive stages which represent phases in child development.

Although astral and etheric forces work continuously through the various physiological components of the physical body, these two layers of being also represent more subjective levels of experience. Thus, as the astral and etheric vehicles grow and finally reach maturity, the child's subjective life of thinking and feeling gradually expands. With the newly developed focus on subjective life processes, objective awareness of the psychic environment fades. The same subtle forces that made the young child psychic are responsible for the natural and normal veiling of these inner perceptions. The psychic child comes down to earth, the heavenly vistas vanish, and now "...he has forgotten everything."

13
Olga Worrall's Secret Childhood

A year before her death in January, 1985, I had the good fortune of meeting Olga Worrall, who had numerous psychic gifts, as did her late husband Ambrose. They endeavored to use their gifts to help as many people as they could, opening the New Life Clinic in Baltimore to offer healing and counseling services. They also lectured widely and gave seminars on spiritual healing and various aspects of the psychic world and psychic sensitivity. They continually maintained that the functioning of the psychic is merely one aspect of a spiritual life, a philosophy which they expounded in numerous books, including *The Gift of Healing* and *Explore Your Psychic World*.

In May of 1983, two friends, Susie Isaacs and Dr. Pascal Kaplan, journeyed to Baltimore to interview Olga about her psychic childhood. Susie Isaacs is the author of four books and many articles on education and parenting. She was hoping to write a magazine article on issues concerning the psychic child. Dr. Kaplan, who had moderated several seminars with Olga, is the director of Searchlight Seminars in California and the author of the book *Understanding Death*. Susie's article never materialized, so she offered the interview transcript for use in this book.

Olga's childhood experiences are fascinating, and her bold and unabashed advice to parents of psychic children enlightening. The following is a transcript of that interview, slightly shortened and edited. The interview begins with Olga describing the dead people who frequently visited her in her childhood.

Olga: It was when I was three years old that I recall first seeing people in my bedroom or in the house, and I would describe them to my parents. And my parents would be startled because these people were friends of theirs in Europe.

SI: The figures were always people your parents had known?

Olga: Yes, that they had known in Europe, but [my parents] did not know that they had died. And a week or two later, they would get a black-edged envelope—they don't do those things any more, but they did then—and it would describe the passing of a person that a week before, at the time of the person's passing, I had described to my parents. And sometimes they would give a little message for my parents. I remember one came and had a little dog with her....I would see them, talk to them, and suddenly they were gone. But at that age I didn't put two and two together and figure out that humans don't fade away.

SI: Did your parents know what you were seeing?

Olga: Well, my parents knew that I was seeing dead people. After all, in the Russian Orthodox church, you know, we believe in communicating with dead people. That's part of our tradition. And so what disturbed them was the fact that *I* should be seeing them. They felt that this was something that was set aside for saints or prophets....

They were deeply concerned about how I would be able to cope with this particular gift in America. In the old country, people would take it in their stride. They'd take you to the church, the priest would bless you and say that you have a marvelous gift, and that's that. And then everybody in the villages in Russia would respect you. They would call such a one either *didot* or *baba* meaning a grandfather of wisdom or a grandma, and they would go visit him. The *babas* would be the healers and would deliver the babies. They would make predictions, too. In the old country they made no bones about it. But my parents knew that, in America, the things that happen in Europe won't go.

SI: Was anyone else in your family psychic?

Olga: Every doggone one in my family has had a psychic experience, and they were all afraid to talk about it. . . . I used to get more spankings because I would tell things. Mother would say, "Keep your mouth shut! You're going to be laughed at." . . . . They went to the church where they had a Mass said, and they lit candles, hoping that God would remove this gift. . . .

PK: But, Olga, how did that make you feel? You had this gift and yet your parents wished you did not have it.

Olga: . . . . What does a five or six year old know when they go to church and light a candle? My father said it wasn't that he didn't honor my gift. He was just afraid when he thought about how the saints were persecuted or stoned when they would have a vision or communicate with the dead.

SI: How did they explain what was happening to you when you were little?

Olga: . . . In those days, they didn't explain anything . . . . You just had psychic ability or you didn't. . . . When I was a kid, I thought everybody could see what I saw, which was very comforting, you know. It wasn't until I was ten years old that suddenly I realized everybody didn't see what I saw.

PK: How did you come to realize that?

Olga: Well, I had a baby brother, and he was six months old, and to all intents and purposes he was a perfectly healthy, normal kid. I had a sister in the spirit world who came to me and said, "Joey is going to die in three days," . . . I ran and told my brothers. They went and told my mother that Olga says that Joey's going to die in three days. Boy, did I get a lickin! Oh, my mother was so annoyed and said, "What's the matter with her? I have a crazy child." Well, the awful thing is that three days later Joey died very suddenly. It was a heart malformation that had not been detectable. . . . Then I was frightened. Not only did I have a spanking before and after he passed away, but I had the strong feeling that somehow I killed him. . . . . I suffered through it until I was about fourteen years old, and then I began to put two and two together

.... I then thought, "Well, maybe [I was] catching the shadow of coming happenings.

SI: Were you still in touch with the same sister [in the spirit world] afterwards?

Olga: Oh, yes. This sister passed away before I was born, and she's one of my closest friends.... She just talks to me and then fades out of the picture. And it's all right, she has to go away.... She's very beautiful—I just love her.

. . .

[Olga told of another sister in the spirit world.]

Olga: When I was about seven years old, I was ironing handkerchiefs and pillowcases... [while] my mother was ironing my father's shirts. Suddenly I saw this little girl. She said, "Mother didn't give me a name." And she said, "I want mother to name me Eva, because that's what she was hoping to name me."

Well, I gave the message to my mother, and my mother almost died.... She had this child who was a six month preemie [and] passed away at birth, and it wasn't baptized.... [My mother] told me [about this] later, when I was about fourteen years old. You know, they didn't talk about babies or anything to girls till they were about fourteen. You were supposed to be modest. But I kept saying, "Ma, tell me about Eva."

Well this is the story. When she was carrying Eva, she said, "If it is a boy, I will name it Gabriel, after its grandfather. If it's a girl, I will name it Eva."... The very night when I had gotten the message, my mother and father went to church and they had a baptismal, and named this baby Eva....

I have five sisters in the other world. Later I met a woman named Belle Cross who had been tested at Johns Hopkins for her psychic abilities.... The first time I met her we were sitting on a sofa, and she said, "Oh, you know you have a sister in the spirit world, and she tells me that you were responsible for having her named. Her name is Eva. And she just loves you; she's so happy that now she has been named and claimed."

SI: How old were you when you healed your mother of kidney stones?

Olga: My mother was facing an operation [for] a floating kidney, not a stone, from having all those children, . . . It was terribly painful. The doctor would come and push it back in again and tape her. He said that she'd have to have an operation to have it sewn back, but it's not always successful. . . . This particular day, she asked me to touch it. She must have been in agony. I did, and that was the end of that. I was about nine years old.

SI: Had you done other things for her before then?

Olga: Oh yes. She'd have a headache, and my mother would say, "Put your hands on my head." I never thought what I was doing was healing. I was just touching. I didn't go into ecstasy, I didn't go into samadhi, I didn't do anything. I didn't know there were such things. I just did it naturally. All I knew was that she got well.

And that's how it went around the neighborhood. When somebody was really sick and they'd had the doctor, my mother would say, "Now, they had the doctor, so you just go in there and put your hands on them." That was my early stage. But I'll tell you, I didn't do it joyously at that time. The joy came later.

PK: When you do the laying-on-of-hands, [do] you feel heat?

Olga: No, not necessarily. Only rarely will I feel something like electrical current go through—very rarely. As a kid, I wouldn't have known what it was. . . . It's just like electricity. We don't know what electricity is, but we use it. . . . And so it is with healing. We don't know what it actually is.

SI: Don't psychic children often feel kind of lonely if they don't have someone to share it with?

Olga: Well, naturally. If you're all alone and something very wonderful happens to you and you can't tell anybody about it, it's not wonderful anymore. . . . When I was younger, my mother listened to me. And then there came a time in life when you didn't want to talk to even your mother, because you're hoping that she thinks you outgrew it, and she's probably hoping the same thing. That happened to me as a teenager.

SI: What advice would you give parents who had a child like you?

Olga: If parents discover that they have a child that sees dead people, they must make absolutely certain that the child really sees these things and has not read books or developed a vivid imagination. You can make sure of this by questioning the child and seeing if there would be some truth to what the child was getting. That's what I liked about my parents, you know. They didn't swallow everything I said. I had to prove it. And then parents shouldn't openly encourage the child. Just say, "Oh, is that so?" People do go to extremes sometimes. If they've heard that some children are psychic, [or] if the child has an imaginary playmate, they [think they] definitely have some kind of psychic ability, when it isn't necessarily so.

[On the other hand] I've seen children with psychic playmates. And I've said to the parents, "Has he ever mentioned a playmate? Well, you know, he's telling you the truth."

We once met a little girl [who] had a playmate. Ambrose, my husband, and I saw the playmate. He was redheaded. So Ambrose said to the girl, "Why don't you describe your friend to me?" Well, my gosh, the kid described exactly what Ambrose and I saw: a red-headed kid about six or seven years old.

SI: Why does a child in the astral come to play with living children?

Olga: Well, just to play . . . . One Thursday morning I saw a man and wife and five kids sitting in the center pew in the New Life Clinic. [One] girl had a big hair ribbon on her head, and I thought, "Well, boy, they're coming back to the old style of hair ribbons."

It turned out both [the man and woman] were Methodist ministers, and they asked if I would come and have lunch with them. Then they wanted to talk to me about healing.

181

They called the kids and [only] four came in. I said, "Where's the little girl who was playing out there with your daughter?" They said, "Well, we didn't see any little girl. We have nobody here, just each of us, two boys and two girls." And then the daughter spoke up, "Oh, that's my friend." The mother and father [being] Methodist ministers, were ready to die. They said, "What's her name?" So she named her friend and said, "She comes and visits me at night, and she helps me with my homework at school." It seems they just had a wonderful time together. I asked, "What does she wear in her hair?" She said, "Oh, she wore a great big hair ribbon."

It was her playmate, her unseen friend. The parents almost died. And I said to them, "Now, listen. Why are you acting up like that? John Wesley had a playmate." And so we talked about it. They asked their daughter, "How long has she been with you?" And she said, "Oh, a long time. As soon as you leave my bedroom at night, she comes, as soon as you put my light out. And when you come back to check, she goes away." The mother said, "Where is she now?" "Oh, she had to go home."

I saw that kid, and the little girl verified it. But the parents never saw her.

PK: When you were a child, did any of your brothers and sisters sympathize with what you experienced and approve of it, or were they all pretty scandalized?

Olga: Well, I had three brothers that were quite psychic. . . . One became a captain in the navy, and when I was older he said to me, "You know kid, you better learn to keep your mouth shut. I see them too. When I go on late watch on the ship's bridge, I see the ghosts of sailors walking around and watching the ship." So he was quite psychic.

SI: Did you have one brother that didn't approve?

Olga: Oh, I had one, two, three brothers that didn't approve. They just didn't want to have anything to do with such things. . . . When you die, you croak, and that's the end of you! And they never changed their minds. . . .

SI: Olga, when you would put your hands on people as a child, did you think that it was having an effect?

Olga: ...I always thought it worked, but my mother kept it very subdued. [It was] just like having curly hair or something.

SI: Was it your mother who told you that God was doing it, or was that a feeling you had?

Olga: Oh, nobody told me it was God. I just knew it. They never told me anything other than to keep my mouth shut about it.

PK: You were telling us that when your brother died and you had precognition of that, there was some difficulty. You said you felt guilty about that. Did you have [any other] feelings?

Olga: Well, the thing that I felt was that I should have kept my mouth shut. By telling my brothers that Joey was going to die, I thought that maybe I had made him die, and that if I had not said it, then he would not have died. But honey, I was ten years old then....[That] experience really shook me....Finally I just came to the conclusion that I had to keep my mouth shut.

SI: Did you stop telling your mother at that point about your experiences?

Olga: On rare occasions I would tell my mother...so she wouldn't get into the habit of thinking that nothing was happening. So periodically, I would share with her something that I would experience....And then I would keep quiet....

SI: When you told her about things before you were ten, did you think she could see them too?

Olga: Oh, at first I thought she did. I'd say, "Ma, can't you see her?" And mother would say, "No dear, I can't see anything."

SI: But when it was somebody that she had known in the old country, would she acknowledge that she thought you had seen something real?

Olga: No, not until they would get the letter from the old country. And then my parents would talk about it to each other. You know they would talk Hungarian between them, but I could understand what they would say....And that's how I knew it was real.

PK: Did you ever have any problems in school because of this?

Olga: No, because I shut it off....It was mainly at night, you know, when I'd go to bed and all the lights had to go out....I'd go off to sleep, and then I'd be awakened. My favorite sister would be standing there by my bedside, and she'd tell me all sorts of things....Periodically, [she] would come and we'd have a nice time....She told me she was Margaret and she was my sister. And we had had a sister Margaret....She'd tell me that she was with me and watching over me, and if I had a difficult problem at school, she'd say, "Well now, if you just attacked the problem this way..." But she never did it for me. She just gave a suggestion, a hint.

SI: We were talking about what advice you would give someone who had a child who was psychic or could heal. Do you think children like that feel different?

Olga: Well, if you bring [such a child] up properly, he shouldn't feel different. It should be just another phase of his life....You don't make a big deal by making him think that he has to excel beyond his capacity in order to get attention. So I would say this: You would be very cautious with the child, and if the child did say, "Oh, mommy, I saw this and that," you would listen very carefully and make sure that the kid wasn't hallucinating. You know, kids' imaginations can really be wild.

SI: How would you tell the difference?

Olga: Oh, you can tell the difference, honey. And, then if it is genuine clairvoyance, just say, "Well, those are things that happen sometimes, but they must not happen all the time." The child's life shouldn't get all mixed up. There's a time for a psychic experience and a time to be normal.

SI: Would you tell them not to talk to other people about it?

Olga: Yes, I would. I would tell them that we don't discuss this outside of the house. You come and tell mother or daddy what you have experienced, but we don't talk about it, because not everybody understands....

SI: Do you think it's ever scary for children to see some of these kinds of things?

Olga: Well, if the child only sees a portion of an experience, it might sometimes frighten him. I'm sure that I had my fears when I first experienced these things. I think we instill a lot of fears by telling the children of the boogie man and whatnot....

If the child saw something that scared him, and I knew that the child did see it, I would tell him, "Well, you know, honey, some people can see beyond the normal range of vision, and you happen to be able to see a little more than we can see. But it's nothing to be afraid of."

I remember as a child, when I saw something scary,...I would have a grand time talking to my [astral] visitors, and finally I'd say, "Oh, I'm not supposed to be talking to you." And I'd pull the blankets over my head, and then they'd disappear. That seemed to break the contact. That was my technique.

A child should not put too much of his time into it. It tends to unbalance a child. And it's so important when children are growing up that they be balanced and that they be in full control and not permit anybody to control them, especially in this....That's why you have to keep a discipline there. They should concentrate on their daily chores and all that, so they don't go mooning about.

I've had letters from people telling me their kid sees spooks and sees this and the other thing, and they've had him to the psychiatrist and all that. And I just say, "Now, you just talk to the child and tell him sometimes you see them and sometimes you don't. You can't live that way. You have to remember that you're in this world [but] a part of you is in the next world. But this world is the most important world now, at this moment."

There's usually no problem because when they go to school, they shut it off so doggone fast it isn't funny. They get friends and their attention is on school, and when the psychic leaves, the kid will say, "Well, so what?" You know, they're not excited over it.

PK: What about the negative things in the astral?

Olga: Oh, there are negatives. Of course there are. But you protect your child with prayers....When children are with me and say they are afraid of these things, I say, "Well, you can't be afraid, because only that which is good comes from God. God wouldn't let a monster or a boogie man come near you."...You just say, "Oh, did you see a ghost? How nice." So we should try not to destroy the psychic in a child, but rather just subdue it a little until the child is able to handle it.

SI: Have you ever had cases of kids coming to you who were possessed?

Olga: Oh, yes. A lot of our poor kids were led astray during the drug era. They'd bring them to the New Life Clinic, and I would raise hell with the kids. I said, "What the heck are you trying to do to yourself by taking these drugs?" Because I was clairvoyant, those kids would listen to me. And I would tell them they could get themselves into real trouble with drugs. In real clairvoyance, you don't trigger it off with drugs, because you are lowering yourself into the gutter of the astral world that way. A lot of these kids stopped taking the drugs. Indeed they did; they listened and they stopped.

PK: Olga, let me ask you about the distinction between psychic awareness and spirituality. Sometimes when a child is having a psychic experience, his parents get it mixed up with spirituality. The essence of what you really care about is letting God take over—recognizing that God's in charge of everything. And it's not the clairvoyant experience that really counts.

Olga: No, the clairvoyant experience is just a little tid-bit, a bonus. A lot of people can be very spiritually oriented and not have a psychic bone in them. And yet, some people can be quite spiritual, decently spiritual, and have psychic ability as well. "Psychic" only means anything pertaining to the soul—the psyche. And it means that certain individuals have a greater awareness or ability to function on that higher dimension. Being psychic doesn't make you more spiritual, and being spiritual doesn't necessarily make you more psychic. But when you get a good balance in there, that's lovely. This is why I feel that when a child does display psychic ability, he should be taught things of the spirit and discipline...so that he will know that he is responsible for his behavior when he's in that psychic state.

PK: One of the things that I've seen a lot of in parapsychology is people separating out psychic experience completely from God and from any kind of spirituality, and wanting to develop it....Could you talk about that a little bit?

Olga: I would say...that if they tried to divorce the psychic from the spiritual, they're going to get into a lot of trouble, because the spirit is lying there dormant, and it's going to pop up. And the kid is going to have a hard time until he becomes aware of his spiritual nature. Then, if he just wants the psychic, he will end up entertaining poltergeists and mischievous spirits. But when he takes the psychic and spiritualizes it, then he has something very precious, and then he can do a lot of good. Parents can help in this process by their own thinking, by their own behavior, and by recognizing the fact that these kids are the sparks of God, and helping them become aware of the part that they play in life by permitting the real spirit to manifest.

But instead, sometimes the parents start abusing the child's talent by telling the child how great it is, and then the child often resorts to trickery. Generally it's the mother. They're very insecure themselves, and when they find the child may have just a touch of psychic ability, they go haywire and start promoting the child, just like a movie star's mother....Every child has a smattering of psychic ability. We all come into the world with it. Some have it to a greater degree than others, and very often the mother with the child that has the least degree of ability will go and promote that to the point where the child has to produce whether it's genuine or not genuine....The next thing you know, the kid will have imaginary visions, and there's a lot of trouble after that, because when the kid gets to be sixteen or seventeen years old, he wants to continue with that adoration and adulation and what not. Then there'll be trickery. And that's why they will become our fake mediums.

SI: What if a child had healing ability? Could the parents in any way encourage him to give the kind of service you did to other people, without going "haywire" in this way?

Olga: No. I think that every case is separate. If a child has any of that gift, you will find that kid will start saying, "I want to be a doctor," or "I want to be a nurse." So let them alone. They will find that this is their outlet, merging from within. So you don't have to worry about it.

And I would never take a psychic kid that had healing powers and say, "Now, you're going to be a doctor," or "You're going to be a priest." Let that child decide. He will go into his own way and you should just be supportive.

SI: I want to ask you about guardian angels.

Olga: I believe that we have a guardian angel from the moment of conception that guides us in the world, watches over us, and then ushers us into the next dimension at death. We should tell our children about the guardian angel. And sometimes I have found that children will have an imaginary playmate who is really the guardian angel.

SI: Do you see them sometimes, when children come to the clinic?

Olga: Sometimes. You'll see them hovering over the children, watching over them. And I know we give them a lot of gray hairs. But nevertheless, God has given us that guardian angel. And you know, among the old country people years ago, every bedroom had a picture in the corner of the room with this huge angel watching two little children that were crossing the bridge. Do you remember that? I have it upstairs in our healing room. That was the picture that was always in the bedrooms of the Russian kids. They always knew that their guardian angel was there.

In the interview, Olga frequently mentioned the trouble children can get into if they are psychically sensitive. She herself went through years of guilt, thinking she had caused her brother's death through paranormal means. She offers sound and practical advice to parents who find psychic talents in their own children. In the next chapter, further practical advice is offered.

14
Helping Kids with Their Secret Life

The previous accounts of children's paranormal experiences have contained some hints about how others can relate to these children, how teachers, parents, and friends can help them to cope with their "gifts." The term "gifts" may seem dubious since these sensory experiences are so often difficult for children. The practical implications of such situations have not yet been clearly delineated, though Olga Worrall in the interview in the last chapter forcefully expressed her ideas on the subject.

I have discovered some helpful and practical principles over the years that deal effectively with the problems of children with paranormal perceptions. These principles are illustrated by the case of seven-year-old Penny, a shy child in one of my second-grade classes. Her shy demeanor was shattered one day when she blurted out to me, "I hate myself! You don't understand; I just hate myself!" These are certainly not the words one expects to hear coming from the mouth of a second grade child whose teacher had just asked her to read to him.

I arranged private conferences with the kids when I wanted to hear them read, so that the less confident readers would not feel humiliated in front of their peers. Penny and I were alone and she was attempting to read, but was making slow and stumbling progress. Her frustration finally reached a peak and she cried, "I can't do this! I can't do this because I hate myself!"

Penny was having trouble in reading, her math skills

were not much better, and her shyness was bordering on a neurotic timidity which prevented her from making friends. I wondered if some psychological factors might be contributing to such a bleak self-concept, so I questioned her about her experiences in first grade, and about her life outside school. I asked if she had friends and whether or not she liked school. But in responding to these questions, Penny didn't give me a clue as to why she "hated" herself.

Since I was in the middle of my Master's degree research on clairvoyant children at the time, I suddenly got the intuition to ask Penny, "Oh, by the way, have you ever seen colored lights around your mom's head?" One cannot imagine the change that came over the countenance of this little girl. Her eyes opened wide and she looked at me with a totally different expression. She replied, "Oh yes, I see those colors all the time. And when I go to bed at night my bedroom is filled with colored squiggles, and when I'm outside I see big cigar-shaped colors in the sky...." She went on and on and on, getting more and more excited as she talked faster and faster. When she finally began to run out of steam, she sighed and sank back into her chair and mumbled, "And that's why I hate myself. Every time I tell my mom about what I see, she gets mad and says I'm lying. And when I tell my girl-friend, Susie, she laughs at me!"

"But I won't laugh at you, Penny," I said. "Please tell me more, I'm very interested in the things you see."

So Penny and I chatted for as long as we could. It was as if she had released herself from a burden that had been weighing her down for years. In the course of just one conversation, she seemed to become lighter, less tense, and more cheerful and outgoing.

Over the next few weeks Penny described and drew crayon pictures of the astral sights that were a part of her daily perceptual experience. She also told me more about the scoldings she received from her mother whenever she mentioned her secret life. Her mother told her she shouldn't lie about the things she saw, and that if she continued to tell such lies she would go to hell when she died. Penny also confided her visions to some neighborhood girls, and they laughed at her and told her she must be cuckoo. Unfortunately, Penny did begin to think she actually must be crazy, and she withdrew into a lonely and private world. Her kindergarten teacher had struggled to draw her into academic activities, but her progress in school was far below average. Her mother became more worried and was considering taking her to a psychiatrist at the time she came to second grade.

After our discussions, Penny began to relax and open up. Always eager to share her visions with me, she frequently greeted me in the morning with questions like, "Mr. Peterson, guess what I saw last night?" Since she no longer believed she was crazy, her self-concept improved immeasurably. She realized that her mother just didn't understand the things she saw and they must be kept secret from most people. But at least she had one person with whom she could talk, one person who believed her.

Penny's poor performance in school seemed bound up with self-doubt and difficulties in understanding her clairvoyance. Now her reading and math work gained ground, even excelled, and her mother became the "president" of the "Mr. Peterson Fan Club." She told my principal that I had taught her daughter to read and write, and must be a genius in elementary mathematics. What could I say? I couldn't tell her that her daughter's academic gains were entirely due to the fact that she had somebody to talk to about her clairvoyant visions.

In my experience, therefore, the first principle in dealing with psychic children is simply to lend a sympathetic ear. One need not offer complicated explanations of their experiences, nor make them feel unusually gifted or "advanced." Rather they should be assured that what they see is real, that they are not crazy. They should be taught that many people don't understand such experiences because they don't personally have them, and that sometimes it is better, as Olga was told, to keep one's mouth shut.

For my thesis, I interviewed a woman named Sonya

who, as a child, had much in common with Penny.
Sonya's comments, which follow, demonstrate the great responsibility parents and teachers have in helping children cope with psychic experiences. The transcript has been lightly edited for readability.

Sonya: You see, to a psychic, that world is just as real as this gross world, and sometimes, of course, you can't always make the delineation between the two.

J.P.: You saw these things from birth—I mean, there was never a time when all of a sudden...

Sonya: ...when it just all of a sudden happened? No, I always knew there was something a little bit different about me, but I didn't really understand that everyone didn't see the same things I did, because it was just so real to me. I would start relating some of the things that happened to me to my mother, and I would ask her what this meant, but she wouldn't understand. I gradually started realizing that she didn't see what I was seeing—that she didn't understand who these beings that came to visit me and entertain me were.

J.P.: Do you remember any specific incident of your seeing anything and asking your mom or some child or your teacher about it and the teacher or your mother saying, "No, this isn't there"?

Sonya: Oh yes. [My mother would say things like] "Oh, it was just something you ate," or "That was a movie you saw."

J.P.: Did you believe that? Did you ever question your own experiences?

Sonya: Of course, because your parents are your authority, and I was very close to my parents. It would sort of satisfy my curiosity, and yet I knew behind all this that there was more.... It's so important for parents to understand what kinds of experiences the psychic child is going through, and that that world is as real as this gross world is to a psychic child. You know, sometimes...the child doesn't understand when he's in one world and when he's in another world, and is very confused by this....

J.P.: You weren't satisfied with the explanations, but did they ever create a conflict of having your experience tell you one thing and your mother and authorities tell you another thing, and being caught in the middle and really feeling awful about it?

Sonya: Oh, yes at school. I didn't do very well in school because there were too many things going on in the astral [plane] around me that were far more interesting than what was happening in the school. You know, I had a hard time focusing in on math and very specific kinds of things when there were beautiful auras around to look at and thought forms floating through the room, and I was very distracted.

J.P.: Do you remember a specific incident in school of, say, being disciplined directly as a result of...

Sonya: No, because I learned very early to keep those things to myself—to keep them quiet and to almost suppress them, and to try and not see some of these things, because people started treating me as if there was something wrong with me. I didn't have many friends because I always had this feeling that I was a little bit different, and that other people didn't quite see things the way I did. I wanted so much to be accepted and to have friends and to be like a normal child that it was very frustrating for me at times. Teachers would accuse me of daydreaming and they were very harsh to me and very negative....They considered me a very sensitive child, and they didn't know how to relate to this sensitivity....they thought I was very moody and very shy. I was afraid to express myself, I never would raise my hand in class, and I would never ask for the answer to a question I didn't understand or ask the teacher to explain something she was talking about, because I was always afraid that I might say something that would indicate to them that I could see something that they didn't see.

J.P.: Did you ever think that other children saw these same things and ask them about it?

Sonya: No, I never did...I just didn't feel that...the people that I was around did. I didn't know anybody that I could really talk to [who] understood the things I was experiencing.

J.P.: But you never tried to tell kids about it?

Sonya: I can't recall anything like that because I was just too frightened of it. I felt this incredible kind of power, this ability to really perceive other things, and I was kind of frightened by it. The only one I tried to communicate this with was my mother, and I knew that I didn't get anywhere there. She was my ultimate relationship, really, because I didn't have other playmates around—they all just kind of stayed away from me.

J.P.: Did you see mostly interesting things and things that made you feel good, or a lot of times did you see bad or frightening sorts of things?

Sonya: Sometimes at night I would see frightening astral kinds of things. Specifically I can't think of anything other than beings and kind of low, astral forms—gross kinds of forms that would frighten me. I remember this one specific time I had been outside playing one night, and I came in and told [my parents] of these things that I had seen. They got very upset and accused one of the neighbors of telling me that these things were there. And they . . . wouldn't talk to the neighbors. I knew that it hadn't come from the neighbors and that I had really seen these things. . . .

J.P.: All in all, though, would you say that your clairvoyant perception was generally a pleasurable experience for you or . . .

Sonya: Oh yes! Oh yes! It was especially pleasurable for me since I was an only child and didn't have other friends. The [invisible beings] really comforted me. . . . Even with the things I saw that were rather disturbing, I always felt protected. I always felt this kind of shield of God around me, and I felt that I had an angel that watched over me.

J.P.: What difference would it have made if your mother had been able to explain these experiences to you?

Sonya: It would have made all the difference in the world, because I could have understood what I was seeing, why I was seeing it, and how to relate to it. I could have done better in school. I could have had friends. I could have understood what I could say and what I couldn't say [to other people].

One of Sonya's most serious problems was learning to

distinguish her inner world from the objective, sensory, outside world. This is a problem not only for clairvoyant children, but also for those who are telepathic. Frequently kids pick up the violent or depressing thoughts and feelings of others and are unable to distinguish these feelings from their own. Adults can help children to separate their own thoughts and feelings from those in the psychic environment. Parents need to learn to recognize moods in their children that may have an external or psychic origin.

When babies or preschoolers are irritable, parents often assume the child is hungry or overtired. They don't realize the problem might be an intense psychic environment, and that the child may be overly sensitive to the influences of that environment. Many settings can be the cause of internal distress for a psychic child. One that comes immediately to mind is the shopping mall. Whining children and shopping malls seem to go hand in hand. The superphysical atmosphere created by the mercantile crowds, particularly in enclosed, indoor malls, can be extremely intense. I call such enclosed malls "psychic pressure cookers." Often the most unpleasant and dense astral matter collects low near the floors of public places, and I feel it is best for a baby out shopping with parents to be carried and enfolded in the protective arms of a parent.

There is more to the astral world than toxic layers of psychic confusion, however, and the child doesn't always need to be "protected" from this subtle environment. Often it is pleasant for a child to be sensitive to psychic planes. It is even possible for the psychic environment to seem more comfortable and familiar than the outer, concrete world. Linda (described in Chapter 5) used the astral plane as a sanctuary from an unpleasant home life. To a certain extent, this can be permitted, even encouraged, for the inner dimensions of life can be nurturing and the child can experience a more holistic and encompassing vision of life there. Experience of these realms can demonstrate to the child that all physical forms are interconnected by flowing currents of living energy, and that these living currents are present in rocks and stones as well as plants, animals, and people. A child who senses these realities would be less likely to feel lonely or isolated in the world. Even a tree, seen from this inner perspective, could make a worthy companion. The inner planes sometimes offer children a psychologically safe place to stand (as Joe Pearce puts it) while they begin to unfold and develop their intellectual and emotional capabilities and talents on earth.

However, perception of the astral world can interfere with a child's job of incarnating on the earth plane and getting both feet on the ground. Parents and teachers must help such children by showing them, as Olga said, that there is a time to enjoy that "other world" and a time to focus on earthly tasks. In some cases the child may need a therapeutic regime, perhaps gymnastics or dance exercises, as physically strenuous activity can help him focus on more material levels of life.

One child I know received the help of a spiritual teacher in this task. Charmian retained the use of her psychic sensibilities into her college years, which itself is highly unusual. She and her mother went to India in 1948 to meet Meher Baba. Her psychic abilities were mentioned, and Meher Baba gently grasped her wrist, saying, "I want you to learn to live in one world at a time." Charmian said it was as if, by that touch, Meher Baba had turned off her paranormal abilities as you turn off a water faucet. Her clairvoyance simply vanished.

Concerned adults should be aware of both the useful and harmful aspects of superphysical sensibilities and be prepared to offer guidance in either direction. Despite individual differences, however, children must learn to differentiate between the two worlds and between gross sensory impressions and psychic ones. It is also important that an attempt be made to keep these two worlds in balance. A harmonious atmosphere in the home and school will help the sensitive child enjoy his childhood years. An adult saying one thing, for example, and thinking and feeling something different is most confusing to psychic children such as Linda.

Even such things as household furnishings can be important. Careful and artistic selection of colors can have a soothing effect. Furniture, paintings, types of fabrics, even selections of books in the bookcase all have an influence, positive or negative. For psychic children, a tidy, uncluttered environment can be a blessing, and it is a help to put books and toys in cabinets with doors that can be closed. Beautiful music and the presence of plants and fresh flowers also can be a pleasant addition to the decor.

I have a story about a little night light which serves to illustrate the importance of seemingly small details of the environment. When I was teaching in a public school, I was speaking with a mother about her second grader when we got on the subject of a younger daughter's nightmares. The nightmares, apparently, had started about two weeks earlier and were a nightly occurrence. I asked if anything special or frightening had happened two weeks ago, but she said no. Then I asked if there were any additions to the decor of her bedroom, such as a new bed or a new picture on the wall. She said everything was the same except that she had purchased a little night light which she kept on in Katie's room all night.

"What color is the bulb in the night light?" I inquired.

"Red," the mother replied.

I suspected instantly that the red night light was the culprit. So I suggested the bulb be changed to green, blue, or white. I had heard that red lights can attract unpleasant astral influences. A week later the mother returned to tell me Katie's nightmares had stopped as soon as the red light was removed. She thanked me profusely, but couldn't imagine why I thought of removing that night light.

There are a myriad "simple little things" that can affect children, though what is important for one may be a minor issue for another. For one child nutritional considerations may be paramount, while for another it may be the style, cut, and color of clothes that are pivotal. Another may be profoundly affected by what he sees on television, or by the electronic output of the T.V. screen itself, while for others careful monitoring of television viewing will not be so important. The type of psychic sensitivity may be indicative of where the thoughtful guardian should try to help. A telepathic child like Linda may find crowds at a ball game or shopping mall psychically toxic, while a clairvoyant child may be fine in crowds. A child who tends to go into deep reveries or to astrally project when alone may need to be gently approached to avoid harshly bursting into his private world. Yet another child may yearn to share special play times and reveries with parents or playmates.

School also presents a challenge for parents and teachers of psychically sensitive children. Many of the children I have met say school has been very unpleasant, but that unpleasantness has often been related to unsympathetic teachers or ridiculing peers. Parents might consider meeting with teachers before the beginning of a new school year to alert them to the special needs of their sensitive child. If the teacher is not responsive, a new classroom could be requested of the principal, or even a new school. Sensitive children often do better in the smaller, more intimate classroom settings of some private schools. The teachers in many so-called "New Age schools" might be particularly aware of the problems of these children. There is no reason why a psychic child should not excel in school if he receives the proper help and guidance.

Parapsychologist Elizabeth McAdams, in a paper on "Extrasensory Perception Research: Difficulties and Implications for Education," suggests that telepathic communication from the teacher to the student may be a useful educational tool (McAdams 1981). My own experience has confirmed a conclusion by psychologist and researcher Dr. Gardner Murphy that there is a strong correlation between creativity in children and their extrasensory perceptions (Tanous and Donnelly 1979). Such conclusions indicate that if teachers and parents recognize the psychic experiences of children, they may discover effective ways to help them to channel their abilities academically. A telepathic child might at least learn to focus on the teacher rather than on the not-so-bright student in the next seat. Clairvoyant children can learn to understand what the colors of an aura mean so they can nurture associations with lighter and more cheerful types of people instead of negative, harsh, or depressive types. More often than not, these are facets of their lives that they have already figured out. The main thing for teachers and parents is to help the children feel comfortable with themselves and free to confide in grown-ups.

It is also important for parents to be careful about the kinds of people who are influencing their children. Many teenage baby-sitters, for example, have their own share of covert anger, resentment, and sensuality. This is normal, as teenagers are coping with difficult astral layers of being. However, the guardians of a psychic child may not wish for such psychic tensions to be influencing their child for an evening.

I think one also has to keep an eye on relatives. If little Susie doesn't want to hug and kiss Aunt Mildred, her wishes should be respected. Perhaps the old aunt has some kind of malignancy or other type of ill-health which makes her aura difficult for a sensitive child. And the uncle who is an alcoholic could be carrying all kinds of unpleasant astral influences. Drug use also is not conducive to a happy atmosphere. I remember spending a holiday with a relative who used marijuana every day in a "recreational" way that he felt was perfectly harmless. While at his house, I had nightmares every night, which was extremely unusual for me. As soon as I left, the nightmares stopped. I am convinced that the drug use in that house had summoned unattractive astral elements that disturbed my sleep. I would never wish for a young child to live in the psychic atmosphere created by drugs, whether the child is psychic or not.

Another common practice in many homes is to use a child's room as a guest facility, giving any visitor passing through town use of the child's bed, blankets, and pillow. Even if the guest is pleasant, the presence of a stranger in the bed can disturb a psychic child's sleep patterns for a long time. Another unfortunate practice is throwing visitors' coats, hats, and purses all over a child's bed. A child's room should be a sanctuary for the child and should be honored and never thoughtlessly violated.

Some children, as already noted, are hypersensitive to influences from past lifetimes. Seemingly irrational fears or passionate interests bordering on obsession may be rooted in past-life memories. The guardian of such a child must be alert to the sometimes awkward situations which arise. For instance, for the little girl in Chapter 8 who became upset at church because she hated organ music, the parents could find a Sunday school class where the teacher played a piano and not an organ.

It is a mistake to read too much into childhood idiosyncrasies, of course. If a child refuses to finish his broccoli, one can not assume some past life experience with poisoned broccoli. The child's emotional reactions should not be allowed to dictate rules of conduct to the parents, though keeping past life considerations in mind can sometimes be helpful. Parents should be sensitive to such considerations, but not go overboard in their interpretations of specific childhood problems.

Some parents do go overboard in their awe of the secret life of their child. Olga Worrall spoke of mothers who push their children into performing psychic feats for relatives and friends. Such parental behavior does not help a psychic child. One woman, Mrs. K., whom I interviewed for this book told an illuminating story. The earliest clairvoyant experience Mrs. K. recalled had occurred when she was three and a half or four. She was playing in the garden when her grandmother came and spoke to her, which was not unusual except that the grandmother had died the previous week. Mrs. K. spoke to the apparition for some time, then ran into the house, saying "Mother, mother, I was just with grandma in the garden!" She related all that grandma had said, none of which was of special consequence. Mrs. K.'s mother was well aware of the realities of psychic perceptions. As Mrs. K. spoke about this experience, she remembers clearly that her mother was thinking at the time, "Oh, how I wish I could see my mother too." Even at the age of four, Mrs. K. suddenly experienced a clear sense of power over her mother, a sense that she had something her mother wanted. She knew that whenever she wanted to assert that power, all she had to do was say, "Oh, I just saw grandma again today." On many occasions Mrs. K. used her "clairvoyance" to get what she wanted from her mother, or simply to assert her own sense of self-importance. She often made up imaginary "visions" and visits from grandma, even though the original experience was a genuine clairvoyant perception.

Mrs. K., now a drug abuse counselor who has raised three children of her own, advises parents never to empower psychic children as she was empowered. "Don't make such a hullaballoo over their perceptions," she told me. "And don't assume that just because they had one psychic experience, they'll be continuously having others. Sometimes kids make up new experiences or even imagine them simply because they know they can get 'strokes' for it."

Through her experience in the drug abuse field, Mrs. K also has concluded that "psychic" experiences are often related to psychological disturbances. "The dividing line between psychic and psychotic," Mrs. K related, "is not always very clear. Some children who claim to have psychic experiences are really simply mentally unbalanced, and for others the psychic experiences themselves can actually drive them crazy." She encourages parents and teachers to help sensitive children learn to cope with the concrete realities of the physical world, and not to avoid such realities by hiding in the psychic world. Mrs. K is concerned that such avoidance can hinder the development of important psychological coping skills needed to survive in the complex, hectic, and stressful modern world.

Often, however, the isolated psychic experiences of children do not seem relevant to the everyday world, and it can be difficult to explain how they fit into the child's life. For one woman, it took fifty-four years for the meaning of such an experience to reveal itself. At the age of sixty-two, Mrs. T was fulfilling a lifetime's ambition as she and her husband, both Presbyterian missionaries, traveled through the Holy Land. As they visited ruins in Aleppo, Syria, Mrs. T's husband sat on a bench near a cliff. From where she stood, the view behind her husband was more than

beautiful; it entranced her. Suddenly she said, "Quick, I need to take a picture, please let me have the camera."
She experimented with different angles, standing now a little to the left, now a little to the right. Her husband, in the meantime, was still sitting on the bench wondering why his wife was so keyed up. Not even in Jerusalem had she been so excited about taking pictures. Finally everything seemed correctly lined up, and Mrs. T took the picture. Later she explained that when she was eight years old she had drawn a strange picture in which the crayons almost seemed to draw the lines by themselves. The picture was of an unfamiliar landscape. For some reason, Mrs. T had treasured that picture, and still had it in a trunk in their attic in New Jersey.

Mr. T did not fully appreciate his wife's story until they returned home and had the photos developed. Mrs. T located her childhood crayon drawing, and when it was compared to her photo from Aleppo, her husband was astonished. They matched exactly—every rock, every tree, the bench, and the hills in the background. The only difference was that Mr. T was sitting on the bench in the photo, and the crayon bench was empty.

Mrs. T did not analyze the significance of this childhood anticipation of the future, and she did not believe in psychism. To her it was simply a mystery which had something to do with the personal, religious significance this Holy Land expedition had for her. As a child, she somehow must have tuned into a moment of great significance for that lifetime and recorded it in crayon. The shadow of an event at age sixty-two was already present somewhere in her mind at age eight.

Another example is in some ways similar to Mrs. T's story. When Jack was five years old, he went on a delightful picnic with his family. At one point he looked up into the cloudless sky and suddenly beheld a vision of a huge reclining woman, seemingly sculpted out of marble. Then, from behind the stone-still figure, a ball of fire emerged, rushing across the sky toward him. For some reason Jack was not frightened, but when the fireball came very near, he ducked his head to avoid it. Then the fireball and the stone lady were gone. It was obvious to Jack that nobody else had seen the vision, so he kept quiet about it. Though he never mentioned it to anyone, it was a memory that was as clear when he was thirty-five as on the day it occurred.

As an adult, Jack became a close friend to a sculptor of some repute. Years after he met Jack, the artist completed a beautiful statue of a young woman reclining. When Jack saw the piece he immediately recognized the marble lady of his childhood vision, and as he seemed so enchanted with the statue, the artist presented it to him as a gift. As with Mrs. T, Jack as a child of five had perceived the astral shadow of things to come. Looking back on this vision now, however, Jack fails to see any great significance to it.

Such isolated glimpses into the psychic world remind us that "there are stranger things in heaven and earth than are dreamt of in your philosophy, Horatio." Perhaps Jack was ripe to be awakened to a more spiritual attitude toward life, and the fulfillment of his childhood vision triggered this awakening. In a general sense I do feel that it is important for children who have had paranormal experiences of one kind or another to be reminded of them as they grow up. Though I do not advocate encouraging or developing atavistic psychism in children, there nevertheless is a significance to their perceptions that may be fully appreciated by the child only long after the perceptual abilities themselves have faded away.

The existence of psychic perceptions reveals levels of life unavailable to ordinary sensory perception, offering explanations for psychological processes and an appreciation of the immense power of thoughts and personal moods. Furthermore, they may demonstrate the fact of life after death and prevent one from harboring fears of the "unknown." From these perspectives and many others, it is a good idea to remind older children and young adults that they had once perceived realms of existence no longer visible to them.

This is one of the reasons for telling children fairy tales and myths as they grow up. Fairy tales can represent pictures and images of inner levels of existence, and their themes often express allegories tracing the descent of a soul from the spiritual world into incarnation as a child on earth. By giving a child a steady diet of such spiritually nutritious stories, several purposes are served. First, the storyteller's message to the child is, "I understand and value your secret life. I know it's real and I can feel it too." Secondly, the archetypes of fairy tales serve to remind children of the inner dimension of life in which they existed before their descent into the concrete world. Such reminders help children to adjust to life here on earth without feeling isolated from the spiritual world. Thirdly, fairy tales offer the hope of spiritual awakening and fulfillment sometime in the future, after years of ordeal, tests and trials, which represent developmental phases of growth. Such stories, along with gentle reminders of early psychic awareness, can serve as a foundation for the religious life of the mature adult.

Through the wise and thoughtful actions of parents and teachers, children can be helped to experience the delights of childhood fully, while at the same time growing toward maturity. Since many children seem to be sensitive to hidden dimensions of life, those charged with their care should themselves become more aware of these dimensions. The secret life of kids compels us to see effective child care in new, non-traditional, and even non-physical ways. Learning to cope with the psychic world can be an adventure in itself, in which parents and teachers discover new realms of life as they learn new ways to meet the needs of these children.

15
Spiritual Practices for Kids— the "New Age" Fallacy

Since my first glimpse of childhood psychism in 1969, I have enjoyed sharing this "secret" with others. Through P.T.A. discussions, seminars, university courses, radio interviews, and magazine articles, I have described many of the experiences now recorded in this book. Though people seemed intrigued by the psychic anecdotes, I have tried to ease my audiences into a consideration of deeper philosophical questions: What do these fascinating stories mean? What do they tell us about the nature of children? Do they offer insight into child rearing and educational practices?

The "secret life" of kids certainly does offer insights into child psychology, educational philosophy, and even religion. Its emergence, development, and eventual disappearance yield many ideas and implications. The nature of the things these children see, hear, or feel (*what* they experience) validates in this skeptical scientific age the ancient wisdom teachings concerning inner dimensions of consciousness. *Why* these kids experience what they experience gives open-minded psychologists new insight into the workings of childhood consciousness. *How* these atavistic psychic faculties emerge and then fade away indicates important directions for the educator of the future.

Often I am asked, "Now that I know about all these important new dimensions of child awareness, what do I do about it?" There are always plenty of people in my audiences eager to answer that question for me. In our supply and demand society, whenever a new problem or question is posed, many new "experts" appear to answer the question, to cure the disease, or otherwise to supply the consumer with the best or even the "only" solution to the problems. This process is apparent in the proliferation of "New Age" educational practices.

The child care-giver who nurtures an interest in the psychic life of children is quickly inundated with trendy practices and techniques: guided imagery, visualization, yoga, meditation, breathing exercises, psychic expansion, psychic channeling, chakra awareness, aura balancing, dream research, past life journeys, out of body trips, color counseling, music therapy, visionary art, crystal sensitization, and the list goes on. My personal view is that the psychological development of the child, as seen from the spiritual perspective, indicates that many of these "New Age" practices may be less appropriate for children than one might think.

"Meditation" is a term used to denote most of the practices listed: yoga, aura balancing, guided imagery, chanting, past life journeys. Why is meditation offered to kids? A popular book on the subject, which also is widely used in "New Age Schools," suggests several reasons. This book, which shall remain nameless, suggests that meditation should be a "way of life" for adults and children, and that childhood meditation facilitates one of the prime goals of education to "orient the mind to the spiritual self." The book claims that it is through meditation that children learn to understand their thoughts and their actions in the world. Further, in this view meditation helps kids feel more of a unity with nature and with other people by helping to dissolve the barrier between the inner and outer worlds, as it dissolves the separation between self and others. Meditation removes ego separation by "untraining the consciousness" of a child. It inspires the "healthiest growth" by allowing the child to transcend all sensory faculties and to know the "real self." Finally, it is suggested in this book that children come into life with the "spiritual eye" open, and normally this inner eye closes down. Through meditation practices, it is claimed, children can be assisted to keep this eye open.

On the surface this sounds reasonable. Everyone wants to raise spiritually aware children who are not petty, violent, nor angry, who are sensitive to nature and their fellow men, and who celebrate the oneness of all life. But are meditation and related techniques the way to accomplish this? The basic psychological goal of a child, as stated before, is gradually to incarnate fully on earth and to consolidate an ego structure which can cope with earthly life. Are these developmental processes of consciousness in harmony with the processes called meditation? It is not an obvious question and it does not have an obvious answer.

Before birth the child-soul exists on the astral plane waiting, so to speak, to be born. But this birth does not take place all at once. It actually takes eighteen to twenty-one years for the child to incarnate fully into the physical body. The emotional self and the mental self only incarnate as the child's astral and etheric vehicles completely articulate with physical processes. As these two sheaths mature, they amplify the child's mental and emotional life, and become completely bound up with the processes of the physical body. They do not really function separately. Consciousness before birth is related to discarnate life on the astral and kama-manasic levels. But when a person perfects a new astral body while on earth, the sanskaras released are part of *physical* consciousness, not some ethereal superphysical state. The adolescent with a fully mature astral body, therefore, is connected only subconsciously to the astral level, and is not in any way developing astral consciousness on its own plane. I emphasize this because it is important to understand that the child's task is to focus consciousness on incarnate life at the physical level.

This new astral body, working through the etheric and physical, represents the ego in incarnation. In order to live on earth, one must possess an ego, whose purpose is to organize, process, and consolidate new learning gained through mental, emotional, and sensory awareness. The ego is the central pole around which all experience is integrated and understood (Meher Baba 1967, II: 59-60).

The psychological task of children, one might say, is to develop a masterful ego—an ego that fully understands the widest aspects of social and cultural life. Such an ego will be able to cope effectively with life, and to become a responsible person in society. As psychologists such as Erik Erikson point out, this consolidation of ego identity is not nearly completed until late adolescence.

What, in contrast, is the task of a spiritually oriented adult? An adult who is aware of the compelling pull of spiritual forces recognizes that the boundaries of his psychological conditioning block him from experiencing spiritual realities. The ego limits perception on every level of life, and it is the ego that separates him from unitary realms of spiritual oneness. The task of a spiritual seeker, therefore, is to loosen the grip of ego conditioning (the sanskaras activated in the present life) and to release spiritual forces which will propel him toward his acknowledged goal.

How does such a spiritually aware adult accomplish this task? Important aids are yoga, meditation, and other spiritual practices, preferably given directly by a spiritual teacher. Various meditations can begin to release the sanskaras which cement the structure of the ego, so that the aspirant can gradually become more aware of his spiritual ideal. The ego then is gradually dissolved. Aspects of this gradual process of ego dissolution have represented the foundation of spiritual study for thousands and thousands of years.

Many New Age educators speculate that spiritual practices started in childhood will provide a "head start" in spiritual development, and prevent children's minds from being conditioned by worldly views, in effect keeping the "veil" from descending so that they might always sense inner realities. Such a philosophy assumes that meditation for kids is crucially important for accomplishing these lofty goals.

I have long felt uncomfortable with this view, and have

been vaguely aware that some spiritually oriented educators, particularly those in Waldorf education, did not approve of meditative practices for children. But it was difficult for me to articulate the reasons for my feelings. In October of 1978, however, at a conference called "Child Quest" at the University of California in Berkeley, I heard a Sufi teacher named Murshid James S.B. MacKie speak on the subject of spiritual practices for children. His presentation helped me begin to clarify the perspective I was already nurturing.

Murshid MacKie summarized some of the points I have already made concerning the tasks of ego consolidation for children, and ego dissolution for the spiritual student. He also pointed out that meditation practices aimed at ego dissolution actually work against the direction of child development. The direction of flowing spiritual force in childhood is from the higher planes "down" toward earthly incarnation, whereas the forces of adult spiritual growth are released from the ego and sent "upward" to connect with higher structures of being.

The basic problem with teaching children spiritual practices, he said, is that these meditations, breath exercises, yogas, and mantras actually *work,* releasing energies that children literally are not equipped to handle. Even many adults cannot accommodate such forces, though within the context of an adult commitment to spiritual life, releasing such energies can be helpful. Also, an adult who practices yoga or breathing exercises does so on the inner compulsion of his own destiny, freely choosing these practices, often under the guidance of a spiritual teacher. A child who is told to meditate in school or who has to do yoga every morning at home after a cold shower is not working from an inner, spiritual compulsion; and some practices such as *Pranayama* breath exercises, I understand, can particularly disturb a child's delicate energy matrix.

Murshid MacKie raised an additional issue at the conference. The energies needed for spiritual advancement, he said, are locked in the superphysical structure of the ego. As the adult "deconditions" the ego, forces are released which make inner connections with the highest mind of the individual, and it is the releasing and channeling of such energies which constitute what is termed the "spiritual path." Many of these temporary ego structures exist for the adult at the astral level. These energies, which are critically important in any spiritually oriented life, can be released and channeled through spiritual practices. But they are not yet present in children because, as previously indicated, children have not yet fully developed their ego, and have not yet consolidated a mature astral vehicle. Therefore, not only would meditation work against the direction of child development, but in a real sense true meditation is not even possible with children because the energy structures needed to "fuel" the meditation are not matured.

Many teachers who advocate meditation for children will argue that it does work, that children love it, and that it can help keep psychic channels open. From the perspective of the present discussion, these three statements are true. Meditation can "work" for children, but it works completely differently from the way it does for adults. Furthermore, I am suggesting, it is more often than not counterproductive and sometimes even dangerous.

Chapter 12 included a discussion of the subtle communication channels of the body known as the chakras. The chakras serve to link various aspects of the mind on almost all levels of existence. In very young children the chakras are hypersensitive to impressions from the astral world and the conscious reception of these impressions is responsible for atavistic paranormal awareness. Lawrence and Phoebe Bendit discussed how the membrane over each chakra matures with age, eventually blocking off the impressions of the psychic world from the child's awareness. Thereafter, the chakras function outside of conscious awareness. Meditative and spiritual practices for children can encourage the psychic permeability of these chakra membranes, especially at the solar plexus, and interfere with correct development of filtering processes. Children can thus be trained to remain open to the psychic world, but is this helpful for them? The astral world is a realm of duality; it contains negative as well as positive influences. A child rendered more open and vulnerable to astral impressions may not be in an enviable position, especially during adolescence. Children are not sufficiently in control of their minds to protect themselves from the powerful negative currents in the astral. Nightmares, terrifying visions, obsession, and even possession can be the eventual outcome.

One teenager I interviewed, Mary, started doing a certain yoga practice at the age of thirteen. She took to it naturally, and the results were almost immediate—she developed healing abilities and clairvoyance. Unfortunately, she began to have frightening visions. One huge, dark, blob-like creature frequently appeared to her at night during her yoga practice or while she was trying to get to sleep. Although it never seemed to harm her, she could not force it to go away. Finally, after two years, the steady procession of frightening visions became too much for Mary. She stopped her yoga and consciously prayed for her clairvoyance to close off, which it did.

I remember once at the summer camp in Pennsylvania, a six-year-old boy started yelling in his sleep. He tossed and turned and cried out as if someone were trying to smother him. His breathing was in gasps and his body jerked convulsively. I called his name but could not wake him up. I shook him and yelled, "Wake up," but there was no response. He just kept moaning and jerking.

The situation seemed so peculiar and dramatic that I concluded this was not a "normal" nightmare, and that a paranormal force might be involved. I put my right hand on the boy's forehead and my left hand on his chest and focused my own mental force for a minute or so. Then I almost shouted, "In the name of God, all spirits depart!" I was only nineteen at the time, and hardly knew what I was trying to do. Nevertheless, the words were scarcely out of my mouth when the movements and moaning stopped and the boy completely relaxed. He let out a deep sigh and started breathing and sleeping peacefully. In the morning he had no recollection of this incident, which I concluded must have involved a malevolent astral being.

Another example in my experience was of a more serious possession and involved another boy of almost the same age. Five-year-old Timmy seemed normal enough. He was affectionate and bright and had high-powered professional parents. One day Timmy became ill with an extremely high fever which lasted for two days. After the fever broke and Timmy recovered his health, he started behaving peculiarly. He had fits of extreme anger and violence and would scream at his parents, using the most vulgar and coarse language. These fits seemed so uncharacteristic of Timmy that his parents became worried. Over a period of several weeks the fits became more frequent until his entire personality seemed to express angry vulgarity.

Much of his violence seemed to be channeled toward family members. One day following a screaming tirade Timmy grabbed a large kitchen knife, ran to his mother with the knife held high, and screamed, ''Mom, kill me! Use this knife and kill me! You must!'' Then he collapsed.

His parents sought the help of a spiritual teacher, who in turn discussed the case with a psychic counselor. They determined that Timmy had in fact been possessed by a malevolent and extremely violent being of some sort. It was also suggested that his momentary desire to kill himself stemmed from an instinctive effort to rid himself of this psychic intruder. The parents were told never to leave Timmy alone and to offer constant support and love. In the meantime, a group of friends gathered daily to pray that the entity be allowed to go its way and leave Timmy alone.

After about a week, the fits stopped, and Timmy seemed gradually to return to his old self. Once Timmy's former personality reasserted itself, he had no further trouble with the paranormal intruder. He went on to lead a normal and happy childhood, and is now at the top of his high school class. Today Timmy has no recollection of the possession; he only remembers that there was a disturbing period in his childhood when everybody seemed to be very worried about him.

I have been told that children can be particularly vulnerable to possession at the ages of four, five, and six. At this time they are leaving the psychic world and coming down to earth, and for a period are in a transitional state. Reportedly, there are discarnate beings who are established in neither the astral nor the physical sphere, but in a sort of limbo state between the two worlds (possibly victims of suicide, drug overdose, or violent deaths) and these sometimes prey on incarnate people's energies in an effort to garner enough psychic force to propel them into the next realm. It is possible for such a discarnate being to cause psychic trouble for a child. It is said that normally children are protected from such violent intruders. Yet a high fever or a violent accident can sometimes affect a child's connection between inner consciousness and the physical body, and this temporary imbalance can open a gateway for an intruding entity.

Another interesting, and frightening, story came from Dr. Allen Cohen. It involved a boy of about six years old who had a severe accident in which he struck his head and lost consciousness for a time. After recovering consciousness, his personality was completely different. Suddenly he became hostile, taking relish in hurting other children, frequently swearing, and engaging in violent temper tantrums. His distressed parents had him in weekly psychotherapy, but to no avail. The unpleasant new personality persisted.

At age fourteen, this boy had another serious accident and was again knocked unconscious. This time when he recovered, his old personality re-emerged. The boy reported that he experienced himself as hovering over his body during the past eight years, watching some other entity make use of his body, and that it was dreadful for him to see how his body was acting under the control of its new owner. Luckily, it would appear, the second accident allowed him to slip back in and reassert his rightful control.

It is not uncommon for head injuries to affect psychic abilities. I have met two adults whose psychism was activated by traumatic blows to the head. One was Geoffrey Hodson, who became clairvoyant after being shelled in World War I. The other was a woman named Irene whose psychic faculties developed when she was fifty-seven after a serious automobile accident.

Spiritual Practices for Kids—the "New Age" Fallacy

Any "spiritual" training children receive which makes their minds blank and passive can, in my view, render them more open and vulnerable to possession. Ouija boards can be particularly dangerous. Such a device in the hands of a child is an open invitation for a passing entity to do mischief. Furthermore, any training in telepathy or past-life reading, in which children are told to be open to inner images, seems to me risky. Children's ego structures are not fully functional, so their "inner images" would as often come from the outside astral environment as from their own minds. And once they passively allow outside energies to be consciously channeled through them, possession could be the outcome. I am even suspicious of art training in which the child is taught to leave himself open to his "intuition" before beginning a drawing or painting.

There are schools that attempt to train children in these passive abilities, including a "seminary for psychic children" in northern California that attempts to open kids up to the astral world. This group also offers seminars for adults on topics such as "how to allow a child to express psychic abilities" and "how to meditate with your child." The view expressed is, "If your child is not already psychic, he ought to be and, with our help, he most certainly will be!"

I have three basic responses to someone who wishes to send his child to such a "seminary." First, developing psychic abilities in a child is contrary to the child's natural growth processes. Natural growth actually tends to close off psychic channels in favor of the subjective abilities to think and feel. Any attempt to open the psychic channels of children artificially can seriously undermine the development of intellectual and emotional competence.

Second, psychic openness in children can be dangerous; psychic impressions can be overwhelming, and there is a danger of childhood schizophrenia from the inner confusion resulting from counteracting the normal filtering system of the chakra membranes.

Finally, there is the ultimate question: what is the value of developing psychic ability at any age? From my own interviews for this book, certain patterns became clear. For one thing, the overwhelming majority of informants found their paranormal experiences confusing and distracting, or even frightening. Another frequent theme is that these experiences interfered with ability to make friends, to do well in school, and generally to feel happy and comfortable.

Joseph Pearce once strongly advocated development of psychism in children. When I first spoke with him in 1975, we had heated discussions. I argued that psychic gifts close off automatically with maturation, regardless of whether or not children are encouraged and told such experiences are valid and real. Joe felt then that it was the general miseducation of children that cut them off from these more fundamental or "primary" levels of life experience. Joe has since come to believe that the best time to reawaken and develop these "primary" levels of experience through "intuition" is during "post-biological development," after biological growth has been completed at around age fifteen.

Other writers question the value of psychic development at any age. Sufi Murshid James MacKie, for example, has written:

> One of the notions that becomes important in my own work is the fact that what (are referred to) as psychic gifts are by no means all the same nor do they all work at the same levels of consciousness. Many abilities which are called psychic gifts are not gifts at all, but handicaps. In discussions of psychism, one frequently finds that all psychic abilities are referred to as gifts. One is invited to consider these gifts as being useful and important. Yet anyone with a rounded understanding of psychic processes knows that many psychic faculties are really handicaps and that using them can be disabling and crippling.

> There are different levels and kinds of knowing and different phenomena involved in the assessment of that knowing. Often qualities of knowing which are popularized in discussions of psychism are really regressive. They represent no advanced integration in knowledge or abilities, but are rather a residue of the very ancient past. To give them great credence seems to me very often a case of going backwards instead of forward in one's own learning. So I

think the notion of levels of knowing is extremely important.

The origin of an unusual ability is important to consider. By "origin" I mean the level of consciousness involved, and the integration of that knowing with other levels of consciousness and with the total product of the person's mind at that time. The notion of levels is very important because the abilities which naturally emerge on a spiritual path would not normally be called "psychic." On the other hand, many of the abilities which are called psychic and are sought after are a product of the astral world and the astral sheath of human consciousness. Those products are sometimes useful and helpful to people, but are extremely difficult to equilibrate, fashion and integrate. And there are many of those levels. Then there are also abilities which occur at levels [that are] called the planes of consciousness. Those are entirely different from the realms of astral experience, and the way in which they work within a personality is entirely different." (MacKie & Duce 1981, 85-87. Reprinted by permission of the publisher.)

Does all this mean that responsible and informed guardians should not attempt in any way to open children to spiritual or religious levels of experience? Not at all. There are many ways children can be helped to retain and develop sensitivity to unseen life processes and crystallize an awareness of fundamental spiritual ideals. Not all "spiritual practices" are dangerous or harmful to kids. Yet, as C.W. Leadbeater pointed out, the best spiritual practices for children are no doubt those in which the parents themselves regularly participate. Nothing can be more helpful to children than the calm, peaceful home atmosphere that can be created through the meditative spirit of the parents. Any spiritual training the parents undergo which helps them to refine their mental and emotional energies works as a great blessing to their children (Leadbeater 1918, 19).

Guided imagery and visualization techniques are popular these days. Often these techniques are used to take children on bizarre astral journeys, to confront projections of their inner being, "spirit guides," or other astral creatures. Although I do not recommend these exercises for young children, there is no reason visualization activities should be neglected. Modern education is far too reliant on auditory memory, and educators do not take proper advantage of other facets of the child's consciousness. Studies have shown that children trained in visualization perform better in school. More learning takes place if more of the five senses are integrated into each learning task. But rather than have children visualize symbols of adult spirituality or visualize some psychic level of life, why not have them use visualization to memorize spelling words or math combinations? The best and most ancient form of "guided imagery" and visualization is, of course, listening to a story. Children should be raised on a continuous diet of all sorts of stories—both in school and at home. I believe that story-telling does more to develop imagination and visualization skills than any other technique, and in the classroom stories can be used as the foundation for an entire educational program. Waldorf Education has aptly demonstrated how stories enliven virtually any aspect of academic training. And in this television age, stories act almost as inner therapy for the children. Constant television viewing has stunted the powers to create imaginative inner images. Television provides ready-made images, so the child's brain does not participate in creating the picture. The result is that familiar dull-looking, deadpan television stare—certainly not an expression that indicates lively and creative involvement.

Oral stories, however, balance the forces of this computer and television age, and indeed can be the primary means for parents to introduce spiritual and moral issues to children. Many fairy tales, myths, and legends deal symbolically with philosophical issues such as reincarnation, karma, life after death, and the reality of inner realms of existence. Many tales and legends strengthen a child's moral nature. Moral development in children—helping them to recognize clearly the difference between right and wrong, good and evil—strengthens the child's sense of self, and strengthens the ego's connection with positive and helpful forces on every plane of existence. Such strong moral development, which can be inculcated largely through the telling of stories which embody positive spiritual ideals, builds a strong foundation for later religious life.

Another helpful way to work with children is to build on their own natural ability to concentrate and observe. Teaching children to channel positive mental energy is entirely different from allowing them to become passively receptive to outer influences. In India, parents sometimes ask their little ones to concentrate on a feather or a flower or some other natural object for a minute or two. Such a practice helps certain children learn how to concentrate.

Krishnamurti always enjoyed sitting quietly with children. He never gave them any technique or guided imagery, but simply said, "May we sit quietly together for a few moments?" He frequently observed how much more easily children from the East sat quietly than those from the West. American children are such fidgeters! In this noisy and frenetic age, helping children experience the beauty of silence is extremely valuable. But such a quiet time of "meditation" is very different from having them visualize their whirling chakras while in a full lotus position.

My colleague and friend from the Association for Research and Enlightenment, Dr. Charles Thomas Cayce, has done a great deal of work with psychically sensitive children. He advocates providing these children with regular opportunities to absorb and experience the beauty of nature. Spiritual realities for them are more connected to the forces of the mineral, plant, and animal kingdoms than to the abstract scriptures of the world religions. Such experiences of nature provide a further basis for later, mature spiritual awakening. He also suggests setting aside regular periods for imaginative activities in the form of creative play, drama, writing, or art.

A final tool that can be used to develop this inner, spiritual side of a child's nature is "pre-sleep suggestion." Dr. Cayce feels that night-time prayers, fairy tales, or Bible stories told before rest establish a potent emotional mood that accompanies a child into sleep, and that such a mood can stimulate higher aspects of the child's consciousness (Miller 1986, 21).

There are indeed many ways in which thoughtful guardians can acknowledge and work with the secret life of their kids. But, as with all aspects of child rearing, careful discrimination is needed to determine the best approach for each individual child. Parents and teachers rarely know what a particular child's destiny will be, so indoctrination into the dogmatic principles of a specific religious philosophy might be entirely inappropriate. It seems to me that a wide ranging, open-minded, and eclectic introduction to various religious views, preferably through the use of simple stories, would assist most sensitive children to appreciate their psychic openness to the spiritual aspects of life.

The most important principle to keep in mind, however, is that just because a philosophy or spiritual practice is good and right for an adult, that is no indication that it will be good and right for a child. One of the most significant advances in child psychology in the twentieth century involves the recognition that children do not think, feel, and learn in the same ways that adults do. Adult powers of cognition develop gradually over the entire course of the first twenty years of life.

The recognition of the secret life of children might well be another revolutionary development in child psychology. Although these widespread, atavistic psychic abilities of children reveal a great deal about the natural relationship of children with inner spiritual realms of existence, one cannot understand them by studying the functioning of corresponding psychic faculties in adults. The mechanism of childhood psychism is unique to children, and it is for this reason that one should not start tampering with and developing additional psychic channels in the child by training them with essentially adult practices of yoga and meditation. Rather, the secret life of kids should be acknowledged in a quiet, relaxed, and natural way. Even if their spiritual vision simply fades as they mature, they can look back later on their childhood as a cherished period of intimacy with all the rainbow-hued forces of life. Rather than wish to re-experience this primitive, though beautiful, perception of life, their warm memories might spur them on to pursue the path of adult spirituality. Then they can be led to the lofty mountain tops of spiritual attainment where they can experience a vision of life which would make their childhood clairvoyance seem like blindness.

16
Children of the Future— What Can We Expect?

It is no easy task to finish this book. Every time I feel that the chapters are completed and the research over, I come across more interesting stories to tell—stories that simply have to be included among these pages. It is astonishing to me that practically everywhere I go, in any social or professional setting, I meet people who have incidents to tell about psychic children. The secret life of kids may be a secret, but it is an unbelievably widespread secret.

In evaluating the importance of psychic faculties in children, it is essential to know how widespread these sensibilities are. Obviously the more common they are, the more significant are their implications in a general understanding of child psychology. The most interesting question of all, however, is the one often voiced by members of spiritual groups: Are children becoming more psychic, and will psychic sensibilities be a more accepted aspect of their consciousness in the future?

One hears talk in our time about the "New Age" or the "Aquarian Age" and about new developments in human consciousness. Esoteric treatises from the early part of this century, for instance, suggest that the people of the earth will evolve to what is called "the sixth subrace of the fifth root race"—the new humanity. Some have suggested that this advancement will come at the end of the twentieth century, as part of a general spiritual awakening—a release of energy from the inner planes that will electrify the mind, heart, and body of all members of the human race. It has even been suggested by not a few esoteric groups that the World Teacher or Avatar will appear to usher in this New Age, and that this event (or "advent") will attract advanced souls from different parts of the universe who wish to be present in human bodies on earth. Many of these advanced souls, I have often heard it said, are now our children.

A prominent feature in this futuristic discussion is the notion that children incarnating in the future will be increasingly sensitive to newly released spiritual energies and forces, called by Sri Aurobindo "Supramental forces." If such a notion has any validity, it indicates that psychic experiences in the New Age may well be a part of all child-consciousness.

Another perspective on this issue was related to me by Rene Querido, director of the Rudolf Steiner College in Fair Oaks, California. According to Mr. Querido, Rudolf Steiner stated that in earlier epochs man's etheric body was more loosely connected to his physical body, a condition particularly noticeable in the head region. The etheric body around the head of early man was very large and poorly articulated with his physical tissue. The effect of this condition was that higher impulses of consciousness channeled themselves through brain processes very differently from the way they do today. Although analytical and logical thinking was not developed, these early races, with their ballooned etheric bodies, had highly developed imaginative faculties and were extremely psychic. Impressions from the psychic planes flowed uninterruptedly into their waking consciousness—though this consciousness was dreamlike in comparison to our present crisp and clear thinking. Early man felt closely bound to the spiritual worlds and, as a result, viewed the universe and its processes in very personal, imaginative, ways. He felt himself to be an integral part of the universe.

Over the millennia, according to Steiner, the etheric body gradually tightened and, by the fifteenth century, had become a molded encasement of the physical form. All physical tissue had an etheric counterpart, and the etheric material around the head extended only an inch or two beyond its physical extension. This etheric "descent" or hardening had a twofold effect on man's consciousness. First it brought about the awakening of modern, intellectual faculties of analytical and abstract reasoning. Thinking became, in a sense, "brain bound." And second, the tightening of the etheric body effectively blocked the free interchange of psychic impressions with brain-consciousness.

The fact that the etheric constitution of a young child is more similar to earlier races of man than to a modern adult has already been discussed, but Steiner observed a related phenomenon. Since the year 1899, he asserted, the earth has entered a new spiritual phase, a New Age. One of the effects of the new currents being released on earth is to begin processes of expansion within the etheric membrane of man. Especially noticeable around the upper portion of man's form, the etheric body, according to Steiner's observations, is opening up and expanding again, and loosening the grip of modern, brain-bound, scientific consciousness. As these processes proceed, human beings will become increasingly psychic and more imaginative. If this is true for adults, it should be all the more so for children. According to this view, children of the future will be more intuitive, more telepathic, more clairvoyant, and more open and malleable in their thinking processes.

Mr. Querido also mentioned in our discussion that this growing expansiveness of the etheric is most prevalent on the American continent, reputed to be the birthplace of this new humanity. This notion is shared by others as well. Geoffrey Hodson thirty-five years ago recognized clear signs of a spiritual awakening in the United States (Hodson 1953).

Joseph Pearce, who graciously penned the introduction to this book, is himself an example of the spiritual awakening which is taking place during this period. In *Magical Child* he evolved new ways of understanding the child in the light of countless recent studies, largely in the area of brain research. But though he recognized the existence of the psychic world of children, he still sought to understand these perceptions through a basically materialistic model. Between the time he completed *Magical Child* and the publication of *Magical Child Matures,* he himself underwent an intense period of personal, spiritual transformation. By the time he completed the second volume, his model of child development had become more infused with spirituality and, incidentally, more in harmony with the model presented in this book. One of the interesting results of his new spiritual perspective of the growing child has been the alteration of some of his earlier terminology. Instead of speaking of the "mind-brain system" as essentially one unit, for example, he now speaks of the brain and the mind as separate, though linked, structures. Another noteworthy change is in his vocabulary describing childhood psychism. In the first book, he referred to atavistic psychic abilities as "primary processes." In *Magical Child Matures,* however, he referred to psychic perceptions as "intuition." "Intuition is our innate capacity for becoming aware of subtle energy as needed for our biological well-being" (Pearce 1985, 70). Although redefining intuition in this way is a bit confusing to those who tend to separate the realm of psychic experience from the realm of intuition, I think Joe's new formulations beautifully indicate the future evolution of childhood psychism.

The development of intuition has often been referred to as the foundation for this theoretical new humanity. Geoffrey Hodson referred to intuitive development when he said: "If one is looking for signs that any particular person is beginning to show marks of that sixth sub-race today, such signs may be found in a growing intuitiveness and in a capacity to lead by love, sympathy and comprehension" (Hodson 1953, 4).

A number of contemporary spiritual tracts claim that this present period represents the end of the *Kali Yuga,* a Hindu term for the darkest, most materialistic of ages. The twentieth century has been called the last stage in this cycle of time *(Kali Yuga)* and the last loop of an even larger cycle of cycles. That is why it is said that humanity as a whole can expect a leap in consciousness. Previous evolutionary leaps in consciousness, for instance, were the transition from a primarily sensory mode to an instinctive and emotional consciousness, and the later transition from instinctive consciousness to an intellectual, analytical mode. The analytical mode obviously is the present state of most of humanity; but that does not imply that people today have all acquired the educated intellectuality that is so revered in America. It merely indicates that in a great many people clear, waking consciousness works primarily through logical thought processes, and that has assuredly not always been the case. The next leap in consciousness, according to this evolutionist view, will be to a much more intuitional mentality. The following quote gives a flavor of the spiritual forces expected to bring about this transformation. Its sentiments are echoed and restated in the teachings of nearly every contemporary spiritual figure:

> Periods [such as the present one] are like the spring-tide of creation. They bring a new release of power, a new awakening of consciousness, a new experience of life—not merely for a few, but for all. Qualities of energy and awareness, which had been used and enjoyed by only a few advanced souls, are made available for all humanity. Life, as a whole, is stepped up to a higher level of consciousness, is geared to a new rate of energy. The transition from sensation to reason was one such step; the transition from reason to intuition will be another (Meher Baba 1967, 111:13-14).

Intuition, according to this formulation, has little to do with psychic sensibilities. Psychic perceptions involve occult modifications in the densest vehicles of consciousness, which allow subtle impressions of the unseen environment to register in the brain and in waking awareness. Intuition relates to internal processes of knowing which have to do with supersensible communication links with one's higher structures. Intuition is a type of "thought-free" knowing that has nothing whatever to do with telepathy, psychokinesis, or clairvoyance. Irene Conybeare, author of the book *Civilization or Chaos?,* called this coming development of intuition an unfolding of the "Divine Mind":

> Every two thousand years roughly, the sun enters another sign of the Zodiac and we are now in the Aquarian Age. Every Age brings with it a new culture. During the Christian era, since the time of Jesus, the lower human mind had developed to its zenith. Now, the Universal Mind is stirring and the New Era into which we are about to enter will unfold the Divine Mind. . . . This implies the immense outpouring of spiritual energy and the quickening of man's higher nature (Conybeare 1985, 10).

Intuition, so conceived, is a direct manifestation into conscious awareness of unitary realms of universal mind.

Although such an unfoldment of "the divine mind" has nothing to do with the seven psychic senses, it does affect one other vital aspect of human consciousness: love. Intuition and love go hand in hand, as each is a direct result of a spiritual experience of the essential oneness of life:

> The coming civilization of the New Humanity shall be ensouled not by dry intellectual doctrines, but by living spiritual experience. Spiritual experience has a hold on the deeper truths and . . . will come into existence through a release of love in measureless abundance." (Meher Baba 1967, 1:24).

Love and intuition are qualities quite different from psychic powers and may be the characteristics that will lead us into the New Age.

This conception of the inner trends of future humanity is corroborated by the Brothers Grimm, of all people. A professor from the Anthroposophical Society suggested that I read the fairy tale called "One Eye, Two-Eyes, and Three-Eyes." This tale is about three unusual sisters. The oldest sister has only one eye in the middle of her forehead; the middle sister has two normal eyes, while the youngest one has three eyes—the third in the center of her forehead. The professor, who had studied the esoteric meaning of fairy tales, told me that this story symbolizes significant events in human evolution. The eldest sister, according to his interpretation, symbolizes the ancient state of clairvoyant humanity. The inner world, revealed through the third eye, constituted the bulk of humanity's perceptual powers. Two-Eyes is the current state of humanity, with the vision of the spiritual world closed down. Three-Eyes, the youngest sister, represents the human development of the future, in which clairvoyant perception through the third eye will become an additional faculty for most human beings. Presumably, children in this coming phase will enter the world psychically open, and rather than losing this ability, will expand and refine it as they mature. Another way of understanding this tale is from the perspective of one child's development during a single lifetime. A child incarnates on earth with his inner eye open through atavistic psychic awareness (One Eye). As he matures, the one eye closes off and normal, worldly vision asserts itself (Two-Eyes). Finally, during later phases of spiritual growth, he regains his psychic faculties without sacrificing clear perception of the physical plane (Three-Eyes). In either interpretation, Three-Eyes is the most evolved.

This fairy tale sounded like a good way to conclude this book. I would gently invite the reader to consider that in the future nearly all children will be psychic, and I would reinforce this prophetic perspective by retelling "One Eye, Two-Eyes, and Three-Eyes." This plan, however, had to be modified because, when I actually studied this tale for myself, I came up with an entirely different interpretation.

In the story Two-Eyes is the heroine, and she is persecuted and ridiculed by her mother and her two wicked sisters because she does not have unusual perceptual powers like they do. They don't even give Two-Eyes enough food to eat. An old wise woman visits her in the woods and supplies her with secret food by means of a magical goat. When the rest of her family discovers the goat, they jealously slaughter it. But again the old wise woman tells a tearful Two-Eyes to bury the goat's entrails in the front of the house and then "your fortune will be made."

The next morning a beautiful tree is found growing in

front of the cottage—a magical tree with leaves of silver
and fruit of solid gold. The mother immediately sends
One-Eye and Three-Eyes up the tree to pluck some of the
golden fruit. But every time they reach out for a fruit, they
grab only empty air. Finally, of course, Two-Eyes climbs
the tree and the envious sisters see that ''the golden apples
did not avoid her, but came into her hand of their own
accord.''

Soon a glorious and handsome knight comes riding up to
the little cottage and asks if he might be allowed to have
one of the beautiful branches from the magic tree. The
mother tries to hide Two-Eyes and have her other daughters fulfill the desire of the knight. But in the end only
Two-Eyes can successfully break off a branch. The knight
instantly falls in love with her and carries her off to his
castle, where they hold a joyous wedding celebration amid
pomp and splendor.

The mother and sisters meanwhile console themselves by
thinking, ''Oh well, we got rid of that stupid Two-Eyes
and we at least get to keep the magic tree!'' But the next
morning the tree miraculously appears just outside of Two-
Eyes' new bedroom window at the castle. The story con-
cludes many years later when One-Eye and Three-Eyes
have fallen on bad times and go to beg at the castle of
Two-Eyes. She recognizes them, forgives them for their
past wickedness, takes them into her heart, and cares for
them for the rest of their lives.

My interpretation of this story would be that it does not
matter whether one has the atavistic psychism of One-Eye
or the more consciously developed paranormal faculties of
Three-Eyes. These psychic powers really can not help one
gather the spiritual fruits of wisdom from the Tree of Life.
Little Two-Eyes, although she did not have flashy spiritual
experiences like her sisters, and so was not considered as
''good'' or ''advanced'' as they, had one thing that they
did not have—love. It was her love that not only allowed
her to collect the golden fruits, but also won for her the
ultimate union with her higher Self, the handsome knight.

What did the open psychic eye accomplish for the other

two sisters? They were both egotistical, selfish, and vain about their "looks," that is, about their psychic powers. Their self-centeredness eventually brought them to a state of complete poverty and destitution. Begging humbly at the Door of Love, however, turned out to be the ultimate key to their salvation. Love in the end takes in everyone and is completely forgiving of the past. If one favors the alternate interpretation that these three sisters all symbolize latent qualities within each human being, then one might interpret this fairy tale's message to be that psychic powers have no value unless they are mediated and mitigated by the force of real love—perhaps even divine love. St. Paul expressed the same message in his letters to the Corinthians: "And if I have prophetic powers, and understand all mysteries and all knowledge, and if I have all faith, so as to remove mountains, but have not love, I am nothing" (1 Corinthians 13:2).

Psychic powers in whatever form cannot in the end be much help to children. If these atavistic faculties of children increase in the future, or come to be retained more frquently in adult life, they still should not be given undue spiritual importance. They should rather be discussed with the children with an attitude of detached interest. Rather than encouraging psychic awareness in children, it would be better, it seems to me, for guardians and caretakers of kids to help children grow in their ability to love. Love holds the answer to almost all personal problems and ultimately is the only solution to the serious global problems which at present seem to threaten the entire human race. Today's children will be tomorrow's leaders, and their vision of world unity and the brotherhood of all humanity without regard to the distinctions of race, color, sex, or religious beliefs (or lack of them) will be the force that will propel all life into the longed-for New Age. Geoffrey Hodson suggests that these children will develop the necessary traits to fulfill their future roles by being educated in love and trained according to new principles of unitary and unprejudiced global consciousness. Only then

will the results of the spiritual plan for earth be assured
and the advent of the new humanity be a reality:

> [This] new humanity will seek unity and cooperation be-
> tween free individuals and nations. The very essence of all
> action in the sixth sub-race will be the union of many to
> achieve a single object, and not the dominance of one who
> compels others to his will. To advance together in freedom
> to a goal that all realize as desirable will ultimately become
> the method of attainment. This tendency to unity of action
> is one of the signs of racial evolution out of dependence
> upon mental processes, analysis, deduction and logic into
> the use of direct intuitive perception (Hodson 1953, 3).

In conclusion, all that can be said for certain about the
future of the "secret life of kids" is probably that it will
become less of a secret. Whether or not more children
come to perceive other realms of spiritual existence, those
who care for children will gradually learn to accept them
for who they are and to love them and nurture them.
Psychic awareness may, in fact, become a natural and accepted part of the perceptual patterns of human beings—
especially young human beings. If such is the case, people
of all ages will no doubt learn to cope more effectively
with these abilities in creative and intuitive ways. Hopeful-
ly, however, it will be the force of love that will dictate
these ways, and not a self-centered yen for personal occult
power. Here, perhaps, it is little Two-Eyes who can show
the way. Whether this inspiring fairy tale heroine most
represents the children of the future or their wise parents,
the Two-Eyes who lives in all of us will come to fully appreciate and understand the expanded awareness of her
sisters One-Eye and Three-Eyes. No matter how well these
sisters have integrated or failed to integrate their supersensible awareness into useful patterns of human growth,
Two-Eyes will nevertheless love them, take them into her
home, and care for them with all her heart.

References

Alter, Stewart. 1979. Mother and child: The ESP bond. *Parents Magazine* (September):34-38.

Anzar, Naosherwan. 1974. *The beloved.* North Myrtle Beach, SC: Sheriar Press.

Armstrong, Thomas. 1985. *The radiant child.* Wheaton, IL: The Theosophical Publishing House.

Bendit, Laurence J. and Phoebe D. 1977. *The etheric body of man: The bridge of consciousness.* Wheaton, IL: The Theosophical Publishing House.

Besant, Annie. 1959. Imagination. *Parents' Bulletin* 24, no. 3 (Autumn):18.

———. 1967 [1904]. *A study in consciousness.* Adyar, Madras, India: The Theosophical Publishing House.

Blavatsky, H.P. 1952 [1892]. *The theosophical glossary.* Los Angeles: The Theosophical Company.

———. 1963 [1888]. *The secret doctrine.* Pasadena: Theosophical University Press.

Bononcini, Annamaria, and Aldo Martelli. 1983. Psychological investigations of subjects who are protagonists of alleged PK phenomena. *Journal of the Society for Psychical Research* 52 (June):117-25.

Buckemuehl, J., et al. 1985. *Toward a phenomenology of the etheric world.* Spring Valley, NY: Anthroposophic Press.

Clarke, E.H. 1878. *Visions: A study of false sight.* Boston: Houghton, Osgood and Co.

Clarke, Mary Whatley. 1983. Children who see with their eyes shut. *Fate* 36 (April):88-94.

Colum, Padraic, ed. 1972. *The complete Grimm's fairy tales.* New York: Pantheon Books.

Conybeare, Irene. 1985. The second coming, an extraordinary story. *Glow International* (August):2-10.

References

Cook, Emily W., et al. 1983. A review and analysis of unresolved cases of the reincarnation type. *Journal of the American Society for Psychical Research* 77 (April):115-35.

Donkin, William. 1969. *The wayfarers*. San Francisco: Sufism Reoriented, Inc.

Douglas, Alfred. 1977. *Extrasensory powers*. Woodstock, NY: Overlook Press.

Ehrenwald, Jan. 1971. Mother-child symbiosis: cradles of ESP. *Psychoanalytic Review* vol. 58, 455-66.

FitzHerbert, Joan. 1961. Extrasensory perception in early childhood. *International Journal of Parapsychology*. 3, no. 3:81-96.

Gibran, Kahlil. 1964 [1933]. *The prophet*. New York: Alfred A. Knopf.

Hall, Manly P. 1957. *The occult anatomy of man*. Los Angeles: The Philosophical Research Society.

—————. 1978. *The secret teachings of all ages*. San Francisco: H.S. Crocker Company.

Hasted, J.B., and D. Robertson. 1980. Paranormal action on metal and its surroundings. *Journal of the American Society for Psychical Research* 50 (June):379-98.

Heindel, Max. 1928. *The Rosicrucian principles of child training*. Oceanside, CA: The Rosicrucian Fellowship.

—————. 1953. *The desire body*. Oceanside, CA: The Rosicrucian Fellowship.

Hilgard, Ernest. 1970. Imaginary companions in childhood. *Personality and hypnosis*. Chicago: University of Chicago Press.

Hodson, Geoffrey. 1953. *America, birthplace of a new race*. Ojai, CA: Parents' Theosophical Research Group.

—————. 1970. *Kingdom of the gods*. Adyar, Madras, India: The Theosophical Publishing House.

Jalango, Mary R. 1984. Imaginary companions in children's lives and literature. *Childhood Education* 60 (January):166-71.

Jersild, Arthur J. 1968. *Child psychology*. Englewood Cliffs, NJ: Prentice-Hall.

Jinarajadasa, C. 1967. *First principles of Theosophy*. Adyar, Madras, India: The Theosophical Publishing House.

Kawaski, Theodore F., and Henry S. Odbert. 1938. Color-music. *Psychological Monographs* 50, no. 2:39-53.

Kiang, Tao. 1982. Sighted hands. *Journal of the Society for Psychical Research*. 51 (June):304-8.

Kyber, Manfred. 1972. *The three candles of little Veronica*. Garden City, NY: Waldorf Institute for Liberal Education.

Leadbeater, C.W. 1918. *Our relation to children*. Los Angeles: The Theosophical Publishing House.

————. 1971 [1903]. *Clairvoyance.* Adyar, Madras, India: The Theosophical Publishing House.

Leadbeater, C.W. and Annie Besant. 1969 [1925]. *Thought forms.* Wheaton, IL: The Theosophical Publishing House.

Leuner, Hanscarl. 1964. *Interpretation of visual hallucinations.* New York: S. Karger.

MacDonell, Arthur A. 1924. *A Practical Sanskrit Dictionary.* London: Oxford University Press.

Mackenzie, Andrew. 1969. Ostensible mother-child ESP. *Journal of the Society for Psychical Research* vol. 45, (Dec.):165-67.

MacKie, James S.B., and Ivy O. Duce. 1981. *Gurus and psychotherapists: Spiritual versus psychological learning.* Lafayette, CA: Searchlight Seminars.

McAdams, Elizabeth E. 1981. Extrasensory perception research: Difficulties and implications for education. *Proceedings of the American Educational Research Association* (April).

Meher Baba. 1967. *Discourses.* San Francisco: Sufism Reoriented, Inc.

————. 1973. *God speaks.* New York: Dodd, Mead and Co.

Meher Message. 1931. III, no. 3 (March):77-78.

Miller, Rhonda. 1986. Are children more psychic? *Venture Inward* 2, no. 4 (July):18-22.

Moncrieff, M.M. 1951. *The clairvoyant theory of perception.* London: Faber and Faber.

Myers. 1983. Sam Lentine. *Fate* (April):76-81.

Nianlin, Zhu; Zheng Tianmin; Luo Xin, and Mu Jun. 1983. The primary measurements of mechanical effects of paranormal ability of human beings. *Psi Research* 2 (March):25-30.

Nicol, J. Fraser, 1979. Fraudulent children in psychical research. *Parapsychology Review* 10 (January-February):16-21.

Nilsson, Lennart. 1977. *A child is born.* New York: Delacorte Press/Seymour Lawrence.

Olenius, Elsa, ed. 1973. *Great Swedish fairy tales.* London: Chatto and Windus, Ltd.

Pavitra. 1976. *Education and the aim of human life.* Pondicherry, India: Sri Aurobindo International Center of Education.

Pearce, Joseph Chilton. 1980. *Magical child.* New York: Bantam Books.

————. 1985. *Magical child matures.* New York: E.P. Dutton, Inc.

Peterson, James W. 1974. Some profiles of non-ordinary perceptions of children. Seminar study, University of California, Berkeley.

————. 1975. Extrasensory abilities of children: An ignored reality? *Learning* 4, no. 4:10-14.

References

Pines, Maya. 1978. Invisible playmates. *Psychology Today* (Sept.) 1981.

Powell, Arthur E. 1973 [1927]. *The astral body and other astral phenomena.* Wheaton, IL: The Theosophical Publishing House.

Practical Sanskrit Dictionary. 1924. London: Oxford University Press.

Rozman, Deborah. 1977. *Meditating with children.* Boulder Creek, CA: University of the Trees Press.

Rucher, Naomi G. 1981. Capacities for integration, oedipal ambivalence and imaginary companions. *American Journal of Psychoanalysis* 41:129-37.

Sarbin, Theodore R. 1967. The concept of hallucination. *Journal of Personality* 36, no. 3 (Sept.):359-80.

Schwarz, Berthold Eric. 1971. *Parent-child telepathy.* New York: Garrett Publications.

Scott, Cyril, ed. 1971 [1953]. *The boy who saw true.* London: Neville Spearman.

Shrager, Elaine F. 1978. An experimental investigation of mother-child telepathy and related personality variables. *Dissertation Abstracts International* vol. 38 (Apr.)

————. 1979. Mother-Child ESP. *Human Behavior* vol. 8 (Jan.) 38.

Steiner, Rudolf. 1959 [1939]. *Cosmic memory: Prehistory of earth and man.* Englewood, NJ: Rudolf Steiner Publications, Inc.

————. 1965 [1909]. *The education of the child in the light of Anthroposophy.* London: Rudolf Steiner Press.

————. 1972 [1928]. A modern art of education. London: Rudolf Steiner Press.

————. 1982. *Man in the past, the present and the future: The evolution of consciousness.* London: The Rudolf Steiner Press.

————. 1986 [lectures, 1921-22]. *Soul economy and Waldorf education.* Spring Valley, NY: Anthroposophic Press.

Stevenson, Ian, and Jamuna Prasad. 1968. A survey of spontaneous psychical experiences in school children of Utter Pradesh, India. *International Journal of Parapsychology* 10, no. 3:241-63.

Stevenson, Ian. 1973. The explanatory value of the idea of reincarnation. *The Journal of Nervous and Mental Disease* 164:307-8.

————. 1974. *Twenty cases suggestive of reincarnation.* Charlottesville: University Press of Virginia.

Tanous, Alex, and Katherine Fair Donnelly. 1979. *Is your child psychic?* New York: Macmillan and Co.

Taub-Bynum, E. Bruce. 1984. *The family unconscious.* Wheaton, IL: The Theosophical Publishing House.

Twemlow, Stuart W., Glen O. Gobbard, and Fowler C. Jones. 1982. The out-of-body experience. *American Journal of Psychiatry* 139 (April):450-55.

Van de Castle, Robert L. 1959. A review of ESP tests carried out in the classroom. *International Journal of Parapsychology* 1, no. 2:84-103.

Worrall, Olga N. and Ambrose A. 1970. *Explore your psychic world.* New York: Harper and Row.

Young, Samuel H. 1977. *Psychic children.* Garden City, NY: Doubleday and Company.

Zuisne, Leonard and Warren H. Jones. 1982. *Anomalistic psychology: A study of extraordinary phenomena of behavior and experience.* Hillsdale, NJ: Lawrence Erlbaum Associates.

About the Author

James W. Peterson has taught elementary school children for sixteen years, in both public and private settings. He has wide experience in both Waldorf and Montessori education and is currently director of the middle school at the Concordia School in Concord, California. He received his B.A. and also his M.A. from the University of California at Berkeley, with his thesis focused on psychic sensitivity in children.

The author is also a faculty member of the John F. Kennedy University at Orinda, California, where he teaches "Psychic and Spiritual Development in Children" and "New Age Education Movements in America." He has published articles in professional journals on child development and psychic senses in children. He lives with his wife in Walnut Creek, California.

6172